sing
New Zealand

sing New Zealand

The story of choral music in Aotearoa

Guy E. Jansen

MASSEY UNIVERSITY PRESS

Contents

Foreword

Guy Jansen is, without doubt, one of the central and key figures in the history of New Zealand Choral Music. My first contact with him was as a student at the Secondary Teachers' College in Christchurch in 1975. After I completed further study in Auckland, and upon my return from the United States in 1986, Guy invited me to work with young conductors at the Inaugural International Summer School in Choral Conducting in Nelson. Guy and I co-directed these summer schools until 2011, when they were handed over to the Association of Choral Directors under the aegis of the New Zealand Choral Federation.

History has shown Guy Jansen's extraordinary contribution to choral music. The formation of the world's first national youth choir in 1979 — the National Youth Choir of New Zealand (ages 13 to 24) — was an initiative of his, and he was its inaugural musical director. For the choir's initial overseas tour, which included singing with Kiri Te Kanawa in London, he made the first arrangement of the New Zealand national anthem to incorporate Māori and English words. He then taught at the University of Queensland, where he established a master's degree in choral conducting, and subsequently he was invited to be conductor-in-residence at Wheaton Conservatory of Music in Illinois, United States. In 2011, he was made a Member of the New Zealand Order of Merit in the Queen's Birthday Honours. In 2013, he was made a Life Member of the New Zealand Choral Federation, and in 2017 he was presented with the Federation's first Distinguished Service Award. His passion, vision and big ideas have set the direction for the future of choral singing in New Zealand.

But what of the future? The New Zealand Secondary Students Choir (founded by Guy in 1986), the New Zealand Youth Choir (founded by him in 1979), and Voices New Zealand (founded by Karen Grylls in 1998) have recently come under the umbrella of Choirs Aotearoa New Zealand. As a result, the first Choral Academy, with all three choirs present, took place in Auckland in January 2019. The academy has accorded us the opportunity to show the work of our vocal and language coaches and our conductors and singers from secondary school to professional level.

There are also the recently established national conducting conferences, Choral Connect, directed by the Association of Choral Conductors, modelled on the pedagogy and choral aspirations of the original summer schools, which Guy initiated. And New Zealand is currently preparing to welcome the World Choral Symposium in Auckland in 2020. This is a festival with 24 of the brightest and best of the world's choirs, including our own New Zealand Youth Choir, and more than 40 eminent choral musicians offering practical workshops, seminars and exhibitions.

Above all, the future must embrace the establishment of a national children's choir and pay attention to the quality of the experience our children have in their choral and musical education.

Very sadly, Guy died as this book was being completed. However, the pages are filled with his entrepreneurial vision, and his passion as an educator and choral pedagogue. Written from his unique perspective, it draws together the stories and history of our musical and choral journey. This is a fine resource and record of our choral history.

Dr Karen Grylls ONZM
August 2019

Introduction

Nau mai, haere mai. Welcome to a story about the beginnings of group singing in Aotearoa New Zealand, how it has developed over the past 200 years, and how the best choirs have become so good.

It has been claimed that gardening is the slowest of the performing arts, but a competitor for slowest could be this country's choral art.

In ancient times, across many continents, our forebears discovered humming and made a range of other vocal sounds. Their descendants and successive generations turned celebratory shouts of joy and cries of anguish into love songs, lullabies, chants of lament and much more. Everyone could take part. Cultural traditions developed; some people danced or moved in procession as they shared their songs — singing and movement were a common combination. Over time group singing developed. From the early nineteenth century it progressed through rank amateurism, easy popularity and well-intentioned passion, offering immediate social rewards and some aesthetic growth. The ease of becoming involved partly explains why group singing in Aotearoa New Zealand is this nation's most popular participatory art form.

The perennial popularity of singing is in contrast to the slow development of a fully mature form of choral music in this country. It has a much longer history than other common musical forms, such as orchestral music (eighteenth century), opera (seventeenth century) and pop music with its attendant technology (twentieth century). The choral world that most New Zealanders are aware of began in communities and churches in medieval Europe, and this mainstream classical tradition is the focus of this book.[1]

The formatting, or presentation, of the classical style has changed over the centuries. Initially, choruses were small groups of soloists with other singers added as needed, but the nineteenth century saw large amateur-based choirs emerge. They were regarded by many as a motley bunch — an unfortunate and unfair generalisation. However, when their often-mediocre standard didn't improve, the opprobrium attached to these large groups remained. So began a volunteer versus elite separation that is seen in choral activity worldwide.

In a little over a century, the public face of the art form changed enormously. The twentieth and early twenty-first centuries saw the emergence of new, smaller ensembles singing a wide range of music spanning many ethnicities and styles. The repertoire included whatever appealed to a director and for which singers would agree to attend rehearsals. There are still large choirs; many are singing fine music to a high artistic level, while others are stuck performing popular warhorses from an old repertoire. But audiences today are presented with a much wider range of choral offerings.

Whether in unison or harmony, regardless of whether musical notation is used or not, and irrespective of qualitative judgements about the experience, singing together has always enjoyed wide appeal. Globally, the spread and diversity of choral activity has been breathtaking.

It is relevant to consider the role choral music plays in modern society. One widely held view is that choral music is significant primarily for its social bonding function.[2] Another view is that it is a compelling and wholesome activity for individual participants. If playing in a brass band is good for the soul ('a boy who blows a horn won't blow a bank'), the discipline of singing in a good choir is similarly useful and empowering.

Another belief still strongly held is that artistic choral music can engender aesthetic growth while imparting pleasure. It is claimed that aesthetic maturity is developed by music like J. S. Bach's *St Matthew Passion*, Samuel Barber's choral version of his *Agnus Dei*, Ēriks Ešenvalds' 'Only in Sleep' and *Spring Rain*, or Colin Brumby's 'Come Away, Death'. Two New Zealand compositions that could be regarded in the same vein are Jack Body's 'Carol to St. Stephen', and Ross Harris's 'Requiem for the Fallen'.[3] There is also anecdotal evidence that choral music provides an accessible entry point into the other arts.

Choral music also provides the ability to transcend the everyday world. According to Austrian-born American sociologist Peter Berger, ecstasy is 'any experience of stepping outside the taken-for-granted reality of everyday life'.[4] He, with others, argued that any life that lacks the capacity for ecstasy, wonder or awe is a profoundly impoverished one. An overwhelming feeling of ecstasy can be experienced through choral singing. Through the discipline of finely wrought rehearsals, techniques are acquired by which the trivial and ordinary are transcended, and the capacity for intense delight is sharpened. There is nothing particularly mystical or unusual about this. Quite simply, quality choral singing provides opportunities to respond to the ecstatic, enriching everybody's lives.

Not surprisingly, Dr John Rutter, one of the world's most prominent choral composers, applauds the worth of choral music. It is not one of life's 'frills', he says, but:

> something that goes to the very heart of our humanity. . . . When you sing, you express your soul.
>
> People . . . pouring out their hearts and souls in perfect harmony is a kind of emblem for what we need in this world, when so much of the world is at odds with itself. . . .
>
> Everybody who has sung in a choir tells me that they feel better for doing it . . . somehow you leave your troubles at the door . . . you walk away refreshed.
>
> Music is like a great oak tree that rises up from the centre of the human race and spreads its branches everywhere. [The values of music shine like a beacon] and choral music must stand as one of the supreme examples of it.[5]

One intention of this book was to determine why some of our choirs have become so good. It quickly became clear that the answer was complex. Interviews with skilled practitioners revealed that, learning from their own experiences, they tended to have in mind a three-point model for success: auditioned, coached voices; quality, challenging repertoire; and a trained, visionary conductor. They omitted a fourth (probably necessary) component, which has mainly been ignored: resonant performance spaces. Acoustically reverberant spaces with high, sound-reflective ceilings are necessary if singers and directors are to find reassurance and inspiration in performance and for audiences to feel sufficiently rewarded.

All four components have played roles in New Zealand choral music's rise to excellence. An aim of this book has been to look for specific evidence that the four

The National Youth Choir performing in the fine acoustic space of the Cathedral of the Blessed Sacrament in Christchurch, 1982. Peter Godfrey is at far left and Guy Jansen at far right. CHOIRS AOTEAROA NZ points have contributed to the high quality of our best choirs. The search involved, for voices, choirs whose members had voice training, conductors who began with a singing background or had developed their vocal expertise, and groups that invited a vocal coach into rehearsals. For repertoire, it involved looking for the effect of musical choices (from mediocre to artistically imaginative), including New Zealand compositions, on discerning choral musicians and their futures. For conducting, it meant looking for the effect of a trained conductor on a choir's performance. With performance spaces, it involved looking for the influence of nurturing acoustics, comparing Wells Cathedral and the Dunedin and Wellington town halls to the more challenging Llangollen Pavilion in Wales, where New Zealand conductor and musical director Karen Grylls had great success in 1999, and contrasting these with the disastrously dry acoustics of many New Zealand halls that have had to be used; and the confronting demands of outdoor singing.

As well as investigating the criteria for successful choirs, it has been relevant to note which individuals have risen to prominence and, more broadly, to see how choral music has been treated in historical works along with its place in the arts today.

Music enthusiasts can be inclined to claim more for their heroes than might be justified, and sometimes the work of other notables in the field is overlooked because of lack of information about them. Of course, there is usually no problem in determining who was 'the greatest of them all'. Phil Garland, called the 'godfather of New Zealand folk music', dedicated over 50 years of his life to collecting, interpreting and preserving the songs of our colonial past; he recorded 19 albums, and received awards for his pioneering work. There were no other front-runners. There was also little debate about Kevan Moore being named the 'godfather of New Zealand music TV' after his unique, creative impact in television musical entertainment in the 1960s and 1970s. In the operatic realm we have been fortunate in being able to accommodate two dames: Dame Malvina Major and Dame Kiri Te Kanawa. It would be a brave person, however, to decide who should be honoured as the greatest in New Zealand's popular music industry.

It didn't take long to find enthusiastic anointing of prominent individuals in the choral sphere. In the late nineteenth century, choral conductor Robert Parker, for nearly 60 years the doyen of Wellington musicians, was described as a 'father of New Zealand music'. In 1936, Victor Peters in Christchurch was said to be as good as the leading British choral conductors of the day. In the same year, Stanley Oliver's Wellington Schola Cantorum was considered by Australia's leading conductor, Sir Bernard Heinze, to be probably the finest choir of its kind in the world. Maxwell

Fernie's Catholic Choir at St Mary of the Angels, also in Wellington, had by the mid-1960s gained a worldwide reputation through its first LP recording.

In 2015, Peter Godfrey was described as the 'father of New Zealand choral music'. Elizabeth Kerr accurately points out that 'our choral tradition was born a century before his arrival [in 1958, from England]'.[6] She quotes John Mansfield Thomson when describing that formative time: 'The colonial choral society was an awesome sight: tiers of ladies in billowing white, bearded gentlemen in black, beneath a panoply of organ pipes.'[7]

Kerr goes on to say that 'Prof', as Godfrey was affectionately known, 'may not have fathered our choral tradition, but has left an indelible stamp upon it'. What may be relevant for New Zealand's large choral community now is to ponder a generous but more precise place for Godfrey. That is also an intention of this book. I worked with him for several years, having initially invited him into the National Youth Choir organisation as Principal Guest Conductor and, like thousands of others, had the greatest of admiration for him.

A new way will be needed to appropriately acknowledge New Zealand's most prominent female choral conductor, Karen Grylls. She not only enhanced the existing choirs she was appointed to, but also thrust her own creation, Voices New Zealand Chamber Choir, into the international spotlight, drawing comparisons with Team New Zealand in the America's Cup and the All Blacks in world rugby. Her successful postgraduate work with a new generation of choral leaders, and her leading, in 1999, of arguably this country's best ever choir to the 'Choir of the World' triumph speaks for itself.

During research, it became apparent that few New Zealanders know that choir singing is this nation's most popular participatory art form or that New Zealand choirs have been very successful in prestigious overseas competitions. This lack of knowledge is reflected in poor coverage of the topic in general New Zealand history books. Historians Keith Sinclair (1959) and Michael King (2003) are virtually silent on the place of music in society. James Belich's two-volume standard history of New Zealand contains references to music ranging from accounts of lively music, opera and theatre when the major goldfields were discovered in 1861 (including the assemblage of circus, vaudeville, folklore and ballads that existed in the goldfields culture) to a reminder that from the late nineteenth century almost 60 New Zealanders had become international opera stars.[8] He documents the over-representation of Māori among professional singers, 'of whom they comprise 32 per cent compared with 15 per cent of the general population'. But in over 1100 pages there are few mentions of group singing.[9]

The arts are referred to in general by Belich. For example, the Wellington Arts Festival is seen as internationally competitive; avant-garde expatriate Kiwi artists, such as Len Lye and Billy Apple, made reputations overseas; Split Enz achieved national icon status by 1984. However, Belich writes not a word about Douglas Lilburn, Dame Gillian Whitehead, Jenny McLeod, Ngāpō (Bub) Wehi, Sir William Southgate or other prominent composers and conductors, nor does he provide any information about choirs and the sizeable choral community that had evolved by the beginning of the new millennium. Standout choral achievers like Robert Parker, Stanley Oliver, Maxwell Fernie and Peter Godfrey are notable for their absence.

More recent histories by Giselle Byrnes (2009) and Philippa Mein Smith (2012) also ignore choral dimensions.[10] There is virtually no mention of choral works in the 2011 book *Just Like Us: Aspects of New Zealand Music*.[11] Peter Lineham (2017) is one of the exceptions among historians, with perceptive, scholarly comments about choirs in colonial society, the many roles of choirs in all church denominations, music being 'a symbol of intellectual cultivation' in the new colony, and a heavy English influence, including 'the Victorian love of ornateness'.[12] Passionate New Zealander John Mansfield Thomson was a knight in shining armour for the choral cause. His recorded talks and writings often illuminate the subject, including entries in his milestone publication, *The Oxford History of New Zealand Music* (1991).[13]

The challenge for historians is to not marginalise the arts, and the fact that they have not adequately described how the arts have contributed to our national life and vision has made it more difficult to discern the distinctive character of Aotearoa New Zealand. William Renwick, scholar and Director-General of Education from 1975 to 1988, often commented on New Zealand's emerging sense of national identity. In an address in which he noted how two very different traditions — Pākehā painting and Māori carving — had influenced each other, he made the observation that 'encouraging the arts in cultural diversity is one consequence of taking multiculturalism seriously'.[14] Renwick would undoubtedly have agreed that before the arts can be encouraged, people must know about them in their diverse cultural contexts and how they enhance our lives in a multicultural society.

Cambridge historian G. M. Trevelyan once wrote: 'Let the science and research of the historian find the fact and let his imagination and art make clear its significance.'[15] We need better coverage of the wide range of the arts now functioning in society, with greater attention given to the influence of social and cultural institutions.

Perhaps the reason a book telling the choral story has not previously been produced is that experienced choral practitioners have been too busy. They are usually drawn into over-engaged, year-round commitments, leaving almost no time for reflection or research. It was only in 2011, when I took permanent leave of the three choirs I was conducting, that I thought I would have the time, inclination and energy to consider taking up the challenge.

Along with prominent figures in choral history, the names of many choir accompanists are mentioned. Good accompanists often don't receive the respect that they deserve, and poor accompanists can effectively derail the best of choirs. Of course, it's not only accompanists but also assistant conductors, vocal coaches, committee members, administrators, managers and musicians who train choruses for operas and musicals, among others, who help the choral industry thrive.

If accompanists have often had a bad rap, conductors have sometimes been completely painted out of the picture. There's an odd practice of naming a choir without identifying its conductor, as though a choir can do a wonderful job without a director. While some ensembles are set up to work well without an obvious conductor, the majority of choirs rise or fall according to the abilities of the person out front, so a conductor's name has been added where appropriate.

Composers and arrangers can also find themselves in the forgotten brigade, with often a choral title mentioned but without the name of composer or arranger. We need to know the composer's name for each choral piece. If it's not given, there can be amusement, frustration or bewilderment — and there's also the small matter of disrespect to the composer.

The narrative is placed in the context of New Zealand's changing social and cultural life and it also takes some account of national personality traits. New Zealanders are often depicted as laid-back, understated, suitably humble, sometimes self-deprecating and not wanting to be taken too seriously, and also displaying a 'can-do' attitude. This theme is taken up again in the final chapter.

Nau mai rā ki ngā kōrero i huataki mai nei i te whitu rau tau ki muri i te wā ko Aotearoa tētahi o ngā whenua takitahi o te ao kia nohoia e te tangata.

So, welcome to the story which began about 700 years ago, when Aotearoa New Zealand was one of the few countries in the world still to be settled.

1

The heritage of Māori song and the birth of a new tradition

Over 700 years ago, groups of people in Aotearoa New Zealand were singing together. The story of choral music in this country begins there, and this chapter examines what that group singing was like, how it developed, and how it has influenced choir music in this country over the past 200 years.

Polynesians exploring the Pacific discovered Aotearoa, 'The Land of the Long White Cloud', in the thirteenth or fourteenth centuries.[1] Some traditions credit the navigator Kupe, in his waka hourua (double-hulled voyaging canoe), with making the discovery. It is likely that many waka hourua made return journeys between Aotearoa and the original homelands in Eastern Polynesia as migration took place.

These first settlers brought with them a culture and a history recorded in whakapapa (genealogy), arts (including carvings of many kinds), and in waiata (songs).

Waiata were at the heart of the settlers forging a life in this new land. Waiata transmitted knowledge and beliefs, and they were used in rituals and to communicate with the deities. Singing was important in 'recording the deeds of ancestors, lamenting losses, calling to a lover or marking the birth of a child', and played a dynamic part in Māori life, for personal, social and spiritual reasons.[2]

Unison chant, deriving from Eastern Polynesia, was the basis of Māori singing. Chants often employed only three or four notes, within a range as small as a minor third. There were many kinds of chants; for example, for paddling a canoe, or for going to war. There were lullabies, waiata aroha (love songs) and waiata tangi (laments). The pātere was a lively genre with usually abusive lyrics composed by slandered women and accompanied by defiant gestures. According to Māori scholar and composer Sir Tīmoti Kāretu, it was revived as the preferred genre of the younger Māori generation in the late twentieth century. Performed mainly on a rhythmic monotone, the pātere represents a vital part of the ancient unison chant tradition.

Classical, ancient Māori chant is collectively described as mōteatea. Over a 40-year period, scholar and politician Sir Āpirana Ngata gathered and recorded hundreds of waiata, and his collection, *Ngā Mōteatea*, was first published in 1928–29. Lullabies, laments and songs of love were the three main categories of waiata mōteatea, but he also included other forms: ruri (amorous songs), mata (prophetic songs), waiata tira (choral songs without actions) and karakia (incantations and prayers).[3]

Harmony (singing in three or more melodic parts) was 'absolutely unknown' in Māori culture.[4] Through most of the twentieth century, Westernised four-part harmony has been a standard part of Māori hymn singing, and of waiata-ā-ringa (action songs), but before Pākehā arrived, it was unheard of.

However, a tradition of singing in groups had developed. This was because a chant required a continuous sound from beginning to end. While a solo singer would need to stop regularly to take breaths, members of a group could breathe at different places to keep the sound going. It was because a group was *always* needed that a Māori solo singing tradition didn't develop. As Kāretu points out, 'a solo singer would never have been able to satisfy the dictates of the art'.

The pre-eminence of chant singing before the arrival of Europeans is clear, and it must have required a very disciplined approach, because each category of traditional chant had its own distinctive melodies and tempi. Some chants were microtonal (a microtone being any interval smaller than a semitone) and these chants must have required intensive listening and practice.[5] Westerners tend to find quartertones or other microtones difficult even to hear, let alone sing.

A Māori group singing a chant would have been heard by the crew of James Cook's *Endeavour* in 1769 when they went ashore in Poverty Bay on the North Island's east coast. Cook was the second significant European explorer to arrive in New Zealand, the first being Dutchman Abel Tasman in 1642, who did not venture ashore. Cook himself found the music 'very doleful to a European ear', and thought that they sang 'in semitones', while his officers were dismissive of the musical ability of 'the natives'. On a later voyage, Cook had on board a young James Burney, son of Charles Burney, the famous English music historian, and Burney thought that there was 'no great variety in the Music'. There were other remarks in a similar vein.

There is a mystery, however, about what was meant by James Burney's comment in 1773 after he heard a performance by a young warrior, Ihaka Te Rangihouhia, and his party: 'Sometimes they sing an underpart which is a third lower, except for the last 2 notes which are the same.'[6] Choral expert Karen Grylls and others interpret the comment as demonstrating singing in harmony.[7] It could be argued, however, that the underpart was a horizontal variant of the chant, not vertical note-clusters or harmony. There are no triads (three-note chords) involved, therefore there is no 'harmony' as traditionally understood; it is made up solely of intervals, which, by definition, consist of two notes only.[8]

Understandably, Burney's Western ears would have perceived the underpart harmonically, not realising that the indigenous people didn't employ harmony, though the aural *impression* of harmony that the Te Rangihouhia performance could have given was real enough. But the motivation of the singers could have had a much different aim: to give variety to the chant and to respect the status of the chant by coming back to it every now and again with unisons.

No Europeans coming in contact with the original inhabitants of Aotearoa could discern the practised microtonal idiom and idiosyncratic musical style that Māori were displaying. And visiting sailors weren't to know that they had come upon a group singing culture, whose songs had for centuries been an integral part of both ceremonial occasions and everyday life.

Māori culture group Ngaru Kaha, from Whangārei, during Waitangi Day celebrations in 2009. ALAMY/PAUL KENNEDY

When the missionary Samuel Marsden sailed from Sydney to New Zealand for a second time in 1815, his right-hand man, John Liddiard Nicholas, wrote a very different account of the singing of Māori who were travelling on board the ship:

> a plaintive and melodious air and seemed not unlike some of our sacred music . . . as it forcibly reminded me of the chanting in our cathedrals, it being deep, slow and extended. . . . It was divided into parts, which the chiefs sang separately, and were joined in chorus, at certain intervals, by the other New Zealanders, while they all concluded it together.[9]

In time, harmonised singing became a part of the Māori repertoire, and kapa haka (performing groups) included songs based on popular Pākehā tunes. Tin Pan Alley in Manhattan, New York, was the source of many popular traditional American songs borrowed by kapa haka groups in the early twentieth century. Māori culture became infiltrated by a Western musical system, but there were differences: finding the harmony of a song was not taught by a tutor but was left to individuals within the group. There was no conductor; the singer's ear dictated where one should go musically. This aural/aesthetic ability is not confined to Māori but has become a marked feature of disciplined, beautiful choral singing at Māori performing arts festivals (see Chapters 7 and 13).

As Kāretu points out, all latter-day performing Māori groups could, in the broadest sense, be called choral groups, including those that sing the waiata-ā-ringa (action songs), which is often performed with the poi, a lightweight ball swung rhythmically on a string. The combination of polished harmony with fluid movement results in a 'beautiful amalgam of sound'.[10] It is finely rehearsed, yet spontaneity is never lost, and the passion and power of the performance is as evident in faces and body movement as it is in the voice.

One of the best-known forms of Māori group performance is the haka. The term kapa haka (which literally means a group of people lined up in rows, or a haka group) refers to the art forms of waiata, poi and waiata-ā-ringa, as well as to haka such as 'Ka Mate!', composed by Ngāti Toa leader Te Rauparaha and made famous by New Zealand's national rugby team, the All Blacks. The haka is a song, or rhythmically shouted cries, accompanied by vigorous dancing, expressing a life force and traditionally used as part of the formal process of challenge and response when two parties meet. There have been many variations of haka and they run the whole gamut of human experience.[11]

TOP 'Messieurs Marsden and Nicholas passing a night with the Zealanders'. Samuel Marsden and John Liddiard Nicholas prepare to sleep with Māori at Matauri Bay, Bay of Islands, November 1814. ALEXANDER TURNBULL LIBRARY, PQ266CHO1838[4405]

BELOW The All Blacks perform the haka before a match against the Australian Wallabies at Eden Park, Auckland, on 15 August 2015. DPA PICTURE ALLIANCE/ALAMY STOCK PHOTO

In 1942, New Zealand poet Allen Curnow wrote tellingly: 'Always to islanders danger is what comes over the sea.'[12]

The artistic danger for the New Zealand 'islanders' was that, at any time after the arrival of Abel Tasman or James Cook, Māori might begin to lose their musical heritage with its microtonal legacy, vocal embellishments and powerful impact. There appears to have been little research on the typical nature of Māori vocal tone, but it is likely affected by factors such as how often the singing voice is used, whether the singing is outdoors (more nasal quality and chest voice) and whether they sing on the larynx or from the diaphragm.

In 1949, Ngata, in an introduction to *Ngā Mōteatea*, lamented this loss, which resulted from the dominance of a Pākehā scheme of education: 'The ear of the Māori has become less and less receptive to the notes of his native music, less discerning of its scale of quarter tones and more inclined . . . to be satisfied with the songs and the music, which the races of the world, except his own, serve out to him "ad nauseum".'[13] While Māori were, in fact, to lose aspects of their traditions, Pākehā settlers were to gain enormously in the long term. Pākehā choirs, trained in an English style, at first did not understand Māori music and as a result brought prejudicial judgements to it. But, over time, early settlers came to appreciate the natural resonance, the rich vocal timbres, and the vitality and innate musicality of Māori music. The taonga of Māori singing came to be seen for the gift that it was.

Samuel Marsden's own story, recorded in his journal, about the first Christian service on New Zealand soil on Christmas Day 1814, is that he began it with a psalm commonly known as the 'Old Hundredth'. This part of our nation's history was begun by a sizeable crowd formally singing together.

> Oihi Beach, Bay of Islands 1814
>
> A very solemn silence prevailed — the sight was truly impressive. I rose up and began the service with singing the Old Hundredth psalm . . .[14]

It was a fine, still morning in a secluded bay in northern New Zealand. The crowd gathered on a white-sand beach, with scarlet pōhutukawa in bloom along the shore. Fantails, tūī, the shining cuckoo and the rasping kākā — New Zealand's exceptional abundance of birds provided a spectacular singing soundscape.[15]

All this was a surprising setting for the birth of a new singing tradition. Slowly,

Samuel Marsden at Oihi Beach, Bay of Islands, Christmas Day 1814. To Marsden's right is Ruatara, a Ngāpuhi leader, dressed in British regalia. PAINTING BY RUSSELL STUART CLARK, ALEXANDER TURNBULL LIBRARY, B-077-006

about 300 people gathered, including Māori and a handful of Pākehā, from a ship anchored in the bay, plus 30 or so from Marsden's brig, *Active*. Many of the passengers would have known the psalm as 'All People that on Earth do Dwell'. There were five missionaries and their wives aboard the *Active*, and some of their children would also have been familiar with the piece. Also present from the ship were Ruatara, a young leader of the local iwi Ngāpuhi, other Ngāpuhi leaders Hongi Hika and Korokoro, and up to four other Māori. They had been to Marsden's Sydney home for extended periods where this, the most common of psalms, would have been sung from time to time. Perhaps that is why Marsden chose it for this first service.

Ruatara had invited Marsden to preach at his settlement, Rangihoua, and he translated the sermon as it was delivered. He and other local Māori would have been keen to make the event a success, and the half dozen Māori who had sung the song before would arguably have sung it with gusto. The de facto 'choir' of the day could also have included some of the crew and companions of Marsden's ship — sailors, sawyers, a blacksmith and a stowaway convict — unauditioned raw recruits who formed a most unlikely ensemble for such a prestigious occasion. No doubt clarity of words and unified vocal tone were absent, as were blend, balance and breath management, or vibratos wide enough to jump through. Certainly the 200-year-old classic psalm would not have been heard in 'a magnificent burst of harmony', such as at an English part-singing festival. If Māori and Pākehā did sing together on that summer morning, the musical offering must have been culturally odd-sounding and diffident. A Māori heritage of sensitive microtone singing was being overtaken by a Western diatonicism. Perhaps, at best, the performance was a kind of ragged, bilingual choral chant.

Regardless of the aesthetic quality and impact of the performance, however, the beach congregation shared in an experience that could legitimately be called 'choral'. It didn't matter whether the unison singing with a little harmony was in tune or out of tune, in time or out of time, even barely audible, or whether Marsden's leadership was musical or merely 'happily enthusiastic'. After all, the 'choir' wasn't rehearsed.

Māori had sung corporately (gathering 'in the bonds of love') for several centuries before 1814. Equally, the Europeans present shared a long history of group singing. Two very different traditions came together on that sunny Northland beach. So, did Christmas Day 1814 witness the birth of a distinctively new choral tradition in New Zealand, one that would eventually blend Māori and Pākehā? Or is that claim too audacious?

In time, the new choral art form being established in New Zealand would feature indigenous and introduced elements, high art and popular art, many musical genres and styles, fabulously deep performances as well as fads and fashions. Choir music would become societally pervasive and widely accepted everywhere.

The basic fabric of Māori communal singing was already in place. The foundations of a European-influenced choral edifice were, however, to be laid slowly; for a long time they would look a little like a patchwork quilt. To understand the beginnings of the Pākehā culture in New Zealand it is to the musical scene in England at the time that we now must turn.

2

Colonial music and choral beginnings

A London-based event in 1784, which has been described as 'the most important single event in the history of English music' and 'almost a state occasion', had a profound effect on choral singing in the nineteenth century.[1] The Handel Commemoration, which celebrated the twenty-fifth anniversary of Handel's death through a series of spectacular concerts, fostered the formation of choral societies throughout England. Handel's highly respected oratorios alternated with other major works such as Mendelssohn's *Elijah* and *St Paul* in well-attended performances.

By the early nineteenth century, singing had become a widely accepted pastime in English public life — in pubs, around pianos in homes, and in choirs and churches. The fresh-sounding hymns of Charles Wesley, Isaac Watts and others were popular in lively Methodist gatherings and other non-conformist denominations. The days had not yet arrived when orchestral music would be more dominant than choral singing or opera; England's strongest roots were in choralism.

Handel's initial performances of *Messiah* in Dublin and London in 1742–43 featured very modest forces, possibly as few as 20 singers and even fewer players. It is thought that Handel saw these chamber-sized ensembles as suited to the buoyant rhythms, brisk tempi, crisp articulation and contrasting textures and phrasings of his oratorio.

By way of contrast, the Handel Festival Choirs (and other combined choirs) in the Crystal Palace, built in London in 1851, sported more than 3000 voices with orchestras of over 500. This tradition of massive performances, beginning in the late eighteenth century, is a world away from the slimmed-down 'authentic' presentations of the late twentieth century. However, the eighteenth-century tradition did help to propel choral music to the forefront of the flourishing commercial concert life of the time. Large-scale works were popular with singers and audiences in concert halls and churches for over 150 years.[2] The enormous impact of Handel's oratorios on the rise of English choral music is confirmed by Handel authority Jens Peter Larsen.[3]

Arguably, it was during the eighteenth and early nineteenth centuries that the arts came of age in Great Britain. In the visual arts, two genres were particularly strong: portraiture (with Gainsborough, Reynolds and others) and landscape painting (Constable and the controversial J. M. W. Turner). Growing British prosperity led to greatly increased production of both fine art and the decorative arts. This was also the time of the Romantic poets — Blake, Wordsworth, Coleridge, Byron, Shelley and Keats — as well as leaders in the English novel, architecture and other art forms.

In addition to being rich artistically, Britain was militarily and politically the strongest power in the world. Victoria's reign (1837–1901) saw great cultural expansion, with advances in science, industry and communications.[4] The people were proud of their national status and of their Empire. This awareness, along with a common heritage of singing and faith, helped build a more or less unified citizenry with an optimistic outlook on the world and its future.

It is unsurprising, then, that New Zealand's early British settlers wanted to continue their involvement in the arts, particularly choral music, and it didn't take long for the traditions of the 'Old Country' to take root in the new world.

Even on the way from Britain to New Zealand aboard the immigrant ships, there

TOP The Crystal Palace, originally built in Hyde Park in 1851, became the most important single location for public music-making in the United Kingdom. Able to accommodate audiences of over 20,000, it was destroyed by fire in 1936. CHRONICLE/ALAMY

BELOW The orchestra and choir of the Wellington Music Festival, 1894. PHOTOGRAPHER LOUISA MARIAN HERMANN. ALEXANDER TURNBULL LIBRARY, PACOLL-3351-1

was a lot of music-making. With a large number of travellers wanting to sing on the long voyage out, groups were set up to sing glees and other part-songs.[5] The *Charlotte Jane* arrived in Lyttelton Harbour in 1851 with a lively glee club drawn from its 151 passengers. In their own small way such glee clubs would contribute to Christchurch becoming the 'most English' of New Zealand cities. Teacher and musician Charles Merton arrived at Lyttelton in December 1856 after a journey of over three months, and 'His face brightened up upon being told we had a Choral Society, and that he was just in time for a concert'.[6] British traditions were always in settlers' minds; for many, English music was an integral part of their culture.

One tradition that did not transfer to New Zealand was the west gallery band, common in English churches until the mid-nineteenth century, when the church organ became popular. These bands began as groups of villagers singing from a gallery at the west end of a church. Later, instrumentalists reinforced the sound, and a number of bands used a vamphorn — a long megaphone — that amplified the voice. The atmosphere was very different from the choir-robed dignity of cathedrals. However, ordinary anthem-singing parish choirs began to be established in New Zealand in the 1860s, at about the same time as they were in England.[7]

Many musical activities flourished from the very beginning of the colony. Music teaching (for example, pianoforte, voice and harp) was sometimes available even when there were few settlers. Private schools were quick to offer music tuition. In July 1857, a Mrs Wilson announced her intention of teaching music in addition to 'the rudiments of an English Education' in a school that she was opening on Willis Street, Wellington.[8] Earlier, a Miss Hurst had advertised a 'Ladies School', where the terms for boarders were £28 per annum with 'Music, Dancing, and Washing extra'.[9] The curriculum of the best provincial (public) schools, which was the same curriculum as that evolving in elementary schools in England, included music.[10] Even such small recognition of music would have contributed to its status, and an appreciation of its importance, and was an acknowledgement of a developing artistic life in the colony. Soon there were soirées at the homes of the more affluent, performances by military bands, hymns sung in churches, and even hastily arranged solo concerts for new arrivals.

The appearance of specifically choral activity came after a critical mass of potential choristers had stepped ashore. Some early settlers had a great passion for choirs. They had brought multiple music copies with them in anticipation of the scores being used with groups of like-minded enthusiasts. In addition, committed singers were willing to attend rehearsals under sometimes very trying circumstances in a new land: 'The establishment of choral societies and church choirs took precedence among the musical activities of early New Zealand life. Busy colonists developed their vocal talents first, and instrumental development followed later — a pattern of musical progress familiar to most civilised countries.'[11]

Some settlers also brought pianos and harmoniums with them. Even though they were expensive to obtain and transport, pianos were part of the furnishings of many colonial houses, so accompaniment for choir rehearsals and performances was assured.[12] Tuning and repair services were rudimentary before 1860, but the industry soon grew.

Over a long period of time, the work of leading choristers and accompanists ensured that the first building blocks of a chorally minded nation were put in place. To appreciate this, it's necessary to trace the rise of choral societies and associated musical leadership from their earliest days.

Soon after settlements began appearing around Wellington Harbour in 1840, the Wellington Philharmonic Society was founded. This group, which presented English anthems along with Handel and Mendelssohn oratorios from 1848 onwards, appears to have been the first choir to be formed in any of the main centres.

A group that was later to achieve 'Royal' status, becoming the Royal Wellington Choral Union, was established about 12 years later. Englishman Robert Parker assumed the directorship of the Choral Union in 1878, and in that same year he performed the Wellington premiere of Mendelssohn's *Elijah*. Parker had left an illustrious career in England, his frail health taking him to Christchurch in search of a better climate. He first held a church choir position, then moved on to St Michael and All Angels in Christchurch three years later, before settling permanently in Wellington.

Apart from cathedral choirs there were many other church choirs through which choristers learned both a love for choral singing and some of the disciplines required. In Wellington there were thriving choirs at Baptist and Congregational churches, and at St John's Presbyterian Church on Willis Street. Later, in 1913, a choir was founded at Wesley Methodist Church, Taranaki Street, by Harold Temple White. Originally from England, White held the position of organist and choirmaster at the Methodist Church for 46 years.

A confident young Danish immigrant formed a choir in 1896. Violinist and music teacher Christian Overbye had trained at the Royal Conservatorium in Copenhagen, and besides taking on pupils and giving concerts in Wellington, he established the Scandinavian Choral Singers. A remarkable photograph overleaf shows the 11 voices being conducted with a baton by Overbye, probably at a Scandinavian Society picnic at Kaiwharawhara Stream.[13]

The Auckland Choral Society (ACS) was founded in 1855 by Joseph Brown, who was its enthusiastic conductor until 1881. Brown had been conductor of the Musical Society at Eton in England and had come to Auckland with his family of nine. The ACS's repertoire was similar to that of the Wellington Philharmonic, with its anthems and oratorios, and was typical of other choirs forming at the time. The music selections of the first five decades of the ACS focused almost entirely on sacred and secular British music, European operatic arrangements, and compositions by a number of Auckland residents.

Under Brown's direction, the choir grew to 200 singers, presenting masterworks as well as traditional glees and madrigals. Brown also formed a choir of 60 picked voices at St Matthew's Church and introduced psalm singing into public worship at St Andrew's Presbyterian Church.

The ACS's second and influential conductor was German-born violinist Carl Gustav Schmitt, who had undertaken musical training in Italy. He was said to be a masterly conductor and 'his kind and genial manner endeared him to members of the ACS and his many pupils'; increasingly larger audiences soon filled the purpose-built Choral Hall to overflowing.[14]

In 1888, Schmitt received the Chair of Music at Auckland University College. He resigned from the ACS 11 years later because of ill health and was succeeded by the rather remote Dr W. E. Thomas, who had come especially from England to conduct the ACS and occupy the university music chair. Other Auckland conductors during the nineteenth century included Thomas Outhwaite, founder of the Sacred Harmonic Society.

Dunedin's Harmonic Society was established in 1856 by a Miss Redmayne and others.[15] The society was amalgamated with another group seven years later, and it gave what appears to be the country's first performance of Handel's *Messiah*. By 1864, after the discovery of gold in 1861, Dunedin had become a leading financial centre, and with increasing commerce and industry came a desire to showcase cultural achievements and offer greater choices in leisure-time activities. With the formation of the (combined) City of Dunedin Choir, the financially buoyant city could boast the 'strongest musical society in New Zealand', attempting major works not approached elsewhere.[16] Early conductors were George West, A. J. Towsey and James Coombs.

Christchurch was the last main centre to begin a choral group: the Christchurch Choral Class in 1857. (The nearby Port of Lyttelton had advertised 'choral classes' earlier, in July 1852, and a fully formed choral society appeared there later the same year.) The Canterbury Vocal Union, which became the Royal Christchurch Musical

ABOVE Scandinavian Choral Singers, with conductor Christian Overbye, Wellington, 9 November 1896. ALEXANDER TURNBULL LIBRARY, 1/2-052222-F

LEFT Carl Gustav Schmitt, the second conductor of the Auckland Choral Society, 1884. PHOTOGRAPHER ROGER EDWARD FENTON. ALEXANDER TURNBULL LIBRARY, 1/1-001194-G

Society, was established in 1860 with J. F. McCardell as the conductor. Meanwhile, church choirs, such as St John the Baptist Anglican Church (St John's) in Latimer Square, were thriving. The first church built in the city, St Michael and All Angels (1851), offered scholarships to attract choristers as early as 1863. The Christchurch Anglican Cathedral was founded in 1864. The Gothic Revival building was consecrated in 1881 with a choir school set up six months beforehand by choirmaster and organist Harry Wells. Outside of the British Isles, this cathedral choir school was the first of its kind and was destined to become influential through its choristers and conductors.

Robert Parker (later the conductor of the Royal Wellington Choral Union) arrived in Christchurch from England in 1869 to take up an appointment as organist and choirmaster at St John's in Latimer Square, where he was said to have greatly improved the choral service.

The Catholic Pro Cathedral (1887), in Barbadoes Street, Christchurch, later made way for the Cathedral of the Blessed Sacrament, designed by Francis Petre. This latter church, whose acoustic properties became legendary, is probably the country's most obvious example of how a fine acoustic space can help to inspire the greatest of choral singing. Choral musicians deserve the profound encouragement of hearing their best artistic efforts in a responsive, beautiful space.[17]

From the early days of the colony, smaller cities and towns established a variety of vocal ensembles, from choral societies and male voice choirs to amateur opera choruses. New Plymouth, Palmerston North, Hamilton, Tauranga, Napier, Hastings, Invercargill, Whanganui and Nelson were all to develop significant choral traditions. Whanganui, for example, had formed a choral society by 1864. The Wanganui Male Choir was founded in 1898 and is said to have 'never gone into recess in the ensuing years'.[18]

In Timaru, another fine building designed by Francis Petre, Sacred Heart Basilica, has also been an ideal venue for choral performances.

In the case of Nelson, the country's fifth biggest town in the late nineteenth century, developments were dramatic. In 1894 a Nelson choir unwittingly determined the course of musical history in their region. The Nelson Harmonic Society had prospered since its formation in 1860 and had found that it was now able to support the appointment of a full-time conductor. This enabled a distinguished 27-year-old German conductor to come across the world to settle in the town of about 7000 inhabitants.

LEFT Michael Balling, 1913. PHOTOGRAPH BY LAFAYETTE, *THE MUSICAL TIMES*, 1913

OPPOSITE TOP The Nelson School of Music opened in 1901. This purpose-built concert hall and music training school was unique in New Zealand. It was refurbished and enhanced in 1984 and 2018, and is now called the Nelson Centre of Musical Arts. ALEXANDER TURNBULL LIBRARY, PACOLL-5744-25

OPPOSITE BELOW The audience and choir at the Church of Christ anniversary celebrations at the Nelson School of Music. Both the audience and choir pose for the camera. PHOTOGRAPHER FREDERICK NELSON JONES, 1913. ALEXANDER TURNBULL LIBRARY, 1/1-011349-G

Michael Balling had been the youngest of a poor Bavarian family, and because of his good voice he had sung in the choir of the Roman Catholic church that his parents attended.[19] Remarkable progress on the viola meant that he had played with Brahms and Rubenstein and at soirées at the Wagner household. Despite his poor knowledge of English, he seized the opportunity to take the long voyage to New Zealand to recover from a breakdown. According to one writer, he almost didn't arrive: 'He booked a passage on the ill-fated "Wairarapa" but at the request of the Austrian consul, delayed his passage two days. When he got to Auckland, he found the flags at half mast, and learned that the "Wairarapa" had gone down with all her three hundred passengers. In the newspapers he read his own name among the list of the dead.'[20] The only trouble with that widely held story is that Balling had set foot in Nelson a year before.

There was fertile soil for him to till in Nelson. Music had played a key part in the town's life since it was established around 1850. Evening musical parties, the good work of music teachers, the formation of orchestral groups, the effectiveness of the Harmonic Society and enthusiasts in the other arts all contributed to a cultivated, 'high art' settlement with several powerful leaders and wealthy entrepreneurs.

Balling established the Nelson School of Music (with the help of a committee of a mere 47 members) and directed it for three momentous years. His plans to form a conservatorium took final shape in his mind on a tramping trip to Mount Cook. Before

F.N. JONES
PHOTO.
CHURCH OF CHRIST
ANNIVERSARY
SCHOOL OF MUSIC
NELSON. OCT. 22.

setting out on the tramp, he had written to the *Nelson Evening Mail*, protesting the exclusive hold of sport on New Zealand life: 'As a foreigner, I am singularly struck by the prominence given to "sport" of all kinds.' He then soberly laid out a proposal to form a school of music and invited townspeople to be part of the adventure.[21]

That enough Nelsonians followed this pied piper's call speaks volumes about Balling's persuasive powers. His musical energy and credibility were evident; the intensity of his playing and conducting within the new school's concerts aroused tremendous fervour and his lectures were very well attended. Three months after arriving, he conducted Mendelssohn's cantata *Walpurgis Night*, showing clearly the effect of his training of the choir and orchestra. With 'the great power and effects . . . produced . . . the result was quite a revelation'.[22]

Also revealing was the maestro's musical credo. Balling spoke of music as above all the arts, and that it did not belong to this earth but was a divine art.[23] Under Balling and a group of influential friends, a three-year course was devised for the School of Music and future directions were set. Choral music by Haydn, Cherubini and Spohr was presented and Wagner was respectfully acknowledged and commemorated. Before permanently returning to Europe, he played a viola solo to the Māori King and, in Whanganui, was struck by the Māori chants of lament that he heard.

Nelson was indeed fortunate to have had Balling as a catalyst and entrepreneur in developing its choral activity, and his benign influence can still be felt today in Nelson and many other towns in New Zealand. John Mansfield Thomson, who thoroughly researched Balling's era, claimed that Balling gave 'a rare insight into the vision that lies behind great music and its creative role in society'.[24]

The momentum built up by Balling was kept going by those who followed him, especially Julius Lemmer, appointed as principal of the Nelson School of Music in 1899. Lemmer's successes were not long in coming. He was the conductor of the large chorus of the Harmonic Society and in December of his first year the chorus gave a magnificent performance. The idea of equipping the Nelson School of Music with a suitable building (rather than the improvised accommodation in the Harmonic Hall) was raised in 1896 as numbers continued to grow. Designed by the noted architect Frederick de Jersey Clere, and unique in New Zealand, a new building was opened in 1901. With its dual function as a high-quality concert hall and music training school, it has set Nelson apart from all other provincial centres, and its acoustically fine auditorium continues to attract leading national and international performers.

Many groups with varying roles and influences played a role in the fostering of New Zealand's early choral life: administrators, choir committees, sponsors, audiences, community leaders and arts agencies, but especially, of course, singers, conductors and accompanists.

The influence of one of these groups has already been noted: the immigrant singers who had brought sets of music copies with them. However, as seen in Nelson, it was the work of conductors that was critical. Conductors were mainly English settlers and they were mainly men. Widely differing levels of choral expertise didn't seem to matter; colonists who were music-hungry appreciated any available leader. Criticism of choir directors was, evidently, not common. Overt grumblings, moans and disagreements were politely put to one side, apparently sublimated in the bonds of shared song.

These early choral musicians, without thinking about the outcome of their intensive efforts, were slowly moving towards the creation of an impressive enterprise: a nation's lively choral soul. Apart from exceptional people like Michael Balling, their work was modest, but more choral action was soon to be encouraged from overseas sources. These influences were to become crucial, partly because local infrastructure for group singing was often lacking. An example of that deficiency was in school singing.

In the first forty or so colonial years, some schools included singing, but the subject was neglected or limited in most state schools.[25] On the surface, the New Zealand Education Act 1877, with its six 'standards' for vocal music, would appear to have been a big step forward. Vocal music had been modelled on the sight-singing and music theory sanctioned in the English curriculum and had the lofty purposes of being a moral force, important for vocal and aural training and a noble recreational activity. But, unfortunately, as inspectors soon recognised, the teaching of the syllabus presented 'almost insurmountable difficulties' to those teachers who had no previous knowledge of the subject, and vocal music was often looked upon as 'an irksome' and 'unimportant kind of subject' by young teachers.[26] Unlike the majority of subjects, it was exempt from examination, and there was large variation in achievement levels.[27]

To be sure, choral music wasn't benefitting from classroom music education. However, it was about to benefit from the visits of groups from other countries.

3

Visits by overseas choirs

Among the choral groups that came to New Zealand in the late nineteenth and early twentieth centuries, overwhelmingly the most influential choir was one from Sheffield in South Yorkshire. But it was not the first choir to visit this country.

Although many internationally famous instrumental and vocal soloists and opera companies visited New Zealand from the late nineteenth century, no vocal ensembles or choirs, apart from small troupes of African-American minstrels performing spirituals, came here until November 1886, when the Fisk Jubilee Singers arrived. This chorale was associated with Fisk University in Nashville, Tennessee. Called 'the finest company of spiritual singers ever assembled', the nine African-Americans, some of them former slaves, stayed for seven months.[1] They journeyed to many centres by boat, train or horse-drawn carriages, in a tour which could only be described as phenomenally successful. They returned to popular acclaim in 1889, 1905, 1918, 1924 and 1936.

It has been argued that the close harmony of the Fisk Singers' spirituals influenced Māori part-singing, a claim that seems quite feasible. It is easy to imagine an empathy between the two peoples — recognising mutual feelings of oppression and each other's musical abilities. The Fisk Singers shared many occasions with tangata whenua; for example, in hospitable gatherings at Greytown's Papawai pā. One tenor in the ensemble, Yale graduate Robert Williams, came back to New Zealand to settle after the final tour, becoming a notable lawyer, long-serving mayor of Onslow, opera singer, and choirmaster at the Methodist Church on Taranaki Street, Wellington.

The Fisk Singers were followed in 1903 by the Westminster Glee Singers, a small group of 12 to 17 singers (partly drawn from Westminster Abbey) who sang part-songs, glees and madrigals. They returned in 1905 to visit many centres throughout the country, and again in 1927. Their tours were said to be highly successful, but it is difficult to ascertain how influential they were; their repertoire may have worked against them in what was still a pioneering environment.

In 1911, the Sheffield Choir toured the country under the direction of Henry Coward. He claimed to have brought some of England's best singers to New Zealand, to perform works by Handel, Elgar and Verdi as part of a six-month trip around the Empire. In the selection of the 200 members of the Sheffield Choir there was an egalitarian element, part of which still resonates with New Zealand attitudes today. The make-up of the choir was seen to be 'a thoroughly representative one. Some captains of industry and gentlemen of independent means were coming out. . . .' and 'also girls who toil for their daily bread for masters whose daughters sing in the same line with the working girls'.[2]

It was another Englishman, Charles Harriss, musical entrepreneur, conductor and first director of the McGill Conservatorium of Music, Montreal, who had actually

TOP Fisk Jubilee Singers. The dress suggests that this photograph relates to the 1905 tour. IRENE COX COLLECTION, ALEXANDER TURNBULL LIBRARY, PA1-Q-242-477

BELOW Members of the Sheffield Choir in the grounds of Sir Henry Brett's house, Takapuna, in 1911. AUCKLAND LIBRARIES HERITAGE COLLECTIONS NO. T0302 conceived the tour. A rather controversial figure, Harriss had also been the moving force behind an earlier Sheffield Choir tour to Canada.

Henry Coward was the more practical visionary of the two men. His burning desire was simply to tour the world with a first-class choral instrument, bearing good musical news from the Mother Country to far-flung colonies. Harriss had a much more elevated view. It has been said that entrepreneurs are, by their nature, different, weird even, seeing things that most of the population doesn't see. What Harriss saw was an idea of 'musical reciprocity in the British Empire' — an ongoing Empire-wide Music Festival no less.[3] He invested £15,000 in the 'Round the World (British Dominions) Tour' and took 12 months travelling to all the countries involved to set up the venture. The two entrepreneurs joined forces, with Coward taking responsibility for programming, auditioning and rehearsing the choir, selection of eight soloists and so on. Harriss was the organiser of the world tour. Through having married a wealthy widow, he could afford to indulge his love of travel, plan grandiose festivals and gala concerts and have his compositions performed and published.

The 200 singers in the travelling choir were made up of 125 from the Sheffield Choir with the rest from Coward's other choirs. The huge entourage left Liverpool in March 1911 to present 130 concerts in 56 cities from Halifax and Winnipeg to Bloemfontein and Cape Town.[4] Sir Edward Elgar travelled with them to Canada and the United States. The singers spent just over two weeks in New Zealand.

Music historian Nick Strimple says that the visit was 'profoundly influential' on New Zealand society, many musicians' ears being opened to the exciting sound of a world-class choir.[5] The visit was still being remembered and referenced nearly forty years later.[6] All contemporary reports seem to indicate that Coward, through this visit, became one of the most compelling influences in developing New Zealand's choral music-making and composing, and in creating audiences for choral singing.[7]

Henry Coward was the son of a Sheffield cutler and became a young apprentice to that trade, working in it for 12 years. His early interest in music developed from a tonic sol-fa class where he enjoyed using his naturally good voice. Family circumstances meant that not only did he have little education but also he didn't learn piano, organ or any other instrument. As a conductor he was largely self-taught, his conducting ability honed by taking the Huddersfield Choral Society, three other choirs in Yorkshire, and the Glasgow Choral Union, all of which had up to 300 choristers attending. From the beginning, he was known to be patient in the face of mistakes and tactful in difficult situations.

Henry Coward, conductor of the Sheffield Choir, 1902.
PHOTOGRAPHER H. JASPER REDFERN, *THE MUSICAL TIMES*, 1902

Early in his career, Coward was told that his choir performances were mechanically perfect but lacking in expression, colour, interpretation and musical quality. As a result, he made a study of singing; vocal standards at his auditions were soon made more stringent, and rehearsal priorities became diction, unity of vowels, absolute precision and dramatic impact.

As his intuitive understanding of the choral process grew, he came to lay great stress on the words, exhorting his members to 'practise reading aloud at least two pages of the part-song words daily'; he even had the words of every piece being rehearsed printed in a booklet so that, 'being available in handy form, they can be looked over at odd moments in armchair, motor, train or tram'.[8] Along with this emphasis, he continued to demand a high level of sight-reading with either the tonic sol-fa system or traditional staff notation acceptable.

At age 27, Coward founded the Sheffield Tonic Sol-fa Association (later renamed the Sheffield Musical Union and commonly called the Sheffield Choir) and was its director for the next 57 years. Losing a position as a school headmaster at the age of 40 (1889), Coward decided to become a full-time musician, completing Bachelor of Music and Doctor of Music degrees at Oxford.

What kind of man was this person who was said to have brought about 'a revival of singing in chorus which has spread through the whole Empire'? Biographer J. A.

Rodgers gave a forthright assessment of Coward's personal qualities: 'Anyone meeting Dr. Coward for the first time, without any foreknowledge of his personality, would find it difficult to credit that this blunt, tear away personage, with the bluff, hearty speech and unadorned manner, could be the famous musical force whose genius for choir-training has stamped itself directly and indirectly upon the singing of a nation.' His rehearsals were seen as unusual but 'masterly':

> The sentences tumble over each other, while the threads of his argument go astray, and half of them are never recovered. Digression is his strong point. . . . He never shoots his bolt too soon. His choir piles Pelion upon Ossa,[9] as in the Amen chorus in the 'Messiah,' but the master-climax is always held in reserve until the moment when it can be superimposed with overwhelming effect.[10]

When Coward took the Sheffield Musical Union to London in 1904, its singing was clearly a revelation to London audiences. It also drew generous commendation from Austrian and English conductors Hans Richter and Sir Henry J. Wood, and the eminent Austrian Felix Weingartner, who once proposed a toast to Coward: 'England has, so far, beaten Germany in choral singing, and we shall have to send our German conductors to Sheffield to be taught how to train choruses.' Coward later wrote a comprehensive and keenly sought-after book on choir training, and continued to assist conductors seeking his help. Attached to the Sheffield Choir from its beginnings were elementary and advanced singing and theory classes, which formed a training ground for many local choirmasters.

This, then, was the man who conducted his choir in over 40 concerts around New Zealand in the winter of 1911: a warm-hearted autocrat, a physically strong, hard-working self-improver, an innovative director who was often hustling but also charmingly genial. He was a church-going family man with an unadorned manner, sometimes laid-back and self-deprecating, who, if he had lived in New Zealand, would have fitted in with, and made a major contribution to, a developing do-it-yourself choral ethos.[11]

As it turned out, New Zealanders were able to be inspired by the results of his years of choral work only by attending his concerts throughout the country — most people did not see his effectiveness in the engine-room of rehearsals.[12] Even so, they were deeply impressed by him, and by the singing of the Sheffield Choir.

Improved travel within New Zealand meant that the Sheffield Choir was able to visit more than the four main centres. The enthusiasm for the choir was such that, after it arrived in Auckland, 'special arrangements' were made for it to visit New Plymouth, Palmerston North and centres south.[13] The choir had six programmes including three oratorios, a patriotic Empire selection and a miscellaneous collection of English part-songs.

Music historian Matthew Leese provides details of what he calls 'rapturous' audiences — from a performance of *Dream of Gerontius* for an Auckland audience of 4000 in a woolshed, to the huge crowds in Dunedin in the Tram Shed.[14] Hundreds were turned away from the Wellington Town Hall concerts, while a reviewer in the Christchurch *Press* wrote of the choir: 'They have sung themselves into the hearts and the memories of thousands here who now have a standard, never possessed before, by which to measure all choral singing.'[15]

There were also criticisms. Pairing local choirs with the visitors was deemed to be a 'deplorable mistake', heightening the differences in training, balance and timbre — in particular, timbral conflicts with the typically open-throated 'Northern' sound:

> A chorus is only as strong as its weakest link, and when there are two hundred weak links the effect must be bad. The members of the Sheffield Choir know 'Elijah' backwards and sing the whole work from memory. It would be infinitely preferable if they sang without assistance from local musicians whose knowledge of the oratorio is at best defective and whose voices are imperfectly trained.[16]

Charles Baeyertz, editor of *The Triad*, also castigated the organisers for over-scheduling the choir (sometimes five concerts in two days). In addition, he was unhappy with Harriss promoting one of his own compositions, which was described as 'terrible' and an 'inferior, derivative' piece, in juxtaposition to the glorious singing of the Bach motet 'Sing ye to the Lord':

> Here there can be no mistake. The sad truth glares and flames. 'Pan' is a series of flimsily disguised plagiarisms from Wagner, Purcell, Handel, Mendelssohn, Sullivan and Saint-Saëns . . . badly put together. . . . The thing is beneath contempt. . . . It is shockingly bad form to insist on the production of his own reminiscent and tawdry music. . . . A splendid organization like the Sheffield Choir should sing only great choral works.[17]

Then Henry Coward came under attack for his poor conducting of a not altogether satisfactory local orchestra. Baeyertz thought, in fact, that Coward was an inadequate orchestral conductor:

> He seldom gave his orchestra a lead at all, and often in recitative he brought in the chords at the wrong time, with effects the reverse of musicianly. . . . Dr Coward is also anything but helpful to his soloists. I have neither space nor patience to multiply instances, but he beat eight in a bar for *O Rest in the Lord*, with the result that this solo was sung at about half its proper tempo.[18]

For Julius Lemmer, Principal of the Nelson School of Music, Coward committed just too many unpardonable conducting sins, including stopping the oratorio in the middle of a recitative and 'naively' informing the audience that he wanted to bring into the performance the (differently pitched) pipe organ:

> The result, of course, was that when after a Babel of heterogeneous A's, the work was resumed, all continuity was lost. . . . Altogether it was a most inartistic and absurd proceeding, and I doubt whether Dr Coward would have dared do a thing like this in England; and if not there, pray why in New Zealand?[19]

On the positive side, however, I have heard three recorded excerpts of the Sheffield Choir and found the singing superb. Even with the patina of age that accumulates with old recordings, one can hear how powerful the oratorio choruses were: virtually flawless in tone quality, with each part sounding as one. I can believe the numerous reports, which Leese mentions, of the choir's excellence inspiring local choirs 'to much higher standards of discipline, ensemble and tone quality'.[20]

The whole country seemed to hear of the choir's world tour; the *Poverty Bay Herald*, for example, headlined a piece with: 'Quarter of a Ton of Music to be Sung in Seventy Cities', and the *Auckland Weekly News* running a headline: 'A great musical revival: New Zealand's latent talent is aroused by the Sheffield Choir'.

It is little wonder that audiences thought that the choir was so good. Today, we might think that we know all about high entry standards for elite choirs. But to join the Sheffield Choir each candidate had to pass tests for power, quality and intonation of voice, sight-reading in tune and time, attend 100 (consecutive) sectional and united rehearsals and

The Don Cossack Choir with the Ngāti Poneke Concert Party, 1937. PHOTOGRAPHER F. MULLIGAN.
ALEXANDER TURNBULL LIBRARY, PACOLL-0229

promise to learn 150 pieces off by heart. The requirement to practise at least 30 minutes daily almost seems an anticlimax.[21]

One group of auditionees was labelled disdainfully by Coward as 'accomplished — very nice singers who were looking for a cheap trip without doing any work'. He called them the 'la-de-dahs', and they were dismissed at once.

Stringent entry conditions for the touring choir should not come as a surprise. Nor should the fact that colonials continued to look to Britain for firm direction, inspiration and resources. The pre-First World War years in the British Isles were musically sophisticated. There were strong concert-giving institutions, a thriving music publishing trade, a developing and impressive music education system and, in other fields, an expansion of the music-hall industry, and awareness of artistic trends on the European continent. These were the years of Kreisler, Casals, Busoni, and Paderewski playing in Britain. Further afield, Debussy, Stravinsky and Schönberg were challenging age-old traditions and gaining coverage in British papers.

The century-long heritage of amateur and professional-level choral singing was part of a rich British musical culture. Methodical, idealistic, socially minded and pleasurable weekly rehearsals like Coward's in Sheffield were a big part of the choral movement's success. Coward was driven by a profound belief in the importance of what he was doing: 'that choral singing is, and increasingly will be, one of the greatest forces in the social and moral uplift of the human race'.[22] That belief, combined with the optimism of the years before the First World War, fuelled a new choral vision and motivated hundreds of conductors and singers in Britain and New Zealand.

Other choirs also visited New Zealand. Between the world wars, two choral groups in particular were said to make an impression on local audiences. The Italian male principals of the Sistine Chapel Choir completed a provincial tour of the North Island in 1925, singing operatic choruses and arias. According to concert-goers in the Wellington Town Hall, they received an enthusiastic reception. A second group, arriving in 1937, had its roots in the Russian Orthodox Church and was keeping alive the grand tradition of Cossack choral singing and dancing. The popular 27-member Don Cossack Chorus sang Russian folksongs, church music and bright, audience-pleasing songs with dances, but it seems to have had less lasting influence.

Ten visits in 50 years by overseas choirs. These overseas interventions, especially the dramatic 1911 tour of the Sheffield Choir, lifted the sights of New Zealanders to imagine what was desirable and possible. The visits presaged invitations to many of the world's best choirs in future years.

4

Thirty turbulent years from 1914

The human cost of the First World War was traumatic for New Zealand. Among all the British Dominions, New Zealand suffered the most proportionally: nearly one in five soldiers did not return home. Of those who survived, many were injured, and some were seriously incapacitated or suffered from shell shock. The loss of most of a generation of young men had a devastating, far-reaching impact on New Zealand's society and culture.

The war had a clear impact on choral activity: fewer people were available to take part, the number of performances was reduced, and the balance between parts in mixed choirs was seriously disrupted because of the loss of male singers. Some choirs disbanded. In 1918, Robert Parker, at that time conductor of the Wellington Choral Society, wrote to an Auckland friend, 'The war, which seems endless, has paralysed our choral world. I am struggling on to the end of the year with the Society, but it is heart-breaking work.'[1]

A psychological cause for the continued decline in choral music after the war was the trauma and mourning of relatives and friends who had lost loved ones, and their consequent lack of desire to sing. New Zealand wasn't about to burst into song about 'a nation of unmarried aunties'. Rather, a sense of fatigue prevailed throughout the country, a feeling not helped by a frightening influenza pandemic two months after the war concluded.

Choral music wasn't highly developed before the First World War, but now it was starting to unravel. In addition to the direct effects of the war, the unravelling process was aided by several other post-war changes. Instead of returning to or joining choirs, some New Zealanders turned to the newly invented gramophone for relaxation, or to moving pictures, the revue, and later ballroom dancing and radio. As elsewhere in the Western world, radio took the country by storm. In 1925, there were 4702 radio listeners' licences in the country; by 1935 there was an increase of over 3000 per cent, and by 1940, a phenomenal 345,682 licences. Alternative new pastimes and the rise of radio listening were catalysts for a slump in choral music-making, which lasted well into the 1930s.

Another factor was the economy. During the 1920s, New Zealand's fluctuating economic fortunes severely curtailed the redevelopment of music and the arts. A post-war boom was brought to a shuddering halt by a sudden recession in 1921–22, and another downturn followed around 1926. Much worse was to come in 1929 and in the early 1930s, when the Depression engulfed New Zealand along with the rest of the world. A wide gap appeared between rich and poor, extreme hardship was common and there was very little disposable income for cultural or social activities. Immigration tailed off, so there wasn't any money coming in with new migrants, and thousands of workers left the country between 1932 and 1935. New Zealand was up against it. It was no surprise, then, that music and the arts lagged badly.

After 1914, conductors, and the few composers that there were, became progressively out of touch with overseas trends. It is not difficult to see how this happened. Conductors of choirs had plenty of existing repertoires from which to select pieces for rehearsal, particularly from the Victorian and Edwardian eras and from previous centuries. The idioms of these selections became familiar and eventually loved by the pioneering choir members who, having less experience than their European cousins, did not expect their conductors to keep making changes. Equally, there was little pressure on composers to produce fresh-sounding offerings. Choirs generally loved Mendelssohn, but they didn't know that he had said, 'The only things that interest me are new compositions.' Conductors and composers were also out of touch because music was very slow to follow other art forms and they were not inclined to challenge the entrenched conservatism of the day.

In the 1920s, some visual artists began to break free from culturally conformist attitudes. One example was a group of Christchurch artists who set up a modernist group in opposition to the conservative tastes of the Canterbury Society of Arts.[2]

Another example of visual artists breaking free from a conservative outlook was the daring interior designers of the Civic Theatre in Auckland, who in 1929 produced an atmospheric 'riot of Moorish, Indian and Persian imagery'.[3]

As had often happened in earlier eras, it took some time for innovations in the visual arts and literature to be reflected in music. Given the tyranny of distance between the old and new worlds, it was a very long time before modernist developments in European art and music became known and taken seriously in New Zealand. Impressionism and Debussy, neoclassicism and Stravinsky, expressionism and atonality: all of these and much more were a closed book to most in the New Zealand choral fraternity between the two world wars. They weren't aware of possibly the most famous scandal in the history of the performing arts: the 1913 Paris riot caused by Stravinsky's *The Rite of Spring*. Nor would they have known about an incident earlier in the same year, at the Musikverein in Vienna, when a concert of experimental works by Arnold Schönberg and his circle was cut short by police breaking up fistfights in the aisles (one 'spectator' said that the most beautiful music all evening had been the sound of people slapping each other's faces). New Zealand was still a very isolated pioneering society.

The few New Zealanders who identified at the time as composers were all apparently out of this modernist loop — knowing little about developments abroad. There also wasn't any help from Alfred Hill, the only significant composer of his time and the only one who had travelled from New Zealand to study music in Europe. The compositional style of Hill, New Zealand's first fully professional composer, remained basically conservative throughout his long career.

Although born in the nineteenth century, Alfred Hill (1869–1960) remained a force well into the twentieth century. His family moved from Melbourne to New Zealand when he was 18 months old, first to Auckland and then to Wellington, where the young Hill attended Thorndon School. He returned to Wellington in 1891 after musical studies in Leipzig.[4] He was active in violin teaching, recitals and chamber music. But principally he conducted choirs and orchestras, having taken over the conducting of the Auckland Liedertafel at the end of 1904. Until he was 41, Hill was largely based in this country, although he travelled frequently between Australia and New Zealand.

Despite his conservatism, Hill was very interested in Māori music. When he set out to tap into the spirit of Māori waiata, poi, action songs and haka for his choral writing, he established a relationship with Māori communities. 'For weeks at a time,' he wrote, 'I lived at Rotorua, Taupo and Ngaruawahia, wandering among these delightful people to collect material.'[5] This research clearly paid off in his operatic cantata *Hinemoa* (1896), a major work at the time and in which a new Māori element was discernible. Audiences warmed to the familiar story of Hinemoa's love for Tūtānekai, and her daring swim across Lake Rotorua to reach him on Mokoia Island. This was followed by the enormously popular (and of its genre, excellent) 'Waiata Poi', along with other choral miniatures. Hill was a quick composer, and his choral works included a mass, a second cantata on a Māori theme, and 11 other pieces, including *Slumber Song*.

Hill has been mildly criticised for an interest in Māori music said to be 'transient' and 'not deeply rooted in his psyche'. In his defence, it can be said that *Hinemoa* was welcomed by Māori involved in the cantata; Hill pushed for the foundation of an Institute of Māori Studies at Rotorua; his first two string quartets were based on Māori themes; and compositions like 'Waiata Poi' (including arrangements for choral groups) were readily 'owned' by tangata whenua. He had reached out to them before incorporating their stylistic elements. It has taken a master's student from Hong Kong to nicely weigh up the situation. Yuen Ching Lam wrote in 2006: 'Whether it was sympathetic interest, the search for novel materials, the need for a unique identity or the combination of all these reasons, the success of "Hinemoa" led to many subsequent Māori-inspired works in Hill's output. It also prompted the development of his relationship with Māori communities.'[6]

In the late 1950s, New Zealand's pre-eminent composer Douglas Lilburn and fellow-composer Ashley Heenan were interested in Hill's typically conservative style of writing and they went to meet him in Sydney. They noted his pioneering spirit that led him to include indigenous elements in his compositions, but his work seems to have had no influence on them. And it has had little influence on other composers in this country, either at the time or since.

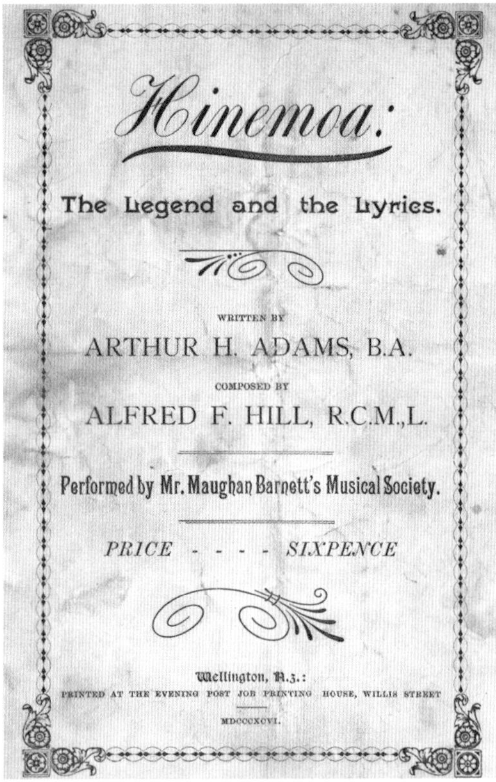

Hinemoa:

The Legend and the Lyrics.

WRITTEN BY

ARTHUR H. ADAMS, B.A.

COMPOSED BY

ALFRED F. HILL, R.C.M.,L.

Performed by Mr. Maughan Barnett's Musical Society.

PRICE - - - - SIXPENCE

Wellington, N.Z.:

PRINTED AT THE EVENING POST JOB PRINTING HOUSE, WILLIS STREET

MDCCCXCVI.

TOP LEFT Portrait of Arthur Henry Adams and Alfred Francis Hill, writer and composer of *Hinemoa*. ALEXANDER TURNBULL LIBRARY, 1/2-111100-F

TOP RIGHT Programme cover for *Hinemoa*, 1896. ALEXANDER TURNBULL LIBRARY, EPH-A-OPERA-1896-01-FRONT

BELOW The stage set for *Hinemoa*, 1896. ALEXANDER TURNBULL LIBRARY, MSY-2498-002

Music historian John Mansfield Thomson tried to find an answer to the puzzle of why the composer's music had 'continually expressed itself in the style of nearly 100 years before — that of the European Romantic composers of his youth'. Thomson thought it sad that Hill had taken 'his training from the mandarins at Leipzig as the final revelation of musical wisdom'. He bemoaned Hill's lapses into Victorian sentimentality. But he couldn't find a compelling reason for Hill's profound conservatism.[7]

By contrast, Victor Peters in Christchurch was a New Zealand-born conductor who did pick up on changes happening overseas. The late Romantic style, still dominant at the turn of the century, was waning and Peters made it his business to obtain samples of works showing new compositional idioms and genres. With the Christchurch Harmonic Society, he tackled Schönberg and other demanding composers with their exacting and oftentimes dissonant, ear-taxing sounds. The choir could manage the difficulties of the music and the sky didn't fall in: Christchurch audiences kept coming to his concerts, and Peters seemed to be re-energised in the process. But the appearances of recent European works in programmes of confident choirs such as this were few and far between.

The entrenched conservatism of the choral world can be seen in the Auckland Choral Society. In 1916, the choir had lost the services of an extremely able conductor, John Maughan Barnett, because the choir's committee insisted on itself selecting concert music. Barnett, who had come to New Zealand from England for health reasons, could have revitalised the choir but disagreed with that policy, particularly considering the unadventurous, even boring, repertoire that the committee constantly chose. He resigned after only two years in the job — a great pity because he was 'one of the country's most talented and versatile musicians'.[8] The Auckland committee seemed oblivious to the fact that their reluctance to accept professional advice had largely contributed to keeping the choral society's programmes dull.[9]

A much more conservative musician who went along with the committee's music selection policy was appointed in 1917 and remained director for 30 years. Joseph Colin Muston, known as Colin, was a busy orchestral and opera conductor in the city and his vocal preferences were for opera rather than choral music. He, like most of his predecessors, had also come from England. He had played violin professionally from the age of 13 and had been deputy conductor of the Leicester Symphony Orchestra.

One of Muston's earliest 'mixed' programmes (orchestral and choral together) with the Auckland Choral Society featured Hill's *Hinemoa*. But the piece had been premiered at the Wellington Industrial Exhibition 21 years earlier and had been since presented in other centres. As historian Adrienne Simpson comments, 'modern compositions, let alone works by New Zealanders, would be rarities over the next three decades' in Muston's programmes.[10]

Muston either ignored overseas programming trends or was ignorant of them, and he showed no resourcefulness in suggesting new repertoire. His stolid, over-careful attitude is a good example of why 'the 1920s and '30s have been labelled the dullest period in New Zealand cultural life'.[11] His purely choral concerts became restricted and repetitive. As good as it is when performed well, the oratorio *Elijah* appeared too many times (seven) over 20 years, and insult was added to injury by another work being presented frequently; as poor as it is even when performed superbly, Samuel Coleridge-Taylor's *The Song of Hiawatha* appeared four times in the same period.

Nevertheless, Muston had many followers. By the time he retired, he was being described as a master musician and was eulogised generously for his devotion to the musical arts in the city. Writers dwelt on 'his enthusiasm and the impact he had made on Auckland's cultural life'.[12]

In the 1920s and 1930s, the directors of New Zealand choirs who were putting their musical pens to paper were almost always writing for only their own groups or for other ensembles well known to them. Edward Douglas Tayler, Vernon Griffiths, Horace Hollinrake, John Bradshaw and Victor Galway all wrote useful, acceptable choral songs, anthems, canticles and other similar work in the English styles with which they had grown up. Evidently, they didn't know much about or weren't interested in what their colleagues in Europe and Britain were currently exploring. Even in the late 1930s and early 1940s the news hadn't got through. The musical doldrums were threatening to become enshrined in a very insular tradition.

At the same time, there was some evidence of positive attitudes, choirs battling to survive and new choral life. In numerical terms, the amount of choral singing was

OPPOSITE TOP The Salvation Army Choir, 1927. PHOTOGRAPH BY CROWN STUDIOS ALEXANDER TURNBULL LIBRARY, 1/1-032829-F

OPPOSITE BELOW Members of the Presbyterian Church Choir in Winton (Southland) pictured in the choir stall in front of the pulpit and pipe organ, about 1916. PRESBYTERIAN RESEARCH CENTRE ARCHIVES, REF P-A 421.1-1

growing, with the formation of Scottish, Welsh and Irish societies, singing circles within Country Women's Institutes (founded in 1921), and other groups as different as workplace choirs, RSA Tin Hat Clubs (from 1933), trained Māori choirs and church choirs. Sometimes choir activity went unnoticed; at other times it was clearly visible. A vivid case in point was when communities were organised to sing together.

Community sings, which began in the 1920s, were upbeat occasions where everyone who wanted to come along sang well-known songs together in town halls or theatres. The informal repertoire comprised traditional, patriotic, music-hall and drinking songs, sea shanties, hymns, rounds, parodies and limericks, as well as drawing-room songs of the Victorian and Edwardian eras. Drawing on strong traditions of social, family and church music, these gatherings were especially popular during the early 1930s, by which time the Depression had hit hard. They attracted thousands of participants and the singing events were often broadcast to large audiences via radio relays.[13]

Regular community singing offered a morale boost during a period of acute social strain. It was essentially a kind of local singing togetherness, good for social cohesion and stability, conveniently intergenerational, inexpensive, easy to organise and, typically, with its homemade humour, banter and tomfoolery, great fun for all involved. Auctions and raffles helped raise much-needed money for charity.

In the same decades, Māori choirs were an element of cohesion and stability within their communities. There were many singing groups on marae, and choral competitions were often a feature of major hui.[14] Those leading the choirs were obviously inspirational and hugely effective.

Missionary influences were clearly seen; some Māori who followed the Christian faith had adopted English-style singing, rendering part-songs and Mendelssohn chorales with great skill and accuracy. This choral singing was said, by a knowledgeable reviewer, to be 'disciplined and formal . . . strongly influenced by Pākehā choral singing . . . occasionally rather mechanical'.[15]

A choral group at the Māori Agricultural College in Hastings showed a strong American influence. The college's music teacher, Walter Smith, although born in Nūhaka on the East Coast and being of Ngāti Kahungunu heritage, had grown up in Idaho, in the United States, and studied at Brigham Young University in Utah. Between 1913, when the Agricultural College opened, and 1931, when it was closed after the Hawke's Bay earthquake, Smith formed and led a glee club modelled on such clubs in American universities. Walter Smith was known in some circles as the 'father of New Zealand jazz'.

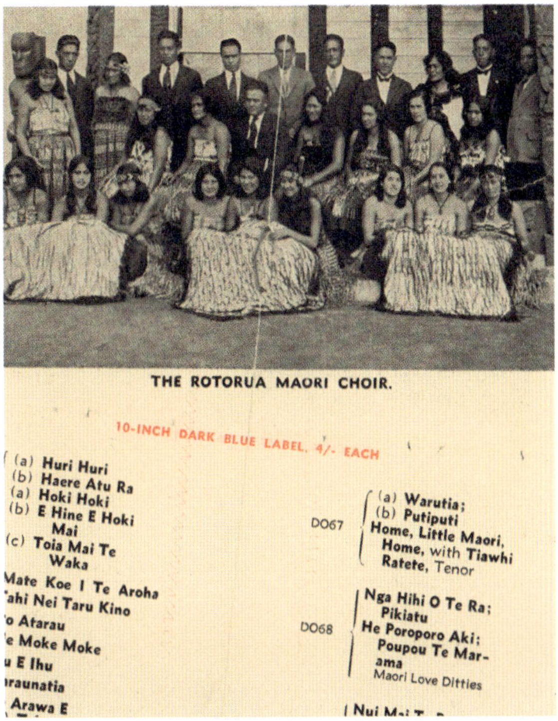

TOP LEFT A songbook used for a community sing in Auckland, 1926. AUTHOR'S COLLECTION

TOP RIGHT The Rotorua Māori Choir LP cover with a group portrait. ALEXANDER TURNBULL LIBRARY, EPH-A-PHONO-1930-01-4

BELOW The Glee Club at the Māori Agricultural College in Hastings, 1918. Conductor: Walter Smith. LDS CHURCH HISTORY LIBRARY

Some all-Māori choirs became nationally prominent during this time, the most well-known being the Rotorua Māori Choir and the Waiata Māori Choir.

The Rotorua Māori Choir was established early in the twentieth century by Anglican clergyman Frederick A. Bennett. Members of the choir, mainly from the local Ngāti Whakaue iwi, had starred in *Hinemoa*, New Zealand's first feature film, in 1914, and they toured the country in subsequent years. In 1930, the choir was recorded by a visiting Australian mobile recording unit of Columbia Records at a meeting house at Ōhinemutu on the shores of Lake Rotorua. In under three weeks 51 titles were set in wax. The recordings included traditional Māori songs, love ballads, hymns, farewells (mostly in a European style), and songs by Alfred Hill. The recordings eventually made it onto LP format but are no longer available for sale.[16]

The musical director for the recording sessions was pianist and orchestral conductor Gil Dech, who felt that because most of the group were accustomed to singing solo he had to train them quickly to sing as a group. He evidently struggled to gain respect as the Pākehā who '[stood] up in front of them waving his arms about'.[17] But, in 1937, choir member Te Mauri Meihana, commenting on these eclectic influences, maintained that the 'Maori spirit' had been kept intact — the spirit of 'yearning for the past; the lament for the days and times that are no more'.[18] The 78-rpm shellac discs, released shortly afterwards, sold well around the country, especially to overseas tourists who asked for recordings of local singers.

It was fortunate that these recordings could be made in New Zealand — other musical acts had to be taken to Australia or England to be recorded. In 1936, legendary All Black George Nepia made a quick recording of 'Haere Ra' in London while on a rugby union tour of England, Ireland and Canada.

The Methodist and Anglican Churches were both active in Māori communities, but Anglican enterprises tended to be well supported whereas Methodist mission work didn't fare as well. From the late 1920s, the recession brought declining support for Māori communities associated with Methodist missions. The communities were demoralised and had very few opportunities for employment. However, the Reverend Arthur Seamer, General Superintendent of Methodist Home and Māori Missions, responded to their needs in a most intriguing way. Seamer's war injuries in 1915 meant that he was in constant pain and physical discomfort, but this didn't stop him from working among Māori in Taranaki and the Urewera and Taupō districts and becoming a fluent speaker of te reo Māori. He utilised a choir that had originally been formed in the mid-1920s around a handful of people who simply enjoyed singing. His reborn Waiata Māori Choir sprang into prominence.

ABOVE A group of Māori performers, probably the Methodist Waiata Māori Choir, circa 1932.
ALEXANDER TURNBULL LIBRARY, PACOLL-0240-01

LEFT Inia Te Wiata (left) as a member of the Methodist Māori Mission Choir, 1932.
ALEXANDER TURNBULL LIBRARY, 1/2-190157-F

With a mixed repertoire of Māori and Western music, Seamer wanted his choir to show their typically European audiences an understanding of Māori history and culture, actively changing the attitudes of both races.

The Waiata Māori Choir (which was also known as the Methodist Māori Mission Choir) grew under his tuition and discipline to become a highly trained, professional Māori group, attracting many talented young singers, such as future opera star Inia Te Wiata. Eventually every major iwi in Aotearoa New Zealand was represented in the choir, and by 1930 it was attracting large public audiences.

This choir was the first large Māori group to present indigenous New Zealand culture to overseas audiences. They made three enthusiastically received visits to Australia and the United Kingdom, where they performed to capacity audiences and were invited to Buckingham Palace. Three 78-rpm discs were made in England during their tour.[19] The recordings help to trace how a lively and constantly changing hybridised music culture was emerging, involving both Western and Māori musical styles.[20]

The choir, which disbanded in 1938, did an enormous amount to popularise Māori music in New Zealand. In particular, it began adapting waiata melodies such as 'Hine E Hine' and 'Pokarekare Ana' into choral arrangements. These melodies became very well known, and this practice became widespread. In 1949, Seamer was made a CMG (Companion of the Order of St Michael and St George) in recognition of his services to Māori and the community in general.

When war was declared in September 1939, there were calls from Sir Āpirana Ngata and the other Māori Members of Parliament for an all-Māori unit to form part of the Second New Zealand Expeditionary Force. The government agreed to the formation of a Māori Battalion, a frontline infantry unit made up entirely of Māori volunteers. Many young Māori men were quick to sign up for military service, and equally quickly a Māori Battalion Choir emerged. Even though proportionately more Māori were killed and seriously wounded than other New Zealanders in the war, the choir thrived until it was disbanded in 1946. The choir gave inspiration to the Māori Battalion and other Kiwi troops and is still remembered today, especially through increasingly popular Anzac Day commemorations and the powerful signature tune 'Māori Battalion March to Victory'.

Choirs in churches had been a stabilising factor in communities since colonial days. Although from 1914 they were affected by the same turbulence experienced by the rest of society, choirs appeared to withstand shocks of loss and disruption with

The choir of the Māori Battalion singing evensong, All Saints Cathedral, Cairo, Egypt, September 1941. ALEXANDER TURNBULL LIBRARY, DA-01474-F

a sense of equilibrium. They were particularly important to the largely church-going population, typically leading hymn singing and offering special music or an anthem, psalm or motet depending on the denomination. Their prominence continued well into the 1950s, when community choirs were becoming more popular than church choirs.

There is no reliable information on the total number of church choirs in this period, so it is difficult to assess the reach of their influence. It seems likely that there were hundreds of active church choirs from one end of the country to the other, in rural areas, townships, suburbs, the hearts of cities and in almost all denominations.

These ranged in ability and value: there were the well-established Christchurch church choirs trained by Robert Parker; Auckland churches Pitt Street Methodist and Papakura Anglican Church; in Wellington, the Terrace Congregational, Vivian Street Baptist and St John's Presbyterian churches; Rātana Church in the Rangitīkei district; Greymouth's Holy Trinity; Invercargill's St Mary's Basilica; and churches in small towns and villages everywhere. This multitude of church-based choirs, both large and small, provided their members with at least a taste of the pleasure and discipline of rehearsed group singing. Congregational singing in turn benefitted from the week-by-week dedication of choristers and conductors/organists. Some groups were of high quality: in 1937, St John's Presbyterian Church Choir was the winner of the choral section of the Wellington Competitions Society.[21]

Well-trained church choirs are said to have raised the standard of the community choirs being established at the same time. These new choirs needed help, many of their singers being inexperienced and requiring musical expertise. Church choirs could provide accurate, strong sight-singers, as well as less sophisticated colleagues who could merely follow the music. New community choirs also needed support from choral enthusiasts who could assist with rehearsal procedures and choral techniques, programme planning, membership policies and choir discipline.

Perhaps the biggest gift from church choirs was their love of choral singing. The contributions of the specialist choirs in Anglican and Catholic cathedrals were particularly substantial and often reminded the public, as well as choral practitioners in general, of the value of choral excellence. The contributions of church choirs to the country's developing choral life in the first half of the twentieth century can now be seen as highly significant.

The New Zealand Centennial celebrations of 1940 commemorated both the signing of New Zealand's founding document, the Treaty of Waitangi, and a century of settlement and government as a member of the British Empire. Fortunately, plans for celebrating the centenary had begun well before the rumblings of a second world war were heard, otherwise the five years of elaborate government planning for the commemoration might never have borne fruit. As part of the celebrations, a Centennial Music Festival was proposed to the government by a 1936 deputation led by Stanley Oliver — a respected conductor recently arrived from Canada — and members of the Royal Wellington Choral Union. They had sought advice from Dr Malcolm Sargent, the eminent English musician who was at the time conducting orchestral concerts in New Zealand.

The official Centennial celebrations were launched on 8 November 1939 by a massed choir of 450 in front of an audience of almost 60,000 at the Cenotaph in Wellington. Stanley Oliver was the conductor of the historic event, for which he had led 'impressive and inspiring' rehearsals.[22] Between speeches, the choir, accompanied by bands, sang the hymn 'Old Hundredth', 'God Defend New Zealand' and 'Land of Hope and Glory'.

In June–July 1940, the Centennial Music Festival featured competitions for choir, string quartet and composition, as well as major choral works presented with celebrity soloists and the country's first national orchestra conducted by Englishman Anderson Tyrer. The hope had been that concerts of choral or orchestral music would be presented in the four main centres and, if possible, in smaller cities and towns, with excursion trains to bring people from outlying places.

Evidence of the strong growth of choral singing in the four main centres was provided by several performances of Charles Gounod's *Faust* in each of them, all involving local choirs. These performances proved to be the highlight of the festival, the *New Zealand Listener* reporting that the name of *Faust* had certainly been put into the musical vocabulary, large and small, of nearly all New Zealanders.[23]

The response to the string quartet and choir competitions disappointed the organisers. Choirmasters, particularly in Otago and Southland, reportedly did not want to 'take the risk of having their choir placed anywhere but first'.[24] There were no such hesitations from conductors of some prominent choirs. The adjudicators placed Christchurch Orpheus Choir first, Wellington Schola Cantorum second and Auckland Dorian Singers third.

However, it was the success of a young New Zealand composer, Douglas Lilburn, in the composition competition that caught the public's imagination and became a topic of nationwide interest. The recognition of his musical voice was seen to be on a par with writer Frank Sargeson's literary voice in his 1940 short story 'The Making of a New Zealander'. Lilburn gained first prize for a 1939 choral/orchestral/soloist work, *Prodigal Country*, which captured his sense of himself as a New Zealander. Anderson Tyrer, chief adjudicator, pronounced that it had 'an excellent vocal line, was never stodgy, and as a whole showed fine writing and judgement'.[25] New Zealand choral composition had come of age.

The piece had to wait many years for a respectful rendition. The highly anticipated first performance, conducted by Tyrer, was disappointing. Compared with vocal music, standards in instrumental music at the time were much less well developed, and it appears that Tyrer's lack of preparation and conducting expertise, shortage of time for rehearsal and the failings of players — particularly woodwinds — were the cause. But *Prodigal Country* is seen as the composer's answer to the same questions of identity that New Zealand writers such as Robin Hyde, Allen Curnow and Charles Brasch were struggling with; in fact the first two sections include settings of poems by Hyde and Curnow. London-based Lilburn's home thoughts from afar are echoed in Hyde's lines used in the work:

Stanley Oliver conducts a choir of 450 before an audience of nearly 60,000 at the Cenotaph, Wellington. The event, on 8 November 1939, marked the start of New Zealand's Centennial celebrations in 1940. ALEXANDER TURNBULL LIBRARY, MS-PAPERS-9204-1-01

ABOVE Members of the Wellington Welsh Society choir, wearing traditional dress, in the temporary 5ZB studio at the New Zealand Centennial Exhibition, Wellington, 1940. PHOTOGRAPHER WILLIAM HALL RAINE. ALEXANDER TURNBULL LIBRARY, PACOLL-0262-01

LEFT Douglas Lilburn in the electronic music studio at Victoria University of Wellington, 30 August 1969. ALEXANDER TURNBULL LIBRARY, EP/1969/3689/18-F

I too am sold into strangeness,
Yet in my heart can only dissolve, re-form
The circling shapes of New Zealand things.[26]

Lilburn's 'overwhelming' successes, along with performances from the winning choirs, were celebrated in a radio broadcast designed to be heard by the majority of New Zealanders. The November 1940 broadcast was, in accord with the prevailing romantic Pākehā–Māori sentiment, billed as 'the first concert of its kind since Kupe touched New Zealand'.

Apart from *Prodigal Country*, Lilburn wrote almost no choral music. There are manuscripts of an abandoned Bachelor of Music exercise (1937): 'Choruses for baritone, male chorus and SATB'; two songs written for educational institutions; and 'The Magpies' for unison men's voices. The only other choral manuscript is a 1942 a cappella work for the Christchurch Anglican Cathedral: 'Magnificat' and 'Nunc Dimittis', commissioned by C. Foster Browne, then Cathedral music director.[27] Douglas Lilburn told me about these canticles when, in early 1982, I asked him to write something for the National Youth Choir. He had publicly forsworn any further non-electronic compositions, but it appeared appropriate for some a cappella music by our 'national' composer to be sung by our national choir. Lilburn politely declined the request and then mentioned with a laugh the pentatonic-mode canticles of 1942, which the Cathedral choirboys had told him sounded like Chinese music.[28]

The imaginative Centennial Music Festival was extremely successful in bringing to the public's attention the man who was to become New Zealand's pre-eminent composer. In another matter, the festival was decidedly unsuccessful. The head of the National Broadcasting Service, James Shelley, had wanted to assemble a Centennial choir of 60 voices, and then follow the BBC's example of establishing a broadcasting choir. He was not able to achieve this aim, probably for financial reasons. Despite that disappointment, the gains of the festival were extraordinary, particularly the deep and lasting impression made by the National Orchestra and the associated choirs and soloists in towns and cities throughout the country. The realisation that ordinary folk could enjoy serious art music added to an awareness of the place that artistic expression could hold in the lives of New Zealanders.

5

Significant choral leaders of the time

The gentle and charming Robert Parker, who arrived in New Zealand in 1869, was the first of a succession of notable choral conductors who significantly influenced choral music in this country for several decades. He had trained with some of London's finest organists, had sung in the choir of St Paul's Cathedral and studied at Queens' College, Cambridge.

On medical advice Parker had moved to New Zealand, first to Christchurch, then briefly to Nelson. Finally he moved to Wellington.[1] There he became the director of music at St Paul's Pro-Cathedral, a position he held for 59 years until 1937. During this time, he directed three other Wellington community choirs: the Choral Union, Choral Society, and Liedertafel, as well as the Orpheus Glee Club and Harmonic Society for shorter periods.

Exceedingly hard-working, Parker was the guiding spirit of the colony's first music festival, held in Wellington in 1888, with performers coming from Auckland and Christchurch. Besides *Elijah* and works by local composers Alfred Hill and John Maughan Barnett, he conducted *The Golden Legend*, an oratorio by Arthur Sullivan, which had had its premiere in Leeds just two years previously. Even though Sullivan's oratorio is not highly regarded today, Parker was, at least, trying to keep Wellington's audiences up to date. The great success of the first week-long festival, launched when he was just 41 years old, led to repeats in 1894 and 1903, all demonstrating his well-honed skills in training and conducting choirs. That expertise included the 'ability to direct a sometimes unsteady choir successfully through taxing works'.[2]

Part of Parker's motivation was his belief that music was beneficial to society's physical and psychic health, had an improving and moral power, was efficacious in the treatment of mental illness and valuable in speech therapy.

Parker's main interest was working with choirs, but he was an outstanding figure in many musical fields.[3] He was a senior music educator and singing tutor, University of New Zealand examiner, and a public lecturer on choral music with a keen sense of historical context. From 1884, he instructed trainee teachers in music, taught singing for several years at Wellington Girls' High School, and composed choral pieces, including a cantata for the New Zealand Industrial Exhibition in 1885. From 1924 until shortly before his death, he was president of the New Zealand Society of Professional Music Teachers (later the Music Teachers' Association of New Zealand), and was chairman of the Music Teachers' Registration Board from its establishment in 1929.[4]

In 1918 a complimentary performance commemorated Parker's fortieth anniversary as a conductor in Wellington and recognised his widespread and profound influence on choral activity. John Mansfield Thomson wrote: 'He was revered by many as the touchstone of musical excellence in Wellington for almost 60 years'[5] and his influence was described as the mainspring of Wellington's early musical activities.[6] In 1930, at 82 years old, he was made CMG, the highest honour that a New Zealand choral musician had received to that point.

LEFT Robert Parker, the 'father of New Zealand music'. ALEXANDER TURNBULL LIBRARY, PACOLL-8018-1-18

BELOW LEFT Programme for *The Creation*, presented by Wellington's Combined Methodist Choirs, conductor Harold Temple White, 1930. ALEXANDER TURNBULL LIBRARY, EPH-A-MUSIC-1930

BELOW RIGHT *The Wellington Apollo Singers Rules*, 1930. ALEXANDER TURNBULL LIBRARY, EPH-A-MUSIC-1930

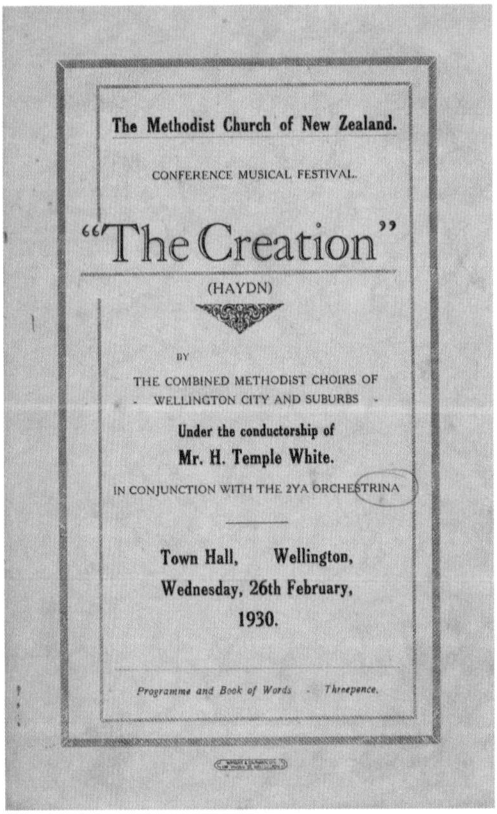

The Methodist Church of New Zealand.

CONFERENCE MUSICAL FESTIVAL.

"The Creation"

(HAYDN)

BY

THE COMBINED METHODIST CHOIRS OF
WELLINGTON CITY AND SUBURBS

Under the conductorship of
Mr. H. Temple White.

IN CONJUNCTION WITH THE 2YA ORCHESTRINA

Town Hall, Wellington,
Wednesday, 26th February,
1930.

Programme and Book of Words . Threepence.

.. The Wellington ..
Apollo Singers

RULES

(Founded 1930)

In 1913, Harold Temple White secured an appointment as organist and choirmaster at Wesley Methodist Church in Taranaki Street, Wellington. Temple White had arrived from England as a 12-year-old in 1893, later training as a school teacher before establishing himself as a (largely self-taught) professional music teacher. With the Feilding Choral Society he had success in provincial music competitions, setting a new standard in 'delicacy, precision, phrasing and modulation'.[7] In Wellington he soon became a familiar figure in the city's musical life. He made Wesley, with its big Gothic-style church building, the centre of many civic musical activities, as well as creating a thriving church choir. A large number of Wellington's leading singers served their apprenticeship in the Wesley Choir and, under Temple White's baton, were also part of combined Methodist choirs presenting oratorios such as *The Creation* in February 1930 in the Wellington Town Hall.

Besides holding the Wesley position for 46 years, Temple White conducted seven other choirs: the Wellington Harmonic Society (which he founded in 1914) until 1957; the Wellington Commercial Travellers' Male Voice Choir from 1918; the Royal Wellington Choral Union from 1919; as well as the Apollo Singers, the Wellington Boys' and Girls' Choirs, and the Tudor Singers, all of which he established in the 1930s. A highlight of these years was a performance of works by Australian composer Percy Grainger in November 1935, in the Wellington Town Hall. Grainger later wrote glowingly, 'I don't know that I can recall any choral programme of my works, in any city of the world, in which every item was rendered with the unvarying perfection attained on November 23.'[8]

Untiring in his work, Temple White especially loved to be involved in the fun of children's choral activities and to be an adjudicator for their music competitions. His intense patriotic and Christian feelings were reflected in his choral compositions. His gentle exterior tended to hide a great strength of character and courage in making difficult decisions on a matter of principle. In 1927, he resigned from the Wellington Choral Union, the region's major choir, because he was unhappy about the committee's lack of consultation over repertoire and soloists' selection. He was, however, very popular with the rank-and-file choir members, who gave him a grandfather clock when he left. He was also well liked by members of the community, playing the organ for regular community singing in the Town Hall during the 1930s, giving free organ recitals and conducting carol services at Christmas. He also served on the Music Teachers' Registration Board of New Zealand, the Music Teachers' Association of New Zealand and the Department of Internal Affairs Music Bursary Selection Committee. Later he was appointed honorary city organist; he was also awarded an OBE. An impressive bust of him was placed outside the Ilott Theatre in the Wellington Town Hall.

LEFT Harold Temple White, circa 1958.
ALEXANDER TURNBULL LIBRARY, PACOLL-6388-37

BELOW The Wesley Methodist Church choir, 1953, with conductor Harold Temple White.
PHOTOGRAPH BY CROWN STUDIOS. ALEXANDER TURNBULL LIBRARY, 1/1-031586-F

Victor Edward Galway was a distinguished choral leader in Dunedin for 35 years. In 1919, when he was 25 years old, he became organist and choirmaster at First Church Otago, the largest Presbyterian church in Dunedin, and for the next 17 years he also conducted the Dunedin Male Voice Choir. In addition, he conducted the Dunedin Choral Society for 10 years.

Galway had been a choirboy from the age of five in Northampton, England, before the family immigrated to Australia. He took up the Dunedin position after completing a Doctor of Music at Melbourne University and holding church appointments at Williamstown Presbyterian Church in Melbourne and St Andrew's Presbyterian Church in Brisbane. Over 70 years later, when I held the choir director's position at the Brisbane church, his influence was still evident.

His new church home, First Church Otago, was a handsome building for him to work in. Built of Ōamaru stone in early Decorated Gothic style, with a finely proportioned tower and elegant spire, the 'Presbyterian Cathedral' was located in the centre of the city and became a sought-after venue for community choral concerts.

But Galway was more than just a grateful recipient of superior work accommodation. In 1925, he became the first music lecturer at the University of Otago, going on to conduct the Otago University Musical Society and giving Dunedin its first performances of works by Purcell and Elgar. Later he became the inaugural Blair Professor of Music at the university and held senior positions at the university and the University of New Zealand.[9]

Galway played an influential, creative and respected role in the musical life of the Dunedin community and his adopted nation. This was a time when local music-making was beginning to be seriously measured against overseas standards, and his work was always of high calibre. A genial and enthusiastic man, and a caring but demanding teacher and conductor, he was called upon to lead the music at important public events, combining his Male Choir with the Choral Society. Alongside organ recitals, his popular public lectures became a notable feature of Dunedin's cultural life, as did his radio broadcasts.

Galway was also a composer and accompanist, and in the mid-1930s and early 1940s, he worked closely with Vernon Griffiths, a former Christchurch Training College lecturer, who was implementing a radical music scheme at Dunedin's King Edward Technical College. Galway composed *Psalm of the Seafarers* for the college, and it later enjoyed a national reputation. Most of his compositions were of choral music, especially for churches. Three other pieces can be found in the *Dominion Song Book Number 13*.

Victor Edward Galway, composer, teacher, conductor and accompanist, circa 1931. ALEXANDER TURNBULL LIBRARY, PACOLL-6303-32

Like Griffiths, Galway was an avid follower of the English musical tradition and ensured that his students — such as future prominent conductors Frank Callaway, John Ritchie and John Matheson — had immersed themselves in the choral and orchestral classics. Galway's provision of a thorough grounding in musicianship, traditional harmony and music literature, as well as his model of choral leadership, was crucial for the success of these three national and international leaders. However, Galway's conservatism often contrasted with the musical tastes of fellow academics.[10]

John Bradshaw came to New Zealand in 1902 to be in charge of music at the Christchurch Anglican Cathedral. He was an extremely stern disciplinarian and never budged from this, but his choice of repertoire was to change after a return visit to England in 1922. More Tudor church music (recently published in reliable editions) was now featured, and he championed the work of his English contemporaries Holst, Elgar, Bantock and Bairstow, who had moved away from the sentimental Victorian chromaticism of their predecessors.

Bradshaw influenced many musicians to follow a conducting career, a tribute to his dedication to high-quality music-making. He imprinted his vision of excellence on several protégés, Robert Field-Dodgson and Clifton Cook being two of the more prominent. Another former choir member, Lin Saunders, later a long-serving music critic, said of Bradshaw: 'In his constant striving after perfection he showed a forbidding exterior to all except those who knew him intimately, but at heart he was deeply religious and humble. . . . His contribution to New Zealand's musical life was significant for, although in each of the spheres in which he worked the foundations had already been laid by his predecessors, he greatly raised general artistic standards.'[11] Frederick Page, who had been a student at Canterbury University College under Bradshaw, was not so complimentary. While impressed by Bradshaw's expertise with choirs, Page regarded him as far too conservative. It is interesting to note that Page, who was later appointed to head up a music department at Victoria University College in Wellington, did nothing to set up a choir at the university in his 25 years at the helm.

Soon after coming to New Zealand, Bradshaw had become conductor of the Christchurch Liedertafel. However, in 1917, he fell out with that group and created the Christchurch Male Voice Choir, going on to direct it for 23 years. This new combination of the voices of boys from the Cathedral Choir and an increased number of men (25) meant that the group could perform a mixed-voice repertoire with or without accompaniment. Programmes ranged from Elizabethan madrigals to stalwarts such as Stanford's patriotic *Songs of the Fleet*, and for many years an immense public following required repetitions of each concert. He also directed the Royal Christchurch Musical Society for two periods, for a total of 13 years.

Bradshaw, who had the nickname of 'Braddy', was one of the most esteemed choral leaders in New Zealand for the entirety of his time at Christchurch Cathedral, until he retired in 1937 after falling out with the dean. He also supported all moves fostering the involvement of children in musical activities, and he participated in several professional music bodies. It was generally acknowledged that Christchurch had the highest choral standards in the country and that Bradshaw was largely responsible. Sir Sydney Nicholson, who had inaugurated a School of English Church Music a few years earlier, visited the city in 1934 and was so impressed by Bradshaw's choir that he exclaimed: 'What an inestimable privilege you ought to feel . . . to have such a beautiful choir as you have here . . . as good a standard as could be found in England'.[12]

Victor Peters, already mentioned for his openness to new European compositions, was among the notable New Zealand-born directors who emerged after 1914. Peters had conducted various other choirs before establishing the Christchurch Harmonic Society in 1927. He turned to full-time music teaching and conducting in 1931. When the economy improved, he made two visits to Wellington with the Harmonic Society. Peters was also the choirmaster at Oxford Terrace Baptist Church for over 30 years, enjoying and employing its superb acoustics. He also took over the Christchurch Liedertafel and taught and conducted choirs at Christchurch Girls' High School.

Taking two years' leave in 1929, Peters earned qualifications from the Royal College of Music (ARCM) and the Royal Academy of Music (LRAM) in London, studied conducting with Malcolm Sargent and Reginald Jacques, and he also conducted massive choirs in the Royal Albert Hall.[13] Peters had seen that singing in choirs was no longer the leading social activity that it had been before the war, so his vision was to re-energise choir singing throughout New Zealand, partly through introducing and promoting an expanding repertoire of contemporary music. From the late 1920s, the Christchurch Harmonic Society performed challenging new works by composers such as Arnold Schönberg and Benjamin Britten.[14]

Among other works that Peters introduced to Christchurch was Constant Lambert's *Rio Grande*, which drew rave reviews in the press. The pianist was Frederick Page, who had suggested the piece. Page later wrote of that 1934 performance: 'Although we were all scared of public reaction, it was modern, it was jazzy, it went well.'[15]

In 1936, Peters took the Christchurch Harmonic Society to Dunedin, where they sang to a Town Hall audience of 3000 for both nights they performed. The *Otago Daily Times* reported that the choir's greatest asset was its conductor: 'His personal influence over his choir has in it something akin to genius, and his control . . . was of a kind to place him among leading British choral conductors of the present day.'[16]

In 1937, Peters took more study leave, to spend six months in England and the United States, leaving the Harmonic Society in the hands of the deputy conductor, George Martin, a fine organist and choir trainer.

LEFT John Christopher Bradshaw, 1922. ALEXANDER TURNBULL LIBRARY, PACOLL-3310-9

BELOW Programme for Christchurch Male Voice Choir, 1930. ALEXANDER TURNBULL LIBRARY, EPH-A-MUSIC-1930

Douglas Lilburn was enamoured of Peters' programmes, and when Lilburn lived in Christchurch from 1941 to 1945, he made a point of always attending Harmonic Society concerts. Lilburn said of Peters' work:

> Contemporary European music, goodness yes. Christchurch was a very advanced outpost. Victor Peters of the Harmonic Society gave one of the very early performances of *Belshazzar's Feast* and the *Rio Grande* of Constant Lambert. He was a terrific conductor. I remember I had to go along as critic to *Elijah*. I thought 'Mendelssohn, my God, what do I say about this!' but I was sitting on the edge of my seat as I listened to these Mendelssohn choruses as conducted by this Victor Peters.[17]

Peters had seen active service throughout the First World War and been severely injured at Bapaume in France. He became one of the greatest of New Zealand's choral musicians despite his disabilities and frequent pain. A long-time choir member and deputy conductor, Malcolm Anderson wrote of Peters that although he was 'only too human in so many ways', he and his wife 'were sustained by a strong Christian faith'. Peters showed a determination to keep learning throughout his life — even though it had been thought in 1915 that he would never walk again. He gained enormous respect as he continued to reach out to choir members and inspire them. He was awarded an OBE in 1949.

The momentum begun by Michael Balling, Principal of the Nelson School of Music from 1893 to 1896, was kept up by those who followed him, and in particular Julius Lemmer, principal from 1899 to 1944. After returning to Germany, Balling was described by Wagner's wife Cosima as 'one of our most gifted outlaws . . . returning home penniless from New Zealand'.[18] He succeeded the period's foremost conductor, Hans Richter, at the Hallé Orchestra in Manchester, where he became a 'power in English musical life'. Later he directed opera choruses on the Continent, was a music director in Darmstadt, a German city known for music and the arts, and he became a regular conductor of Wagner's cycle of four epic operas, *The Ring*, at Bayreuth, Germany. He died in Darmstadt at the age of 59.

The Nelson Male Voice Choir was founded in 1932, the Nelson Civic Choir grew out of the Harmonic Society, and Polyhymnos and other choral ensembles appeared later. They all enjoyed the privilege of singing in the purpose-built School of Music auditorium.

LEFT *Portrait of Victor Peters*, by Evelyn Page, circa 1930. UNIVERSITY OF CANTERBURY ART COLLECTION, UC-UCF-08, COURTESY ANNA WILSON

BELOW Programme for the Christchurch Harmonic Society's Wellington concert, 1937, featuring conductor Victor Peters. ALEXANDER TURNBULL LIBRARY, EPH-B-MUSIC-CHS-1937/79

An Auckland initiative, which stood in contrast to the Auckland Choral Society's earlier conservatism, came from Albert Bryant, a farmer who had studied music in Leipzig, Germany. In September 1935, while organist and choirmaster at Pitt Street Methodist Church, he formed a specialist group, the Dorian Singers, which soon became a fine chamber ensemble of soloists. Their quality repertoire would not have been so successful with a larger choir of less experienced singers. Bryant and his select group of 32 received critical praise. He conducted the Dorian Singers and the Royal Auckland Male Choir in a work at the national Centennial celebrations in 1940 with Scottish soprano Isobel Baillie and the remarkable New Zealand bass Oscar Natzke.[19]

Bryant remained conductor of the Dorian Singers for just six years — until 1941 when he was called up to serve in the Second World War. He handed the group over to Harry Luscombe who, a year earlier, had conducted his own works, *Centennial Ode* and *The Burial of King Cormac* — the latter based on an Irish legend, for baritone, chorus and orchestra — with the choir.[20] Luscombe set about increasing the choir's size and broadening its repertoire.

From 1945 to 1950, Bryant served as organist and choirmaster at St Paul's Cathedral in Mulgrave Street, Wellington. He later became the organist for St Peter's Cathedral in Hamilton. There he formed another choir which would present the Bach *Mass in B Minor* with the Auckland Dorian Singers, by then conducted by Peter Godfrey.

The contributions to New Zealand's choral culture made by individual leaders such as Parker, Temple White, Galway, Bradshaw, Peters and Bryant were matched by the creditable work of two sets of musicians spread through the country: performing artists and the often-unnoticed private music teachers.

Good vocal and instrumental performers influenced choral singing. For its size, New Zealand was producing an exceptionally high number of divas and celebrity soloists, including Rosina Buckman (1881–1948), Oscar Natzke (1912–1951)[21] and Inia Te Wiata (1915–1971), along with Frances Alda (1879–1952) and Dame Joan Hammond (1912–1996), both Christchurch-born Australian-raised operatic sopranos. By displaying high artistic endeavour to the public, these performers inspired and encouraged choristers.

Overseas vocal soloists brought to New Zealand were also influential. Immediately after the 1940 Centennial concerts in Wellington, celebrated British soloists Isobel Baillie, Gladys Ripley and Heddle Nash (in addition to New Zealander Oscar Natzke) set out on a concert tour of provincial towns in both main islands, accompanied by a

Albert Bryant, 1955.
ALEXANDER TURNBULL LIBRARY, EP/1955/2170-F

pianist and four first-desk string players from the Centennial Festival Orchestra. This was the first of tours of recitals and plays under the auspices of the Community Arts Service that would become a feature of small-town and rural life after the war. This group undoubtedly made a profound impression on receptive listeners in all parts of the country.

Private music teachers also added to the advance of choral music. The results of their often-unseen efforts were steadily raising levels of musical knowledge and music literacy. Learning the piano or another instrument or voice slowly helped to create more musical environments, and sometimes this teaching fostered an awareness of opportunities to perform — including joining a part-singing choir. Future choral leaders were standout beneficiaries of the work of these teachers; private teachers were often the only source of musical skills and, indeed, any training for conductors. A Music Teachers' Registration Bill was passed by Parliament in 1928; the government of the day clearly thought it important that the professional interests of the small army of private teachers should be safeguarded.

In the midst of the years of upheaval, turbulence, challenge and promise from the start of the twentieth century, public schools were one institution that could possibly help to bring the country together — perhaps through singing in classes and assemblies as happened to some degree in Britain during the Second World War.

With the passing of the Education Act 1904, which had made singing in primary schools compulsory, it appeared New Zealand might move towards becoming more of a singing nation. In fact, the attention given to singing was less uniform than in any other subject. 'Lamentable lack of interest', and 'Singing is still the Cinderella subject', reported school inspectors. The 1904 Act appeared to be toothless. The news wasn't all bad, however; there was some concern for the proper treatment of children's voices — for example, that downward scales should be largely employed to counteract the upward forcing of the chest voice. But just as singing in schools had generally been disappointing during the pre-war period, the decade 1915–25 was said to resemble it. Actually, it was reported to be worse in some districts. It wasn't to improve until the late 1930s and early 1940s.

Yet there were always brighter moments brought about by the committed, enlightened efforts of special individuals. In the Wellington Town Hall in 1915 a choir of some 700 children gave an outstanding performance the like of which Robert Parker had not heard since the hall had opened 10 years before. The improvement in the quality of tone in that time was said to be simply amazing, and the work by Parker and others had borne fruit. Singing classes for teachers had helped and were still continuing in 1916.[22]

It was not before time, then, that Minister of Education Sir James Parr announced in 1925 that arrangements were under way for the appointment of a Supervisor of School Singing.[23] It was a turning point in the official recognition of singing as a valuable activity in schools as well as the community. The Education Department had earlier rectified a similar deficiency in the field of physical education, when a Physical Education Branch was opened in 1912. Since then physical activity had begun to flourish; now it was singing's turn.

While some other improvements were noted, such as songs printed in the *School Journal* gradually making their way into schools, the Chief Inspector of Schools, T. B. Strong, realised that one of the biggest problems to be overcome was the lack of systematic instruction on a definite plan, progressing from year to year.[24] Strong's observation was astute. This obstacle has continued to hamper the creation of lively school singing traditions ever since.

From 1936, it was theoretically easier for teachers to meet curriculum responsibilities in subjects like singing because of the abolition of the Proficiency Examination at the end of primary school, which liberated teachers and pupils from the restrictions of meeting narrow exam standards. They were now meant to have more time and energy to devote to music and the arts and crafts. The two game-changing policy-makers behind this were Peter Fraser, Minister of Education in the 1935 Labour Government, and his Director of Education, Clarence Beeby. Fraser was interested in bringing about a changed spirit in schools, freeing them to provide all children with a well-rounded education to the fullest extent they were able, and Beeby drafted the policy statements for him. In due course the Fraser initiatives would be seen as a crucial moment of change in the education sector. In the meantime, there was little improvement in primary school singing.

Class singing and choirs in secondary schools were still in their infancy. Little had changed for decades, except when interested teachers or school heads acted on their own initiative. In official documents there are references to agriculture and needlework but no mention of music, physical education or drawing as either compulsory or recommended subjects.

This gloomy nationwide state of affairs in school singing wasn't specifically related to the economic and social circumstances of the day. It had been a common complaint of inspectors, leading educators and private music teachers for probably 30 years or longer that there was a lack of leadership in the subject of music.

Despite these circumstances, group singing survived the economic difficulties and almost lethal blows to societal institutions of the turbulent period after the First World War. The memory of past performances and training can remain strong with choir members, and social bonding and an optimistic spirit are quickly revived even without recognised leadership; the singing voice is never far away. How fortunate that the vocal gift has always been the democratic instrument par excellence: freely available and nurtured in all cultures.

6

Bonanzas unheralded, unsung, 1925–45

Turbulent social setbacks and economic difficulties had plagued New Zealand since 1914. Everywhere, people were pushed into improving their situations by their own efforts — pulling themselves up by their own bootstraps. This extended into the choral world. If choirs were to be put back together or improved, conductors and committees needed to be self-reliant; there was no one else to help. This process may have reflected a resilient 'can-do' attitude, a dogged determination to achieve against the odds.

At the same time, some unexpected good fortune was to strike in the years 1925 to 1945. This consisted of seven bonanzas: six remarkably fine musicians arriving on our shores, and the broadcasting boom making the sound of choirs and singing programmes available to all. This sudden increase in choral wealth slowly lifted the gloom that had settled over New Zealand for more than a decade. In particular, the six musician bonanzas revitalised choral singing in the main centres. But the first to arrive also had a larger, nationwide contribution to make. He was Edward Douglas Tayler from Lancaster, England.

Sir James Parr's 1925 announcement of the appointment of Tayler as 'Supervisor of School Singing to the New Zealand Government' was a seminal moment in the history of choral expansion in this country. That is partly because of a successful recommendation made by Tayler that appointments should be made to the training colleges of four English musicians: Horace Hollinrake to Auckland and Vernon Griffiths to Christchurch in 1927, followed by Ernest Jenner to Wellington and J. Crossley Clitheroe to Dunedin in 1928. Three of these were to have a substantial influence on future choir directors, with one of the three to have an enormous impact on the way choral music was viewed within the community. But Tayler's appointment as supervisor was also important because of his own contributions.

Selected in London by composer and conductor Sir Walford Davies, E. Douglas Tayler, FRCO, ARCM, was considered a brilliant choice for the New Zealand post. He had a special interest in choral singing, with useful experience in two choral positions in England and as an examiner in singing for the Royal Schools of Music. His 'solemn conviction' was that New Zealand had retarded its spiritual development through lack of song.[1] He set about trying to build the teaching of sight-singing in primary schools ('instruction in which must be given') and he tried to establish 'sound methods of voice-training'. He encouraged singing in every way possible; for example, he arranged for 1000 senior students to attend the final rehearsal before each concert given by the Wellington Royal Choral Union.

There is no doubt that Tayler worked hard in his national position. He visited hundreds of schools, the training colleges and Rotary clubs, and addressed public meetings around the country. That he had laudable aims and materials is also indisputable. However, his idealistic scheme was beyond most regular classroom teachers, and it was only towards the end of his tenure that the necessary third-year music specialists were being trained to assist in each school or cluster of schools. He had taken on 'an impossibly huge task'.[2] His legacy, though, is significant. As well as raising awareness of a new national scheme in music education, he developed two initiatives which were to have a widespread influence on choral music-making: promoting radio broadcasts to schools,[3] and establishing the *Dominion Song Books* (which included Māori songs and musical notation) for use in schools. Above all these, however, it was his recommendation for the appointment of four other English musicians, and his leadership throughout the country, that had many beneficial downstream effects.

Why then, in view of his hard work and signal contributions, did this visionary and friend of choral music have just five years and two months in his honourable position? The answer is found in the changing economic circumstances of the time.

While New Zealand had emerged from the Great War in reasonable economic shape, a downturn hit New Zealand one year after Tayler had taken up his duties (1927) and this became a full depression from 1929. The nation's severe woes meant cutbacks everywhere. Government departments were shut down, all four teacher training colleges were closed and in 1931 Tayler was asked to resign. He sailed for San Francisco with his family and became a professor at the University of California Berkeley, but died in August 1932.[4]

His resignation affected the four men appointed to the training colleges. As a result of a reshuffling of positions, Clitheroe returned to England, Griffiths went to Dunedin and about a year later Jenner was offered a position in Christchurch. Hollinrake, fortunately, was able to stay involved in Auckland. But, in the reshuffle, Wellington missed out.

Unlike Tayler and the other English musicians appointed in 1927–28, Horace Hollinrake was fortunate in being able to stay in the one city all his working life. The music department at Auckland Training College had remained open and he continued to teach there part-time. Hollinrake was to contribute at all levels in the Auckland area, including leading many summer schools, workshops and extramural classes.[5] By 1935, after eight years in New Zealand, he was teaching at both the training college and the university, where he was given a professorship at the age of 31.

Before he left England, the young Hollinrake had acquired useful experience for his future position in New Zealand. At age 15 he had been appointed organist at a Priory church in North Yorkshire, where he was a 'wonderful influence on the boys and men, raising the whole tone and spirit of the members and infusing his own keenness into them'.[6] At Cambridge University's Selwyn College, founded as a memorial to New Zealand's first Anglican bishop, he was in charge of the chapel choir for four years and received various scholarships and prizes. He also had administrative responsibilities and took addictively to the river, becoming a distinguished member of a crew in the College Boat Club. Musically, his tuition was the best available: his composition mentor for three years was Charles Wood and his professor was Sir Charles Stanford. To find work, he chose to follow Bishop Selwyn and take the long sea voyage to the Antipodes, marrying just days before his departure. He was 22 years old.

In Auckland he led a renaissance in choral singing in primary and secondary schools. Dorothea Franchi, a graduate of the University of Auckland, said that watching Hollinrake work with children 'was almost a magical experience, he had them in the palm of his hand'. Lin Saunders and other critics praised his music festivals highly, with 'some 5000 children taking an active part in music of first rate quality'.

Hollinrake's views on choices of children's repertoire are clear in the 24 selections in *Dominion Song Book Number 2*, which he compiled.[7] This book, as well as his fourth book, *Eighteen Classical Songs*, was distributed widely and used by conductors of school choirs for several generations.

An immensely popular Auckland Secondary Schools' Festival, established in 1931, ran under Hollinrake's direction for 25 years. Sometimes waiata and poi dances by the Queen Victoria Maori Girls' School and the Hukarere Girls' College of Napier were added into festival programmes. Partly because of parental support, the festivals had helped maintain civilian morale in wartime, but the 1945 festival, the most memorable of them, was something very special. Many people had to be turned away from what was 'one of the city's leading musical events'. A member of the choir later recalled that the music soared. 'The last item on the programme was Chapman's "Let all the world in every corner sing".[8] As it ended, "Holly" [Hollinrake's nickname] pointed his baton to the ceiling and 600 young voices were lifted for the final triumphant note. It was a moment you knew everyone in the hall would remember.'[9]

Festivals like these, which came to be regarded as an obligatory component of the educational system and were willingly endorsed by heads of schools, would be carried on after Hollinrake died.[10] Principals could see that young choristers sang for the joy of singing and for mutual entertainment, that singing was removing social barriers and was freeing students from constraints experienced in other areas of school life. The *Auckland Star* indicated further benefits for the over 9000 attending annually: 'Through their choral singing they learn to know and love music, often carry it on actively into their later lives, and always come to music with sympathy and understanding.'[11]

ABOVE Combined Children's Choirs, Auckland Town Hall, on the occasion of one of their school term festivals, 1946. ALEXANDER TURNBULL LIBRARY, EPH-A-MUSIC-1946-01-03

LEFT Vernon (Thomas) Griffiths was a former lecturer at the Christchurch Training College and was involved in the development of music training at Dunedin's King Edward Technical College. PHOTOGRAPHER F. E. MCGREGOR. CANTERBURY MUSEUM, 1983.237.5244

Vernon Griffiths, a Cambridge graduate like Tayler and Hollinrake, was expected to return to England after losing his position at Christchurch Training College, but instead he accepted a position as music master at Dunedin's King Edward Technical School (later College). From March 1933, he developed part-singing in assemblies and had hundreds of pupils singing in large choirs or playing in a massed orchestra.[12] His enthusiasm and success at King Edward Tech should have been no surprise. He had been a teacher in two schools in England (declining a full-time position at Cambridge): as senior music master at Downside School in Somerset, followed by a similar post at St Edmund's School, Canterbury.[13]

Griffiths' work at the school attracted national and international attention. Teachers passing through the Dunedin school were inspired to mount programmes as robust and inclusive as those Griffiths had pioneered. Frank Callaway, later Sir Frank, a world figure in music education, professor at the University of Western Australia and the leading choral conductor in Perth, became a colleague of Griffiths at the school and later took over the musical leadership.[14]

Ralph Lilly is probably the shining example of a music specialist who used Griffiths' methods and music to great effect. At Nelson College the whole school performed as a large four-part choir with pipe organ, and 50 boys comprised the Nelson Cathedral Choir at most services.[15] Other successful choral directors influenced by Griffiths included Clifton Cook at Christchurch Boys' High School and Leonard White at Papanui Technical College. The Griffiths Scheme was initially developed in the North Island by the first assistant and music teacher at Hutt Valley Memorial Technical College, Rudolph McLay, where it was later continued by music specialist David Sell. Elements of the scheme were implemented by Grahame Lilly at Naenae College, and by conductors at Hawera Technical High School, Feilding Agricultural High School and elsewhere.

Vernon Griffiths became frustrated at the lack of interest shown by the Education Department in his internationally recognised King Edward Tech curriculum. In a letter to Frank Callaway, he wrote, 'It would be comparatively so easy to organise a wonderful scheme for training school music directors. . . . It is as hard as ever to make any impression here on the leaden mountain of complacency and indifference . . . they don't want anything new in New Zealand. Take away "New" and "Zeal", and you have taken away a lot!'[16] It is tantalising to think how much choral music in New Zealand communities might have been fostered by national implementation of the Griffiths Scheme — or something similar. Even if not every school principal had supported the new plan, its effect would have influenced several generations of secondary school students. Imagining how the scheme would have been implemented

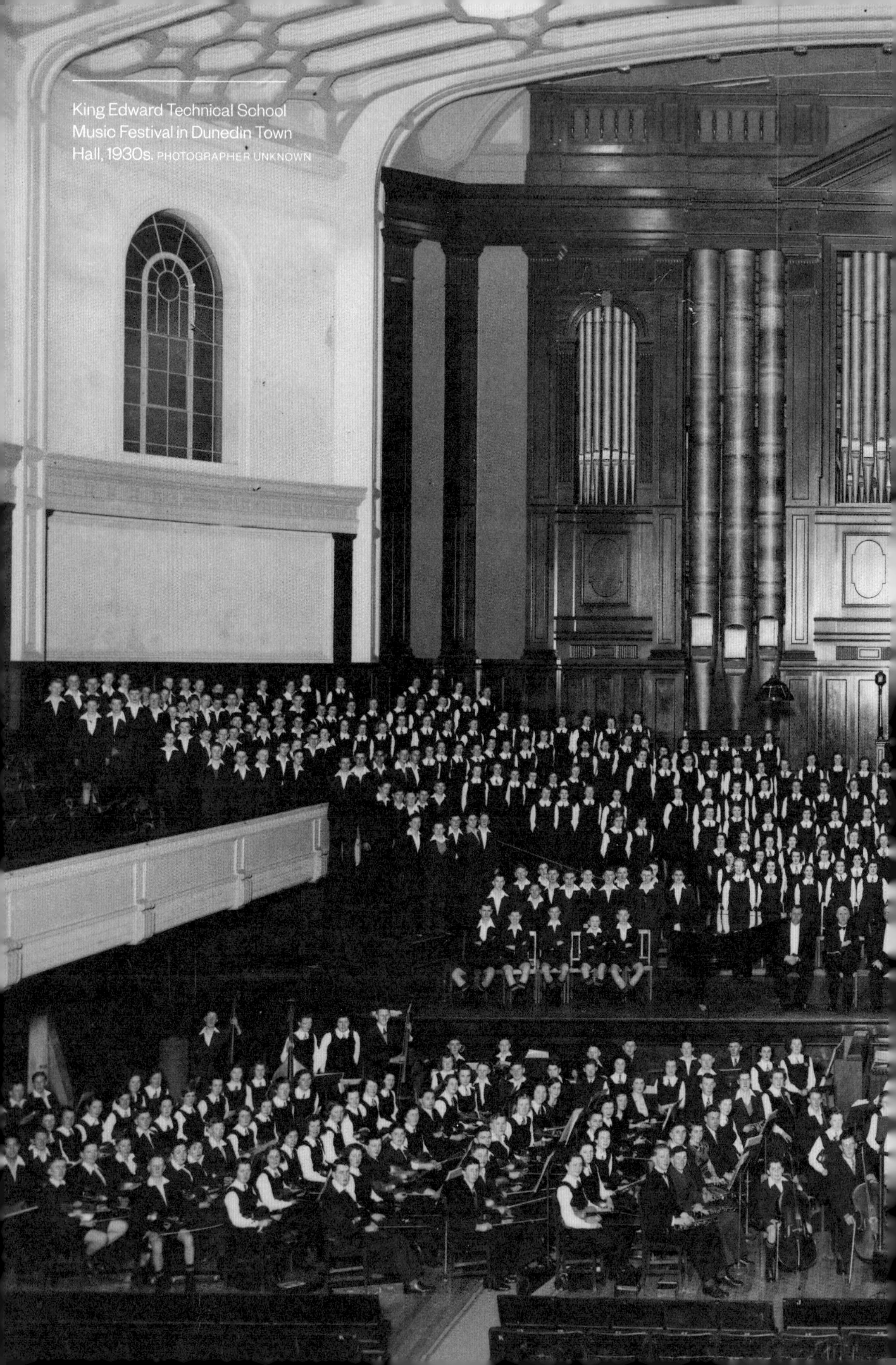

King Edward Technical School Music Festival in Dunedin Town Hall, 1930s. PHOTOGRAPHER UNKNOWN

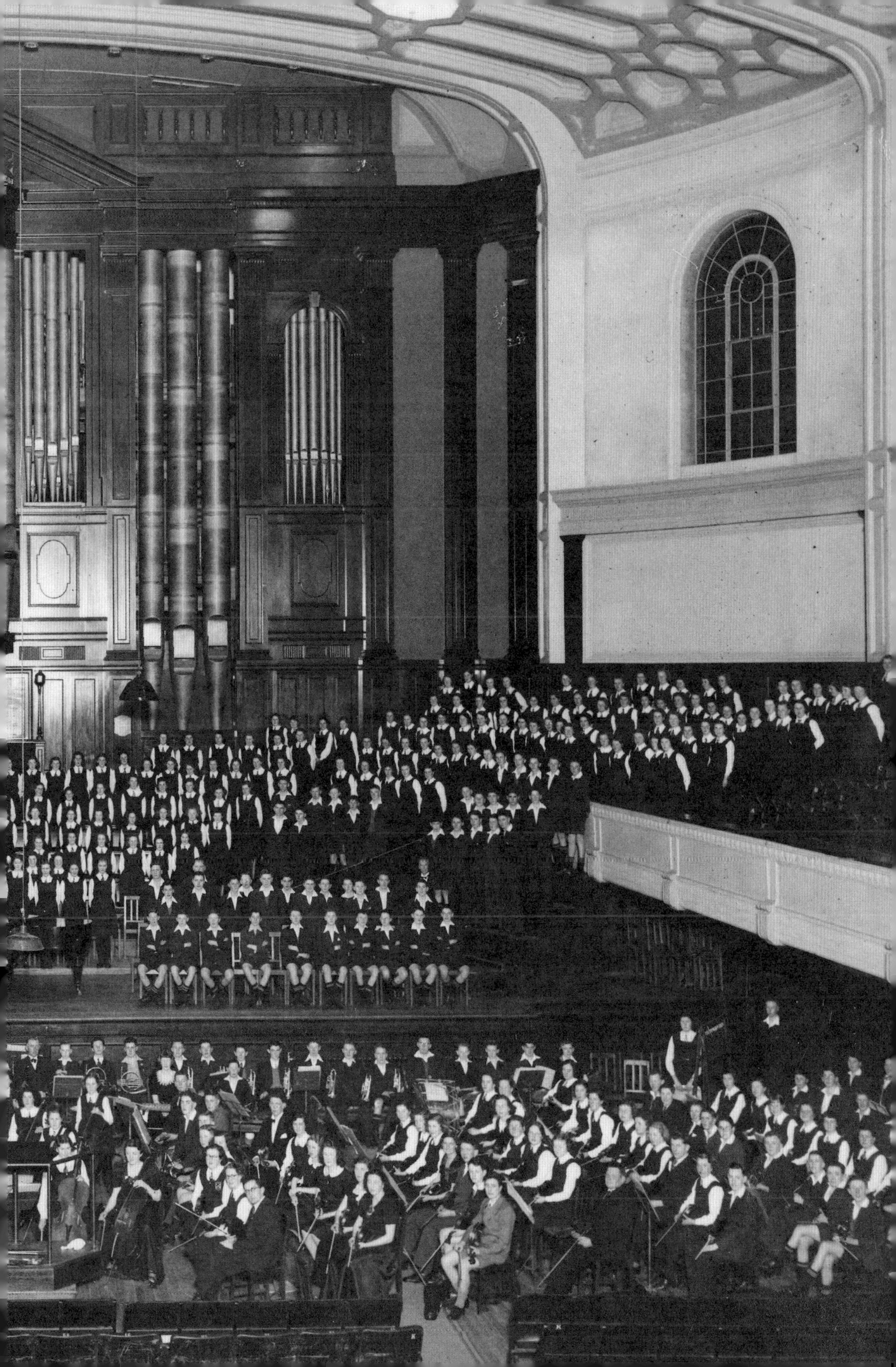

is not a latter-day pipe dream. From the 1930s to the 1970s, strong music leaders were certainly able to coax whole schools to sing in parts. 'Griff', as he was affectionately known, said that almost everyone had a usable voice; his pioneering work clearly showed the efficacy of group singing for the average student.[17]

Ernest Jenner was the third of the Englishmen who decided to stay in this country after losing their jobs at the height of the Great Depression. A year after the closure of Wellington Training College, Jenner was offered a position at the reopened Christchurch College and he stayed there until retiring in 1954.

At Wellington Training College, Jenner had helped to bring about a rising standard of singing. Moving south, he became an expert in the field of sight-singing, using tonic sol-fa and French time names, and creating simple methods to help classroom teachers. His articles and books on the subject were highly respected and his *Dominion Song Book, Number 9* (1944) was a powerful beacon of light for primary schools. Rhythmic flow was a critical musical factor for him: he expressed sentence-rhythm by using rhythmic curves or thickly printed bar-lines 'preceding the points of rhythmic culmination'.[18] A beautiful example of this approach is his setting of 'Who Would True Valour See'.[19]

As a choral practitioner, Jenner held positions as choirmaster at Sacred Heart Basilica in Wellington, St Michael and All Angels, the Royal Christchurch Musical Society and the Liederkränzchen in Christchurch, all the while using his prodigious piano technique in recitals and chamber music and also as a concerto soloist.

Jenner probably contributed most of all as the gifted teacher of the hundreds of future teachers and conductors of choirs that passed through his classes at the training college. These were primary and secondary teachers and music leaders-to-be. As someone who worked in the music scene in Christchurch for six years in the decade after he retired, I was aware of his profound influence. The cognoscenti spoke in reverential tones of his enormous passion for music generally and for singing in particular.[20]

Jenner's musicianship and artistry were also utilised by the Archbishop of Wellington when he commissioned a course for Catholic schools. The course covered voice production and stylistically varied singing for various parts of the liturgy.

In addition, Jenner made a major contribution to school radio programmes. For a quarter of a century, from 1931, he presented broadcasts that were popular with the children for whom they were designed, as well as with thousands of adults listening in. Responses to a 1935 3YA station questionnaire showed that 'a very large following of parents' found his talks stimulating and educative.

LEFT *The Dominion Song Book Number 9: The Pupil's Own Song Reader*, compiled by Ernest Jenner, 1944. ALEXANDER TURNBULL LIBRARY, MUSIC BOX DOM [1955]

BELOW Ernest Jenner, May 1951. PHOTOGRAPHER MR WOOLETT. ALEXANDER TURNBULL LIBRARY, F-34465-1/2

While the rise of radio listening generally was a catalyst for a slump in choral music-making after the First World War, there were targeted radio programmes that actually advanced choral singing, and these quickly became popular. One of them was the Friendly Road Children's Choir. It tapped into a country-wide involvement of children in school and church choirs.

Thomas Garland, broadcaster and children's choir specialist, established and conducted the Friendly Road Children's Choir in Auckland in 1933 as part of a non-denominational radio church, the Fellowship of the Friendly Road.[21] The radio church was a prominent public voice in support of a Depression-hit population. The choir sang for Sunday morning radio services led by Methodist missioner Colin Scrimgeour (Uncle Scrim), and along with other choirs gave concerts to full houses in the Auckland Town Hall until the early 1960s. The Friendly Road Choir rode out the sometimes stormy waters of Uncle Scrim's political activities and was listened to by thousands of children and adults throughout the country.[22] Over 1000 visitors a week, particularly from country districts, called into the radio church's home — the 1ZB Club in Queen Street, Auckland — and Uncle Tom (Garland) was there to greet them. Within its wide concert repertoire, Garland included many Māori songs.

The country's first adult choir broadcast was heard from the Wellington Town Hall Concert Chamber on 8 November 1933. Over 80 people had rehearsed under Thomas Wood, 'L.A.B. Specialist in Voice Production and the Art of Singing', during the winter months. Purportedly, 'thousands of Wellington citizens and many members of the Radio audience residing in all parts of New Zealand' then asked the 2ZW Broadcast Choir to remain 'on the air'. Accordingly, a Sunday evening programme was relayed on 3 December of the same year from Nimmo's Buildings on Willis Street, Wellington. Items ranged from 'Lullaby' (Brahms) and Molloy's 'Love's Old Sweet Song' to 'Mother England' from Bullock's *Dogs of Devon*, along with customary piano and vocal solos, one performed by Thomas Wood himself.[23] Thus was marked the formal beginning of choral music on the wireless and, later, television, the internet and social media.

From the mid-1930s, the regular broadcasting of choral material fed a steadily growing awareness of choral singing within New Zealand. Just three years before New Zealand became one of the first countries in the world to broadcast Parliament (1936),[24] the National Broadcasting Service began playing orchestral and choral recordings on its powerful national station, 2YA, and other stations.

Some programmes were a succession of short items (three to four minutes on each side of a 78-rpm shellac disc), but the new long-playing records (available from the early 1930s) and overseas transcription programmes soon enhanced listeners' experiences and transformed the broadcasting industry.

Another factor in advancing choral singing was broadcasts to schools. They began after 1932, when the government established the New Zealand Broadcasting Board, and continued to 1979. The broadcasts encouraged regular classroom teachers to take singing with their pupils. Most of the work had been done for them — so long as they remembered to turn on the radio at the right time each week and did the follow-up work required. Better selection of songs taught in schools was hailed as a special benefit. Thomas Young remarked in the *Education Gazette*:

> In our New Zealand schools one of the greatest needs is to build up a repertoire of suitable worthwhile songs . . . which will form the basis for the growth of musical taste. In this direction the National Broadcasting Service performed a valuable service in providing free collections of songs annually.

There was critical comment about a real need for 'children's songs about our own country', while Māori music was thought to be neglected by Pākehā New Zealanders because they had not taken the trouble to learn the language. Certainly, the repertoire had a dominantly international flavour: of the more than 600 songs promoted between 1943 and 1979 only 34 were of New Zealand origin, of which 20 had Māori titles. The broadcasts drew on the expertise of leading primary school teachers and teachers' college music staff.[25]

Thomas Young's national singing broadcasts on Thursdays at 1.30 p.m. were especially noteworthy. The choirs that he formed from the early 1940s are even now, nearly 60 years later, recalled as 'so important, so special'.[26] From 1936, Young had been the music lecturer at Wellington Teachers' Training College (following Ernest Jenner), and the process of using a school choir for his broadcasts was simple. He merely walked from the teachers' college across Kowhai Street to Kelburn Normal School for rehearsals with a composite Standards 4 to 6 class specially selected for their voices.

Tom Young had a great rapport with people and was able to motivate children to sing in classrooms all over the country. He spelled out his teaching plan in 1940: '(1) to introduce a new song in each lesson using the echo method; (2) to give help to

teachers who wanted to impart a knowledge of sight reading to their classes; (3) to explain the main features of music written in simple time'.[27]

One of the reasons for Young's success was that he had an excellent assistant both at the training college and for the broadcast choir. Pupils in the composite classes thought that her name was 'Miss Gay'.[28] This mystery woman, who came across from the training college three times a week to practise the week's songs and who was also at the 2YA studios on The Terrace to keep the children in order and at the ready, was actually Miss E. Conway. She is one of the unsung heroes in the propagation of superb choral singing in this country — deeply respected and keenly remembered by many but whose contribution is largely unacknowledged.

A large number of parents and other adult listeners found Mr Young and Miss Conway's sensitive and dynamic work stimulating, and they expressed their appreciation of the broadcasts and other choral offerings on national radio. My personal experience bears this out. Until 1945 our family lived in the country at Western Lake, nearly an hour's journey from Featherston in the South Wairarapa. On afternoons my mother, a trained singer, would listen not only to Parliament on our battery-powered wireless

OPPOSITE LEFT Souvenir programme of 2ZW Choir, 1933. ALEXANDER TURNBULL LIBRARY, EPH-A-RADIO-1933-01-FRONT

OPPOSITE RIGHT Thomas Young at Queenstown, circa 1960. ALEXANDER TURNBULL LIBRARY, F-114421-1/2

ABOVE Tom Young's Kelburn School Radio Choir, 1944. COURTESY OF DENISE WILSON

but also to the classical repertoire on 2YA and the regular school music broadcasts, especially enjoying Tom Young's Kelburn School Choir.

Of the 26 children in the 1944 broadcast choir photo above, most of the names have been identified by one of the members: Denise Wilson (née North) — who has been a prominent contralto soloist and member of four chamber and community choirs.[29] It seems that many of Young's former choristers have since played important parts in the development of adult choirs, or the musical life of their communities, or in encouraging their own and other people's children to take up the choral pastime that enriched their lives so much.

At the same time, there was a contrary viewpoint from influential choral musician Vernon Griffiths, who expressed grave doubts about the worth and effectiveness of radio in education. The work of Jenner, Young and others, however, demonstrated what a boon the medium was for music appreciation and school singing programmes particularly. The *Education Gazette* commended the 'special value' of carefully planned radio lessons, stating, 'We are apt to lose sight of the fact that we need instruction if we are to appreciate any of the fine arts, and not least the art of music.'[30]

Two other outstanding musicians arrived on our shores during the first half of the twentieth century. They were Stanley Oliver in 1934, who would win an international reputation with a new Wellington choir, and Georg Tintner in 1940, described as 'a brilliant musician of world class', who would take an Auckland choir to new heights.[31]

Stanley Oliver had a dramatic start to his New Zealand conducting career. In March 1934, the 43-year-old stepped ashore in Wellington on the way from Canada to visit an uncle in Melbourne. After conducting at a public concert in the city, he was offered the conductorship of the Royal Wellington Choral Union, a position he eventually held for 17 years. This confident English-born Canadian had grown tired of 23 years of cold Canadian winters and he found a warmer, ready welcome in New Zealand.

In his early teens in Kent, England, Oliver had already trained two church choirs. In Canada, he had been director of the vocal and choral departments at a liberal arts college for women, organist and choirmaster at the largest Protestant church in Montreal, and artistic director of the Montreal Mendelssohn Choir. During his Canadian years, various noted conductors and composers, including Sir Henry Coward, Ralph Vaughan Williams and Gustav Holst, had written to him congratulating him on his work.

Oliver set up a voice-training studio in Wellington and within two years initiated Schola Cantorum, a chamber choir modelled on the world-famous Schola in New York. He invited 25 singers, including several of the city's leading soloists, to gather with him in Begg's Piano Salon in central Wellington to form a choir for the study of 'Modern Works'. A Wellington reviewer would claim within a few years that Mr Stanley Oliver 'has provided the best small choir we have ever known'.[32]

Lin Saunders, in critiquing two Schola recitals in Auckland, said that the choir could hold its head up high in any part of the world, noting the conductor's fine use of tone colours and an 'acute musicianship and pitch sense'. He hoped that the choir would return to Auckland, 'to give us more of these ennobling performances'.[33] Sir Malcolm Sargent, who conducted one of the first concerts in 1936, said that it would already 'be Grade A in any city in the world'. Within three years of the choir's formation the *Dominion* and *New Zealand Free Lance* were reporting: 'Such distinction in style and tone is something new to Wellington';[34] 'No one has ever exhibited such keenness and enthusiasm for the choral compositions of modern composers';[35] 'His Baton will Begin Centennial Celebrations . . . he will conduct massed choirs . . . before an audience expected to be of between 50,000 and 60,000 people'.[36]

The secret of Oliver and the Schola Cantorum's success is multifaceted. The choir's preparation was one key. The body of singers met for 'study and enjoyment'

Stanley Oliver, circa 1955.
PHOTOGRAPHER UNKNOWN

with no set concert schedule. Disciplined rehearsals and starting on time were a priority. The singers worked hard, eagerly and loyally, 'like galley slaves', going home 'mentally tired out, if not physically exhausted'. Oliver had chosen well — inviting the right people — even if one-third did leave after one year.[37]

The Schola's fresh repertoire is another key. Unfamiliar works, full of modern chromaticism and intonational challenges, were very soon the usual fare in rehearsals.[38] 'After five seasons the choir had undergone an intensive course in contemporary music with benefit to its musicianship, together with an advanced study of choral technique which enhanced its reputation for singing.'[39] In time, concert-goers learned that Schola concerts would always be substantial, stimulating and widely talked about. They particularly appreciated the way in which the choir exemplified the stylistic differences between historical eras.

Another reason Oliver was seen as a great gift to the country was his optimism and constant encouragement, mixed with a relentless aim for high standards. Choir member Harry Brusey's honest comment about him was, 'This man had drive, and we were driven. The impression remains, though we know him better now, of a ruthless, outspoken, scathing and relentless conductor with an ear as keen as a razor blade.'

Yet another reason the Schola caught the public's imagination was the perceived relevance and topicality of its programmes. A concert in St Francis Hall, Wellington, on 1 June 1939 featured Vaughan Williams' cantata *Dona Nobis Pacem* (in English 'Give Us Peace', first performed at the Huddersfield Festival three years earlier) as part of a

TOP Stanley Oliver and Schola Cantorum in the Wellington Town Hall. ALEXANDER TURNBULL LIBRARY, PACOLL-5595-01

BELOW 'Mr Oliver'. Cartoon by A. S. Paterson, *The Dominion*, Wellington, 19 June 1934. ALEXANDER TURNBULL LIBRARY, MS-PAPERS-9204-1 socially conscious programme just three months before the Second World War began. In an obviously heart-warming presentation, the disquieted audience appeared to be 'in complete sympathy' with those who sang and played.[40] All felt the need for peace in our time to be 'urgent, necessary and greatly to be desired'.[41]

Georg Tintner arrived in New Zealand from Vienna, via London, in 1940. Later he was to draw the Auckland Choral Society out of its doldrums and lead it to achieve remarkably high standards.

In his native Vienna, Tintner had been a singer in the Vienna Boys' Choir, the only Jewish boy ever accepted into the prestigious group. He had heard Lotte Lehmann and Richard Tauber sing in opera and recital, he had heard the 1932 premiere of the Alban Berg *Lyric Suite*, seen Toscanini, Furtwängler and Bruno Walter conduct Mahler, Beethoven and Bruckner, had written instrumental compositions, and felt all of 'the tremendous creativity and ferment that was going on' in pre-war Vienna.[42] Later, he had been a conducting student of Felix Weingartner and assistant conductor of the Vienna Volksoper (the People's Opera). Being Jewish, he had found living in Austria in the 1930s to be 'marvellous and alarming at the same time'.[43] 'When he lost his Volksoper position after the annexation of Austria in 1938, Tintner began proceedings to sue the Volksoper for breach of contract, but soon came up against Nazi intimidation and viciousness. Many years later he said of the incident, '"Please do not believe that I was courageous. I was simply crazy."'[44]

Wanting to leave Vienna because of the persecution, he could not gain entry to other countries because he had no connections, no reputation and no money. Richard Hoffmann, a former student of his who had become a New Zealand resident, became his lifeline. In 1938, it was arranged for Georg and his sister to immigrate here. Arriving in Auckland in 1940, he became a New Zealand citizen, conducted the Mt Albert Presbyterian Church choir, gained a little work as a piano recitalist, composed,[45] and, with his wife Sue, established a poultry farm in Waitākere, west of Auckland. Later, in 1946, he would become the dynamic conductor of the Auckland Choral Society, winning the position over dozens of other applicants. That story is told in a later chapter.

7

After the Second World War: A new world beginning

Unsurprisingly, there was a renaissance in choral singing immediately following the Second World War. Energy pent up by the suppression of so many freedoms during the war was bursting forth in every field of human endeavour — economic, political and social. Choir directors and committees, motivated by the enthusiasm of returning members, and inspired by the creative energy around them, were dreaming of new achievements.

Refreshed choral passion appeared as part of the vision of a dynamic post-war world full of limitless possibilities, with far more time for leisure activities now that the war effort was over.

Over a dozen leading musicians, including five of the specialists from overseas mentioned in the previous chapter, had already begun to change the face of choral activity in New Zealand in the years before 1940. A rebirthing process had already been occurring before 1945 in literature, painting and instrumental music, led by imaginative artists, entrepreneurs, publishers and enthusiastic followers. What happened after the war in the choral sphere was echoed in the arts generally.

New Zealand writing hadn't withered during the war. The 1940 Centennial produced a flood of books, and, before that, novels such as John A. Lee's *Children of the Poor*, Robin Hyde's *Check to Your King* and John Mulgan's *Man Alone* had found English publishers. Some older books, for example Satchell's *The Greenstone Door*, had been reprinted and the publications of Caxton Press had helped create an audience for verse. A wide range of other literature appeared, from Ronald Meek's *Maori Problems Today* and Stella Morice's children's book, *The Book of Wiremu*, to *We New Zealanders*, A. R. D. Fairburn's ponderings on our national character.

From its outset in 1939, when founded by arts activist James Shelley, the *New Zealand Listener* had made the arts, particularly writing, a major focus, publishing works by leading figures such as James K. Baxter, Janet Frame and Maurice Shadbolt.[1] *Landfall*, Charles Brasch's enduring quarterly, began in 1947, publishing short stories, poetry, reviews, and addressing all the arts in various ways.

In the visual arts, because painters were prevented from travelling to Europe to study (shipping dangers cut off travel to Europe during the war), artists like Rita Angus, Toss Woollaston and Colin McCahon explored the landscapes of their native country, to find ways 'to abstract rather than report'.[2] They were to find the most telling of symbolic images, but although there was generally keen interest in New Zealand painting, their idioms were not readily grasped by members of the public. Traditional work in oils and watercolours dominated art exhibitions. Sculpture, pottery, wood carving and craftwork were comparatively invisible.

Live theatre had suffered great damage with the advent of 'talking pictures', but there had been a charmed period until the late 1930s with touring companies performing musicals like *Chu Chin Chow* and *The Desert Song*. By the end of the 1940s, musical comedy was revived with shows such as *Oklahoma* staged by vigorous local amateur operatic societies.

A spirited home-grown drama tradition also developed, but it came a little

ABOVE The chorus of the Kiwi Concert Party performing in Egypt during the Second World War.
ALEXANDER TURNBULL LIBRARY, DA-01436-F

LEFT An unidentified children's choir singing at James Smith's department store, Wellington, 1959.
ALEXANDER TURNBULL LIBRARY, EP/1959/4301-F

later than the growth in fiction, poetry and painting. By the late 1940s and 1950s, Wellington's Unity Theatre was to provide many of New Zealand's emerging actors, playwrights and directors with an apprenticeship in theatre skills. Bruce Mason, Richard and Edith Campion, Nola Miller, George Webby, Sunny Amey and others were key players. Unity's repertoire of plays was said to cover 'almost the entire corpus of modern drama'.[3]

In the music sphere, the decade 1929–39 had been a lean time for New Zealand instrumentalists; many players had found work as teachers (private and at schools) or they took non-music jobs. By 1930, theatre musicians faced a very uncertain future because of the departure of silent films.[4] Some instrumentalists obtained regular work and broadcast contracts with newly formed YA radio station orchestras, while others decided to take on advanced training to prepare for professional playing after the war. In 1932, the formation of the British Music Society — a group that promoted chamber music through its branches around the country — provided work for a few.

During the war, however, some instrumentalists thrived; there was no shortage of work for dance band musicians in the cabarets and halls throughout the nation — especially once American troops arrived for rest and recreation at Paekākāriki and other centres in 1942. Instrumentalists also joined the Kiwi Concert Parties to provide entertainment for servicemen and -women. Pipe bands and brass bands carried on their publicly applauded work, and 25 brass bands were equipped for service in the Middle East and the Pacific.[5] During the war, some women's bands were formed for the first time and the Air Force and Army Bands gave performance opportunities to leading players. It was claimed in 1945 that brass band music, along with the pipes of the many Highland associations, made up New Zealand's real music. Many small centres had developed bands from the beginning of the century or even earlier, and besides municipal bands there were workplace groups such as the Wellington Tramways Band, the Wellington Waterside Band and the Roslyn Mills band. Brass bands were to win multiple honours overseas in the years ahead.

Historian F. L. W. Wood described musical activity among the people as intense, though uneven. The limitations imposed by wartime constraints, he said, were severe, but music struggled on and thrived where there was enthusiastic, informed leadership. The little South Taranaki town of Hāwera, for instance, could muster an orchestra of 50 thanks to an enthusiast, H. C. A. Fox, who had taught most of the players, including the leader, his son Louis. The small town also sported four flourishing church choirs, one conducted by Louis Fox, a Male Voice Choir (also conducted by Louis), several school choirs, a children's choir (The Hawera Midgets), and a smallish Orpheus Choir.[6]

One common problem was the lack of focus for local talent — no national conservatorium or regional conservatoria, no national orchestra — along with a cultural cringe that lauded overseas recognition rather than local achievement. Wood observed:

> Connoisseurs deprived of first-rate orchestras and full of intolerance for anything New Zealand could possibly do, turn into gramophone fans. The highbrow collects records as a philatelist collects stamps. . . . And alongside the classicist is the swing fan who scents new records with the same clairvoyance. There are many young men and women who listen to the performance of the best American swing orchestras with a critical ability based on real knowledge both of composition and performance.[7]

He also wrote that 'an astonishing number learn to sing or to play the piano'.[8] With more children than ever learning instruments, many of whom sat English music exams, music teachers were busy. Surprisingly, there was also more money around to buy sheet music and recordings. But demand exceeded supply. Second-hand instruments and accessories were scarce, and the importing of pianos had stopped early in the war.

In this period choir directors continued as best they could, keeping their choirs going even if they were overshadowed at times by the spurts of progress in instrumental music and other art forms. Wood reported that 'there are choirs all over the country'.[9] Most towns still had a choir, and the main centres had more than one, but since many of the male personnel were serving overseas, sopranos and altos often overwhelmed the tenor or bass sections after mid-1941 (depending on what the latest military service ballot had thrown up), and the quality of choral presentations was highly variable.[10]

Notwithstanding the challenges, Handel's most popular oratorio, *Messiah*, was likely to be performed as the Christmas season approached. Sometimes such large choral masterpieces had to be reduced to small-scale means: J. S. Bach's massive *St Matthew Passion* was presented in Christchurch Cathedral, not with the requisite double chorus, double orchestra and 10 soloists over several hours, but with a smallish choir, a few soloists, an organ and piano, in one and a half hours. 'This is all we can afford ourselves in New Zealand, but it is surprising how a competent presentation with these means can give us a sense of the immense wealth of the music; a less competent performance would bring us, instead, to a realization of our music poverty.'[11]

Wellington, however, had managed to stage a complete performance of the same *Passion* the previous year (1941) in the Dominion Museum Hall. The committee of Stanley Oliver's Schola employed only one outside soloist (using choir members for the other parts); they included an hour's tea break during the performance and made a net profit of £2-13-5 (around $500 today). The inventive Kiwi 'can-do' mentality was taking hold.

Following the celebrations and post-war adjustments after Victory in Europe Day on 8 May 1945, the general population began to realise that a new day was dawning in many areas of life. The thousands of returning soldiers and nurses also quickly sensed a new beginning.

People became aware of the growing presence of high quality in many parts of the musical spectrum. Events such as the announcement of the first rehearsals and premiere performance of a national orchestra (October 1946 to March 1947), along with the visits of the Boyd Neel String Orchestra in 1947 and the Boston Symphony in 1960, captured the imagination of music lovers and arts enthusiasts. The energy and enthusiasm of the first conductor of the national orchestra, Anderson Tyrer, was undeniable, but his musicality was questioned by Stanley Oliver, J. C. Beaglehole, and other individuals and organisations. It wasn't until the appointment of James Robertson (1954–57) and John Hopkins from 1957 that choral music was well served by the orchestra's conductors.

Hitler's exiles — performers, teachers and music administrators fleeing Germany — had brought in a new wave of knowledge, skills and standards. Part of their legacy would be as catalysts in forming an indigenous and influential Chamber Music Federation. Regional arts festivals, which presented professional-level music, drama and other arts in one package, were developed in the 1950s. The enlivening Cambridge Music Schools, beginning in 1946, always included an enterprising choir and featured, especially, a composers' class, the first of which was directed by Douglas Lilburn.

In the post-war years, a greater number of choirs incorporated New Zealand compositions in their repertoires and some of them commissioned works directly from composers. To some extent following the lead of earlier composer Alfred Hill, chorally attractive, and not infrequently demanding, choral works were produced by Edwin Carr, David Farquhar, Ronald Tremain, Jenny McLeod, Jack Body, Christopher Blake, David Griffiths, Douglas Mews, Dorothea Franchi and others.

Popular music introduced new genres and directions. In 1946, the strong influence of popular music was presaged with the launch of the *Lifebuoy Hit Parade* on ZB stations. When the startling film *Blackboard Jungle*, with its soundtrack of Bill Haley's 'Rock Around the Clock', reached New Zealand cinemas in 1955, the age of rock 'n' roll had arrived. Added to this were many popular entertainment phenomena such as the Howard Morrison Quartet (1958) and the modern folk music revival of the late 1950s and early 1960s, including the discovery of our own folk songs by Rona Bailey, Les Cleveland and Neil Colquhoun. The result was a heady mix of juxtaposed musical genres and a dozen new directions. The lid was off a modern Pandora's box. Choral arrangers increasingly brought a selection of this material into their repertoires.

Schools played their part in this new world. The recommendations of the Thomas Report, an influential investigation of the post-primary curriculum, were implemented in 1946, making music a compulsory core subject. Music specialists were to be appointed to all secondary schools; many didn't yet have one.[12]

A generous scheme of in-school group tuition of instruments had been announced in 1945. Within a decade this was to lead to a remarkable growth in school orchestras and bands.[13]

Free tuition in musical instruments for primary children came about in 1960, in conjunction with the provision of pools of orchestral instruments in each Education Board district. Children were permitted to borrow an instrument for a limited time. Suddenly hundreds of nine to 11-year-olds became part of a larger, national music-making community. Structured Saturday morning schemes where children could join orchestras were encouraged. Christchurch soon had four graded orchestras and Wellington had up to 250 children taking part.

Clearly, musical progress was being made, but the noticeable lack of national leadership in music education since Douglas Tayler's departure in 1931 had long been a sore point with many in the musical fraternity. In the Department of Education, Philip Smithells had been appointed to lead Physical Education in 1939 and Gordon Tovey had become the Arts and Crafts Supervisor in 1942. But there was no such appointment in music.[14] Music's turn didn't come until Philip Skoglund, Minister of Education in the 1957–60 Labour Government, told his department and the public that he was 'particularly keen that music in schools should be given more attention'. It was his intention that a director of school music 'would travel around the schools and help in the organisation and encouragement of music'. In 1958, a position of National Adviser on School Music was advertised widely, and in 1959 William (Bill) Walden-Mills, director of music at King Edward Technical College, Dunedin, moved to Wellington to take up the position. He brought with him experience of music

ABOVE William Walden-Mills plays the guitar for a group of school children. ALEXANDER TURNBULL LIBRARY, PACOLL-5771

LEFT William Walden-Mills, National Advisor on School Music from 1959. ALEXANDER TURNBULL LIBRARY, PACOLL-5771 advisory work in Norwich, England, and six years of teaching in Dunedin. If there is a question as to why a New Zealand-born person wasn't appointed instead, an answer might well be that there was no well-trained, experienced and qualified primary or secondary music teacher available. No specific secondary school music training existed at the time.

What Wellington received was a slight, moustachioed figure with a rather military manner and sometimes controversial ways, who had come from a traditional English background. But as an amenable 50-year-old with endearing energy and a warm sense of humour, Walden-Mills was willing to fit into and accept what departmental inspectors wanted him to concentrate on. The firebrand Vernon Griffiths hadn't been acceptable to the Department of Education, but Walden-Mills was.

Once in his new position, Walden-Mills was surprised to find himself immediately assisting in the selection of members for the first National Youth Orchestra. This bold concept, of an orchestra for the best of the emerging orchestral players nationally, had been discussed by James Robertson in 1955 and 1958,[15] and a year later was formally established by new National Orchestra conductor, John Hopkins.[16] The year 1959 also saw Walden-Mills conducting a first national secondary schools orchestral holiday course in Auckland. With choirs as his first love (he had been very popular with the Dunedin Choral Society and had already formed a small adult chamber choir, the Renaissance Singers, in Wellington), it is not surprising that Walden-Mills came up with the idea of a choral singing course similar to the orchestral course in which he had already been involved. He invited Spotswood College, in New Plymouth, to host the first course in August 1966.

The importance and wide-ranging ramifications of this initiative will be made clear in the next chapter. But a national youth choir to match the National Youth Orchestra would have to wait another quarter of a century.

Along with the growth and expansion of music-making and singing nationally, there was new development in the already strong music of the tangata whenua. As a result of a new focus on nurturing Māori song and dance, choral singing in the 1960s became one of the features of kapa haka competitions.[17] A national event, Te Matatini, emerged in the late 1960s, and became a three-day biennial festival and competition in 1972.[18] Its disciplines included whakaeke (entrance song), mōteatea (traditional or contemporary chant), waiata-ā-ringa, poi, haka and whakawātea (exit song).[19] National respect, recognition and international acclaim developed for these

First National Polynesian Festival Competitions, Rotorua, 1972. Waihirere team from Gisborne (Māori aggregate winners). PHOTOGRAPHER R. ANDERSON. ARCHIVES NEW ZEALAND, AAQT 6539 W3537 1/R5206

The Tongan Choir from Holy Trinity Anglican Church, Otahuhu, singing at the Church of the Holy Sepulchre in Auckland during the visit of Archbishop of Canterbury Justin Welby. ANGLICAN CHURCH IN AOTEAROA, NEW ZEALAND AND POLYNESIA / LLOYD ASHTON 2014

disciplines as well as for cultural traditions such as pōwhiri (welcoming ceremony) and tangihanga (rites for the dead), and Māori festivals generally.

Lively Pasifika choral traditions with differing vocal styles were also being recognised. By 1972, there were over 50,000 Pacific Islanders living in New Zealand (up from 3600 in 1951); this led to a growth in the number of Samoan and Tongan church choirs.

Various churches, including St Paul's Presbyterian in Christchurch and Taranaki Street Methodist in Wellington, became the home for these communities. In addition to singing in church choirs, this new force was felt in school and community choirs. Singing has always been a big part of Pasifika cultures, with choir night and choir competitions a special feature of Pasifika church programmes. Later, its resonance and colour dramatically enriched the sound of the New Zealand Youth Choir and the New Zealand Secondary Students Choir.

Pasifika singers had a growing impact on the New Zealand scene. When bass-baritone singer Joel Amosa won the 2018 Lexus Song Quest grand final, his victory was the fifth time in 10 years that a New Zealander of Samoan heritage had won the competition.

The steady stream of Pacific Islanders into New Zealand after the Second World War was matched by the thousands of immigrants arriving from other countries. They had heard of employment opportunities, had often met New Zealanders, or had relatives here. Many came for a 'better life' — usually understood as a healthy lifestyle, a sunny climate and an egalitarian society. Over 100,000 took advantage of the full assisted-fare scheme offered by the New Zealand Government for 30 years from July 1947. Some of the new arrivals were conductors and more would have been singers: more than 66,000 English immigrants settled here between 1945 and 1971.

The influx created a hunger for cultural pursuits, and in the post-war environment New Zealand was increasingly able to meet the demand.

8

The main cities take centre stage

In the 1850s and 1860s choral societies were established in the four main cities. In 1864 a choral society was formed in Dunedin, which in 1871 became the Dunedin Choral Society. It continued to perform during the Second World War with singing teacher Alfred Walmsley conducting a choir of about 85 members and their own orchestra. It sometimes combined with the Returned Services Association Choir and with the Royal Dunedin Male Choir, which had (and still maintains) an unbroken record of performances since its founding in 1886.[1]

The Dunedin Choral Society had had a chequered development over its first 50 years after it was formed in 1871. Historian Jenny Burchell identifies 'trouble spots where they appointed a conductor who was perhaps less musically competent than a large number of the choir, or where committee and conductor lacked focus'.[2] The magazine *The Triad* (edited by C. N. Baeyertz in Dunedin and read throughout the country) provided acerbic criticisms of performances.

New life was brought to the choir when William Walden-Mills was appointed conductor in 1953. He advanced the choir's technique and musical expression and expanded its rather conservative repertoire. He was followed by Peter Platt, who introduced many new works (by Carl Orff, Benjamin Britten and Sergei Prokofiev) and included the city's first performance of the Beethoven *Choral Symphony*. The Choral Society, which has since changed its name several times, adopted the name Schola Cantorum in 1967 when Jack Speirs took over and merged it with the University Union Choir. Speirs auditioned the choir vigorously, streamlining it to 60 very well-trained choristers and expanding the repertoire still further.[3] Dunedin was fortunate to have these three choral leaders during the post-war period.

St Paul's Cathedral, Dunedin, has had a notable history of church music, with its choir known for its high performance standards and wide repertoire. Victor Galway, Charles Collins and Donald Byars all held the director's position with distinction, Byars raising St Paul's to become 'one of New Zealand's finest choirs'.[4]

Later, in 1985, Raymond White took the choir to Europe, the first New Zealand cathedral choir to visit there. The influence that St Paul's has had on choral singing in this country is indicated by the number of future National Youth Choir members that have come through the choir. Tecwyn Evans, Diccon Sim, Martin Snell and Tony Sandle all appear in the photo overleaf. Composer Richard Madden was assistant choirmaster of the Cathedral, and Peter de Blois, later a deputy conductor of the New Zealand Youth Choir, was a leading member and organ scholar in later years.[5]

Notwithstanding the musical achievements, it hasn't always been sweetness and light in cathedral choirs, with relationships between choir directors and clergy sometimes less than cordial. Historian Peter Lineham summarises some of the rivalries and disputes:

> At Dunedin Cathedral, the director of music, Raymond White, was dismissed in 1998. His successor was also dismissed. Similarly in Auckland there was a struggle between Michael O'Connor, the dean at the newly enlarged Holy Trinity Cathedral, and Indra Hughes,

The Cathedral Choir of St Paul's, Dunedin, in St Paul's Cathedral, London, in August 1985. Front, from left: Alan Firth, Kelly Gillian, Jonathan Huntley, Derek Cutfield, Jonathan Shine. Second row: Kendall Henderson, Dominique Peyroux, Dominic Fitchett, John Matthewson, Gregory Peyroux, Luke McKinlay. Third row: Martin Shelton, Rupert Henderson, Philip Thompson, Matthew Smith, Damian Peyroux. Fourth row: Raymond White (musical director), Richard Madden (assistant choirmaster), Andrew Letham, Tony Sandle, Martin Snell, Mark Simpson, Timothy Snell, Stephen Smith, Gerald Madden, Diccon Sim, Adam Butler (organ scholar), Tecwyn Evans. PHOTOGRAPHER DONALD EVANS. COURTESY RAYMOND WHITE

> musical director, and in 2000 choir and director left and formed the highly regarded independent Musica Sacra. These stories could be repeated many times over at the parish level with devastating consequences.[6]

Knox Presbyterian Church in Dunedin has also had a noteworthy choral record. With its Scottish Free Church heritage of having no instrumental music in worship, a precentor led the singing when the church was opened in 1860. The second precentor started a singing group to help the singing of psalms and biblical paraphrases, and a formal choir appeared in 1865. Opponents of the 'kist of whustles' (case of whistles: a pipe organ) were not won over until nearly 20 years later. A choir of about 65 established a high reputation with frequent performances in venues away from Knox Church. During Paget Gale's time as organist and choirmaster from 1905, anthems were sung regularly at Sunday morning services, and his choir was said to be capable of rivalling the Anglican Cathedral's choir. Later choirmasters (and they were all men) included Roy Spackman, and Peter Warwick from 1971 to 1985. After Warwick's death, Roy Tankersley, Bruce Aitken, Peter Stockwell and Karen Knudson introduced a large range of substantial musical settings, major works and New Zealand compositions.

Everyone knew it already. Stanley Oliver and others had spoken of it. Christchurch's choral culture was the best in the country. The heritage of Bradshaw, Peters, Jenner and others was crucial in forming future musical leaders and helping to draw music students to the city. This legacy lived on through a new generation of choral musicians.

After nine years in Dunedin, Vernon Griffiths returned to Christchurch in 1942. While teaching in Dunedin, Griffiths had added a Doctor of Music degree to his qualifications and had been invited to apply for the position of professor at Canterbury University College. By 1946, he had revitalised the undergraduate music courses and established a master's-level musical leadership course with a specific aim of providing training for working with choirs. In a revolutionary move, he founded the Addington (Railway) Workshops male voice choir in an attempt to introduce music into the lives of industrial workers. But this move was not out of character for Griffiths. Egalitarian attitudes coloured his ideas about life, composition and national culture. Believing that almost everyone had a 'usable' voice with which satisfactory results could be quickly

TOP Performance of the Royal Christchurch Musical Society, 1920. PHOTOGRAPHER STEFFANO WEBB. ALEXANDER TURNBULL LIBRARY, 1/1-005543-F

BELOW The Dunedin Choral Society, 1947. CAMPBELL PHOTOGRAPHY, DUNEDIN. HOCKEN LIBRARY, UNIVERSITY OF OTAGO, S13-587

achieved (in comparison with instrumental training), he poured his compositional energies almost exclusively into choral music.

In Christchurch, he continued to compose choral works for adults and children, including cantatas and major pieces for choir and brass band, as well as compiling eight volumes of the *Dominion Song Book*.[7] His books were specially intended for many groups, including the armed forces, Diocesan Choral Festivals and Bible Class Massed Choirs, but they were most valued in post-primary schools.[8] It is interesting that his compositions rarely reflected the horror or harshness of his own experiences among the poor in Norwich, and as an officer in the trenches in France, from which he was invalided home.[9] Always genial and gracious, 'Griff' was one of the country's most well-known musicians and made a huge impact on choral music in New Zealand, particularly nationally at the secondary school level.[10]

John Ritchie was appointed a music staff member at Canterbury University College in 1946, succeeding Griffiths as professor of music in 1962. Ritchie's amiable ways and leadership abilities saw him serve a short period as acting vice-chancellor of the university and a longer time as secretary-general and president of the International Society of Music Education. But equally impressive is the comprehensive list of his choral compositions, as well as the range and versatility of his other works.[11]

One piece is a five-part, a cappella setting of metaphysical poet Richard Crashaw's 'Lord, When the Sense of Thy Sweet Grace'. Written in 1954 for Christchurch conductor Peter Zwartz, it has been singled out as a masterpiece. Ritchie said of the text: 'Even though the language is recklessly romantic, rich in exaggerated religious image, it still to me possesses the reality of religious art. . . .' Peter Godfrey included it in his programmes and his Dorian Choir made the first recording.

Ritchie conducted several Christchurch choirs, working with the Addington Workshops male voice choir around 1962. In later years he wrote the haunting song cycle *Canary Win* for one of the prominent woman conductors of the time, Nan Anderson, and her women's choir, the Cecilian Singers.

William (Bill) Hawkey, pianist and organist, joined the University of Canterbury music staff in 1962, having conducted the University Madrigal Singers from a year after its formation in 1952. With the Madrigal Singers, he had astutely tapped into the market for traditional hymns with an LP recording as part of A. H. & A. W. Reed's Kiwi Sacred Recording series.[12] For several years he had also been the accompanist for the Christchurch Harmonic Society. All this activity began as a result of the young Timaru-born Hawkey getting his big break from Ernest Empson, his Christchurch

LEFT William Hawkey, director of music for the Christchurch Harmonic Society from 1960 to 1974. ALEXANDER TURNBULL LIBRARY, EPH-B-MUSIC-CHS-1937/1979

THANKSGIVING
JUBILEE
1927-1977

Victor Peters

The Christchurch HARMONIC SOCIETY

William R. Hawkey

CHORAL MATTINS
AT 11 AM ON SUNDAY
21ST AUGUST 1977
IN
CHRISTCHURCH CATHEDRAL
CHRISTCHURCH,
NEW ZEALAND.

Dobbs Franks

BELOW Programme of the Christchurch Harmonic Society's jubilee concert in 1977, featuring three previous conductors of the society — Victor Peters, William Hawkey and Dobbs Franks. ALEXANDER TURNBULL LIBRARY, EPH-B-MUSIC-CHS-1937/1979 piano teacher; the perceptive Empson had encouraged him to go to the University of Canterbury to study music.

Hawkey was a charismatic figure who breathed new life into the Christchurch choral scene. He was a vigorous and astute choral professional who, after becoming conductor of the Harmonic Society in 1960, won the confidence of the New Zealand Government to have the choir represent the country at the first Commonwealth Arts Festival in London in 1965. Hawkey's programmes in England and Europe included Christchurch originals such as Ritchie's 'Lord, When the Sense of Thy Sweet Grace', and the director's own 'The Avon', but the highlight of the choir's tour was working with English composer William Walton on a performance of his celebrated cantata *Belshazzar's Feast*.

Hawkey had utilised his considerable entrepreneurial skills to get 153 Harmonic choristers to London and back in the earliest days of international jet travel. But he also had the wisdom to gather around him an expert committee.

In his Christchurch concerts, Hawkey introduced music that was unsurprising to concert-goers around the world,[13] but he didn't shirk tougher assignments such as Michael Tippett's *A Child of Our Time*. Tippett's secular oratorio was written with a sense of outrage in response to Nazi atrocities, including the *Kristallnacht* pogrom of 1938. The choir would have found it challenging rhythmically and demanding in its subtlety of expression, but they conquered the difficulties. The choir also continued the tradition of complete presentations of Bach's *Mass in B Minor*. Hawkey's initiative of placing a 'Young Performers' segment in his concerts, bringing several chorally minded schools to the public's notice, restored a linkage that Victor Peters had established with Christchurch Girls' High School while choir director there. Among the schools invited was Southland Boys' High School, under director Kennedy Black. In addition, Hawkey organised a Christchurch choir for disadvantaged people of all ages.

Given one of three national 'Outstanding Young Men' awards in 1967, Hawkey was later awarded an MBE. In 1976, he left for Australia, where he later became director and professor of music at Australian National University and was the founding director of the Canberra School of Music Llewellyn Choir.

Born in London, Robert Field-Dodgson learned all the fundamentals of choral singing as a chorister at Christchurch Cathedral Grammar School from choirmaster J. C. Bradshaw. He completed a Bachelor of Music degree at the University of Canterbury under Vernon Griffiths and became a fine pianist, organist and singer.

Also a charismatic figure in the music world, Field-Dodgson was appointed conductor of the Royal Christchurch Musical Society (RCMS) in 1949 at the age of 23, and director of music at Christ's College in 1952. Upon appointment to the RCMS, he bravely auditioned *out* of the choir some long-standing singers who were not up to standard. At his first concert, the same rejected, angry singers sat at the front of the balcony of the Civic Theatre and booed loudly as he came onto the platform. Such are the perils and vulnerabilities of public music-making. In 1956, Field-Dodgson received a state bursary to study with Sir Adrian Boult in London.

Field-Dodgson's RCMS was New Zealand's first large choir to travel abroad. In 1962, three years before Hawkey's tour, the choir travelled to South Australia to be part of the Adelaide Festival, singing Walton's *Belshazzar's Feast* and Antonin Dvořák's *Te Deum* with the London Philharmonic under Sir Malcolm Sargent.

Another invitation in 1971 took the RCMS to Sydney and Melbourne. As a deputy conductor of the choir, I was privileged to be part of that tour and took part in a performance of Verdi's *Requiem* in the Sydney Town Hall, which has one of the largest pipe organs in the world. I was standing alongside one of the massive organ pipes, the 64-foot pedal reed (an important place for a second bass to stand, naturally), and while beginning to absorb the pipe's vibrations, I remembered that a climactic moment, marked in the score as *ffff* (quadruple forte), was soon to arrive. Little did I know what an unforgettable, physically moving, indeed primal, experience it would be! The 'Dies Irae' (Day of Wrath) section of the *Requiem* was launched ferociously by the conductor, using the large choir of mature voices, full symphony orchestra and an organ registration to maximum effect.

Field-Dodgson had an extraordinary breadth of knowledge of the arts, and as a choir director was known for his sensitive and compelling rehearsals. He conducted the RCMS for 41 years and his years of leadership were recognised with an MBE. No other large choral society in New Zealand has ever had the same conductor for such a length of time. Field-Dodgson died at the age of 73 in Christchurch.

Rivalries between choirs were also a feature of the Christchurch scene. The arch-rivalry in sport between the Boston Red Sox and the New York Yankees was surely matched by the long choral rivalry between the Christchurch Harmonic Society and the Royal Christchurch Musical Society. Both choirs were around 150 to 200 voices; both choirs had a good cross-section of the adult choristers in the city and environs (with the Harmonic recognised as having the better sopranos and the Royal the better altos); both choirs had outstanding directors; both choirs wanted to sing similar masterworks; and both needed to attract big audiences in order to pay for performance costs. If the Royal sang the Brahms *Requiem* in English, the Harmonic, not wishing to be seen to be competing directly, would sing the same piece in the same year in German. If the Harmonic gave a first New Zealand performance of a major work (Walton's *Belshazzar's Feast*, 1955), then the Royal would also give one (Herbert Howells' *Hymnus Paradisi*) in the same year. It is a comment on the availability of so many mature singers, and the willingness of a city to support two large choirs, that both choirs survived for so long with almost no crossover of membership.

The Primary Schools' Music Festivals, begun in 1939, had been a big factor in helping Christchurch build its reputation as the country's choral capital. George Martin, a primary teacher and church organist, received support for a Christchurch Schools' Music Festival and was appointed musical director. The first festival, made up of 25 school choirs, had been held one month before the outbreak of the Second World War in 1939, and was very successful. However, because of his Christian pacifist leanings, Martin's tenure was short-lived. The Canterbury Education Board decreed that as a conscientious objector Martin was no longer suitable to lead the project. Headmasters objected to this action and said that if Martin was not acceptable, they would close the festival down, which they did.[14] After the war, Hugh Findlay, and then Keith Newson (1949–70), conducted the event.[15] Pianists filling the important role of accompanist included Charles Martin.

The rise of suburban groups such as the South Brighton Choral Society and the Risingholme Community Choir, and the appearance of workplace choirs in the Hays Department Store and the Addington Workshops, is evidence of how choral singing began flourishing again in Christchurch communities after the war. In 1949, the Civic Music Council inaugurated an annual festival of community choirs, an event which has continued ever since, featuring traditional songs, sea shanties, spirituals, anthems and similar repertoire, and sometimes more extended pieces.

Male voice choir singing continued to be advanced by the Liedertafel (in existence since 1885), and women's choir singing by the Liederkränzchen. The two cathedrals maintained their own traditions, and several thriving church choirs continued to enrich worship, including Oxford Terrace Baptist (George Macann and David Sell), Durham Street Methodist (Wallace Woodley) and St Barnabas Anglican (Vic Ellena). All this community activity, together with the strength of choral singing in schools, encouraged people to become involved in singing in general and choirs in particular.

A bright new day dawned on Christchurch's choral scene in 1972 when the new Town Hall's purpose-built concert auditorium was opened. The city's two large choirs had successfully introduced new, exciting and important repertoire in the 1960s, such as Orff's spicy *Carmina Burana*, the often-neglected Dvořák *Requiem Mass*, and Schönberg's *A Survivor from Warsaw*.[16] But the choirs had always had inadequate performance spaces, particularly because of the size of orchestras required. This problem was solved on 30 September 1972 with the opening of the new auditorium. There was a palpable sense of euphoria in the choral music community.

Now began the challenge of filling the 2500-seat facility to offset hall and orchestra hire fees, and all the other expenses of presenting a modern choral concert. This was at a time when insufficient financial support, including lack of substantial sponsorship, meant that rising orchestral costs and the extremely high cost of some new music were cramping the activities of New Zealand choral societies.

A new Christchurch publication helped build national choral morale. *New Zealand Choral News* appeared in 1970 from the University of Canterbury Registrar's Office. William Hawkey was the prime mover and choir member Ann Schrader was the first editor. It was Schrader's belief that reading about each other's choirs would build good morale. She argued that the inspiration of choirs performing music to a very high standard would help committees facing the demands of rising costs and the constant need for new members.

In its third edition, in May 1971, Schrader wrote of the imminent overseas tours of the Royal Christchurch Musical Society and the University of Auckland Choir as an effective answer to the claim that choral music was mainly an amateur enterprise. She thought that, like the amateur bandsman, the amateur choir singer had a dedication to their art that took them to the front in the international arena.

A year and a half later the *Choral News* listed all its subscribing choirs and conductors. This list provides a snapshot of some of the most active choirs in the country and tells us something of those who were adding to 'the quality of life' — a phrase often heard at the time from politicians.[17]

Schola Cantorum, which had been formed in 1936 and continued until 1955, was a central part of Wellington's renewed musical life after the Second World War. True, it had given fewer concerts in the latter stages of the war, but rehearsals had continued, so it was well placed to assume its leading role when peace was declared. Its standards had remained extraordinarily high. In 1947, it gave New Zealand's first full performance of Bach's *Mass in B Minor*. By 1948, a *Dominion* reviewer was enthusing: 'One has to hark back in the memory to the Sheffield Choir to recall choral singing comparable to the Schola Cantorum. . . . The music of the Vaughan Williams mass was alive with radiant hues, as varied as a summer garden.'[18]

Music critic Owen Jensen was of a similar frame of mind in 1950: 'The Schola Cantorum has so far outstripped other choral work in New Zealand that we are left without any reliable measuring rod of their excellence. Overseas critics . . . have confirmed our pride in an organisation which has demonstrated convincingly what fine musicianship and patient effort together can accomplish.'[19]

Along with great musicianship and patient hard work, the Schola's continuing success was due to Stanley Oliver's conducting abilities (especially the use of his hands and arms) and his overall direction of performances. Oliver's technique was said to be masterly, with 'the generous sweep of his baton and the expressive persuasions of his left hand' controlling, interpreting and inspiring.[20] This came in a report of a 1951 presentation of the *Mass in B Minor*. The audience was said to be 'transported from "the mundanity of just another Saturday" to the unmistakeable, inimitable atmosphere that pervades something that is of God'. The 'magnificent contribution' of the director was undeniable.[21]

By 1954, Owen Jensen had decided that 'the Schola Cantorum has exercised a considerable influence on the musical life, not only of Wellington, but of the whole country'. 'Early on . . . 300 [attendees] would have been regarded as satisfactory. . . . Now, anything under 1200 may cause dismay. And that's a very good audience anywhere for music.'[22] But none of this increased income from box-office success went to anyone in the choir. For the whole of its history, payments were made only to soloists and orchestral players, with neither conductor nor accompanist receiving fees.

Returning to Melbourne after a visit to New Zealand, the Australian Sir Bernard Heinze was motivated to say: 'I consider the Schola Cantorum of Wellington, New Zealand, to be probably the finest choir of its kind in the world. It should be brought to Australia as soon as possible.'[23] It never was.

The probably very flimsy claim that Oliver's star shone brighter than the All Blacks' is based on a newspaper's positioning of an article about the Schola Cantorum. The 1951 clipping shows how the *Auckland Star* gave priority to Harry Brusey's book on the Schola's history over an aticle entitled 'Success Predicted for All Blacks'.[24] Even if too much is made of this editorial decision, and even if there is a degree of reading back into history the current standing of the All Blacks, nevertheless a story of a

Accompanist Writes History Of Choir

"This is for study and enjoyment. We may give a concert if and when we feel ready to do so." In this spirit the Schola Cantorum held its first meeting in Wellington in 1936, and it is still the policy of the choir, which is in Auckland this week-end to give two concerts in the Music Festival.

Sir Malcolm Sargent, who conducted its first concert later in 1936, said that it would already "be Grade A in any city in the world."

Stanley Oliver, its founder and permanent conductor, is a Canadian who had been two years in New Zealand when he invited 25 singers to join him in this enterprise.

Among them were some of Wellington's leading soloists, and all of them had had considerable choral experience. Later the choir grew to more than 30 in number, but the standard of individual excellence stays as high as ever, and admission is still by careful invitation.

In a booklet just issued, Clement Howe, who has been the Schola's accompanist throughout, writes a history of its 15 years. He had included a full list of the music performed in this time. It is an impressive list of pioneering in contemporary music, but its first New Zealand performances include also Bach's Mass in B Minor.

Contemporary music was the choir's main study for the first four years, after which it turned increasingly to the classical and polyphonic period. Aucklanders who heard the Masses of Palestrina and Vaughan Williams given by the Schola in St Matthew's Church during last year's festival realized that they had attained equal excellence in both ancient and modern music. Mr Howe, by the way, regards that St Matthew's concert as the Schola's peak performance of all the years.

No Rules

"I have been asked about out rules and regulations," writes Mr Oliver in the foreword. "We have none. In a co-operative effort such as ours, rule-making is the first sign of disintegration. Rules and regulations soon become the negation of loyalty to a common aspiration."

As outsiders see it, the Schola Cantorum's outlook is as exceptional as its music. Study and standards have come first, profit-seeking engagements last. No fees have been paid to its members, though the choir has paid large sums to outside soloists and its orchestral members are always paid. The choir members, many of them professional singers, pay a subscription to the Schola, and the conductor and accompanist accept no fee. Buying music has been a considerable item.

Mr Howe passes briefly over the financial aspects, because it is not the Schola's policy to ask public sponsorship. But it is interesting to find that on this basis has been built the finest ensemble work that any group of New Zealand musicians has yet achieved.

Mr Oliver has only twice handed over his baton—once to Sir Malcolm Sargent and once to Mr Andersen Tyrer. "The standard expected was high and the pace terrific," Mr Howe writes of their early rehearsals with Mr Oliver.

"This man had drive and we were driven. The impression remains, though we know him better now, of a ruthless, outspoken, scathing and relentless conductor with an ear keen as a razor blade."—D.F.T.

Success Predicted For All Blacks In Australia

WELLINGTON, Friday.—The prediction that the All Blacks will do very well on their Australian tour was made by members of the University team which returned to Wellington today. They said they saw the All Blacks at practice yesterday and reported them all fit and well.

During their own tour, said the manager of the team, Mr R. G. Bush, of Auckland, the forwards proved themselves superior to the Australian forwards and in both Tests got control in the second half.

The Australian students seemed to rely on about six backs and, when one of them was out of action, they did not know who should fill his place.

R. A. Jarden, who, with J. N. Tanner, was remaining in Australia to join the All Blacks, was sensational, said Mr Bush.

The way Jarden was going he should be one of the All Black Test wingers. Members of the University team picked Dick Tooth, Cyril Burke and John Solomon as likely backs for Australia.

Tooth, they considered, would probably be first five-eighths against the All Blacks. Apart from C. R. Moore, who dislocated his collarbone last Wednesday, there had been no

ACCEPTANCES FOR WAIPA CLUB'S WINTER MEETING

At the Waipa Racing Club's winter meeting, to be held at Te Awamutu next Saturday, the Arapuni Hack Handicap has been made two separate races, with divisions in each. Divisions have also been necessary in the Wairini Hack Handicap.

The doubles totalizator will be operated on the Woodstock Stakes and the Orakau Hurdles.

Acceptances:—

10.45 — ANDREW KAY MEMORIAL HACK STEEPLECHASE, £375, about 2½ miles.—Euryalus (9), 9.10; Betterboy (8), 9.9; My Boy (19), 9.2; Hazara (3), Whawhairelhi (15), Pin-Up (10), 9.1; Superb (11), Regal Fame (18), Yusuf (5), Bainbridge Gunner (4), Regal Chase (12), Roll Over (17), Hardrada (16), Trench Hunter (1), Turoto (13), Sharlina (6), Bellnamara (2), Arrowtrack (7), Miss Nasrah (14), 9.0.

11.35 — FIRST ARAPUNI HANDICAP, £270 (or £360 if run in two divisions), 1 mile.—First division: Treasure Fox (12), 8.10; Cecily (5), 8.3; Valla Vale (9), 8.1; Treval (1), Bofors (4), Gay Calorie (13), Pictavia Lass (10), Eagle (8), Art Shade (3), Glen Gavin (17), Seahaven (2), Royal Fox (6), Valtavia (11), 8.0. **Second division:** Regal Fair (8), 8.5; Careless Talk (2), 8.1; Little Rita (3), Arigna (10), Prince Contact (6), Hiko (4), Subscriber (9), Lady Evrus (11), General Supreme (13), Greek Act (5), Portland Bay (12), Flamboyant (7), Son (1), 8.0.

12.25—WOODSTOCK STAKES, £550, 1½ miles.—Big Notes (19), 9.0; Con Spirito (5), 8.9; Carnegie (1), 8.8; Kilfenora (14), Reliance (9), 8.3; Roista (4), 8.2; Gay Coronach (8), 7.12; Frontier Mac (10), 7.7; Sleepy Duke (3), 7.4; Grande Fille (16), Tactful Lad (17), 7.2; Gay Spion (15), Gavinmor (11), Terminate (18), Radiant Fox (2), Clear View (12), Gay Sari (6), Soeur de Beau (7), Lord Treasure (13), 7.0.

1.10 — W. G. PARK MEMORIAL STEEPLECHASE, £750, about 3 miles.—Redingote (8), 11.6; Dukeron (6), 10.8; Ohuka Fox (3), 9.10; Corsair (1), 9.9; Moutoa Lord (2), 9.5; Euryalus (10), Betterboy (5), 9.2; Paul Gregor (9), Pleasant Bay (11), 9.1; The Call (4), Sharlina (7), 9.0.

1.55—ORAKAU HURDLES, £525, about 1½ miles.—Moutoa Lord (3), Fort Knox (8), 9.13; Happy March (2), 9.9; Kyrat (10), Bustany (1), Dr John (7), 9.4; Barry's Girl (5), Sir Oswald (9), Hazara (4), Ututere (6), 9.0.

2.45—SECOND ARAPUNI HANDICAP, £270 (or £350 if run in two divisions), 1 mile.—First division: Silver Archer (2), 8.10; Glencrana (12), 8.1; Jovial Quest (1), Cimbal Song (8), Sir Cimbrone (10), Spiteful Lad (13), Sleepy Beau (3), Highland Rose (9), Catriona (4), Valda's Praise (7), Bramble Thorn (5), Intercede (11), Bainbridge Pat (6), 8.0. **Second division:** Chief Admiral (10), 8.5; Gold Cloud (5), 8.1; Wotan's Gold (9), Royal Tradition (8), Nepkin (3), Prince Aga (13), Gold Spray (12), Indian Charm (2), Red Rastus (6), Regal Motion (7), Admiral's Yarn (1), Gold Scorn (11), Guardsman (4), 8.0.

First in each division, £135; second, £30; third, £15.

3.30—HAIRINI HACK HANDICAP, £320 (or £440 if run in two divisions), 1½ miles. First division: Special Script (6), 10.2; Lone Star (13), 9.2; Bolton (8), 8.9; Brer Mark (3), 8.2; Treval (2), Malla (14), Intuition (1), Egyptian Prince (12), Knight's Star (10), Proficiency (7), Grey Moments (11), Leon Fox (15), Hillcrest (9), Lady Leonie (16), Sunny Baron (5), 8.0. **Second division:** Lekas (2), 9.13; Silver Archer (7), 8.10; Malbomie (4), 8.4; Balham (3), 8.3; Shikari Lad (14), 8.1; Barry's Girl (5), Belle Lorraine (11),

LEFT Choral news trumps the All Blacks. *Auckland Star*, 9 June 1951. AUCKLAND LIBRARIES HERITAGE COLLECTION

BELOW Members of the Schola Cantorum at rehearsal, 1955, with Stanley Oliver at far right. ALEXANDER TURNBULL LIBRARY, EP/1955/0514-F

Wellington choir that had wowed Auckland several times was the editor's choice for the flavour of the page.

The *Southern Cross* had figured out that not only did the Schola Cantorum take a special place in the country's musical life but also that its conductor was 'one of the few musicians in New Zealand to devote his energies to the performance of contemporary music'.[25] The *Auckland Star*'s view was just as clear-cut: 'Four parts of the "Western Wynd" mass by . . . John Taverner were perhaps the highlight of the Schola's visit. . . . What Mr Oliver has built here has already become a legend of musical achievement in New Zealand.'[26]

Another report mentioned the mainly British and American repertoire, and talked of 'the Schola's brilliant versatility and the continuing enterprise of its conductor'.[27] Then there was a story about an Australian company that made the first LP recording of any New Zealand organisation because the ensemble had won a world reputation, and another about the BBC broadcasting a programme in honour of New Zealand National Day, 'the main feature of which was a series of items by the Schola Cantorum'.[28]

The Schola's last appearance was on 11 December 1955. Oliver had arranged for a new choir to be established in its place — a larger group to be called the Phoenix Choir, of which he was to become honorary music adviser. The Phoenix went on to sing major works with the National Orchestra under James Robertson and to present unaccompanied music with Harry Brusey.

Upon his retirement, many in the musical world paid tributes to Oliver and his chamber choir. However, an equally generous tribute from the man himself is a telling clue to understanding choral development in this country. It was about the calibre of New Zealand choral singers that he had worked with. Oliver had cultivated 'the wide fields of choral music in Canada before he came to New Zealand in 1934', but he said of the Schola Cantorum that he had 'never before worked with a more cooperative group nor a more competent one'.[29] Oliver died in 1964.

The Oliver phenomenon gave Wellington and New Zealand many taonga over a 20-year period: not-to-be-missed concerts, greater public awareness of choral works of art, intelligent rehearsing, the sharing of international best practice, and many more.[30] But the power, beauty and widespread acclaim of Oliver's groundbreaking achievements are now virtually forgotten.

In Wellington the demise of Oliver's Schola created a huge void for its expert choristers and the concert-going public. Not long afterwards, the flagging Royal Wellington Choral Union presented its last *Messiah* and it finally dissolved in 1959. While this was happening, Malcolm Rickard's new Orpheus Choir was becoming better known, growing in numbers and expanding its repertoire. At the same time, Maxwell Fernie was beginning a 40-year directorship of the St Mary of the Angels Choir, and had become a mentor to young musicians, including Anthony Jennings, who were to become future leaders in the city.

In writing about the post-war times, Simon Tipping says that 'there was a feeling abroad that somehow a better world should emerge from the chaos and loss of the Second World War, and clearly music was to be part of it'.[31] Tipping was therefore not surprised to find that in the Hutt Valley in early 1947 a newly formed music society had produced a vocal group. American Horace Hunt and New Zealander Len Schwabe had brief tenures as musical directors of the vocal group, which was under the chairmanship of Harry Brusey.[32] In 1949, Malcolm Rickard, a local conductor making a name for himself in Wellington and Eastbourne, was appointed. When, in 1952, the vocal group's parent body was dying, a separate organisation was set up and the newly born Orpheus Choir was on the way to becoming 'one of the foremost large choirs in the country'.[33] Rickard would be at its helm for 34 years.

In 1955, Rickard travelled to England on an Imperial Relations Trust bursary to hold discussions with the BBC on professional matters (he held a senior position in the New Zealand Broadcasting Service) and he was also able to hear many choirs and attend the Three Choirs Festival in Gloucester.

The works that Rickard's deputy, Ivan Hills, conducted while Rickard was overseas are indicative of the less demanding music featuring in the very early programmes of the Orpheus choir and in other choirs of the time. Hills rehearsed and conducted Stanford's *The Revenge* and Edward German's 'Just So' songs, putting them alongside Edward German's 'Merrie England' and 'Tom Jones', and other choral songs of that genre. This was the only concert that Ivan Hills conducted in his 39 years as deputy conductor. His long service as a deputy (and later associate) conductor is probably a New Zealand record.[34] A soloist in a later performance of these works was baritone Peter Nisbet, who became, many years later, general manager of the New Zealand Symphony Orchestra.

By 1958, the Orpheus Choir had increased in size to over 80 singers and the choir's repertoire had expanded to include standard oratorios such as *Elijah* and *Creation* and, naturally enough, *Messiah*. With higher standards of choral work, it had developed a handy relationship with the National Orchestra. In addition, it was enjoying financial assistance in the form of broadcast fees. Under the guidance of Director of Broadcasting James Shelley, broadcasting became New Zealand's principal cultural patron with the aim of developing 'artistic endeavour and civic consciousness

Malcolm Rickard was the conductor of Orpheus Choir, in Wellington, for 34 years. Photograph taken for the *Evening Post* in 1959. ALEXANDER TURNBULL LIBRARY, EP/1959/1561-F

of towns and districts' throughout the nation. The patronage of YC stations, which was welcomed by many major choirs, was to continue through the 1960s and well into the 1970s.[35]

In 1929, at the height of the Great Depression, a young accounts clerk who had been educated at Marist Brothers' School in Newtown, Wellington, and later at Wellington College, had secured a choirmaster/organist's position at a city church. Maxwell Fernie began work at St Joseph's Catholic Church next to the Basin Reserve.

Eight years later, in June 1937, at the age of 27, Fernie began a community vocal group, the Aeolians, named after Aeolus, the Greek God of the winds. In choosing this name for the group, was Fernie thinking of the sighing, musical tone sometimes produced by the wind, or was he having a gentle dig at Wellington's reputation as the 'Windy City'?

His very full first concert included Henry Purcell's 'Nymphs and Shepherds', Edward Elgar's 'As Torrents in Summer' and Michael Arne's 'The Lass with the Delicate Air'.[36] A year later the *Evening Post* was reporting under 'Current Entertainments': 'Purcell's dainty melodies, country songs of different vintage, and familiar numbers of Handel, Schubert and Sir Edward Elgar were all sung in skilful and attractive manner by the Aeolians.'

As well as presenting their own concerts, the choir was invited to sing on radio (stations 2YA and 3YA), and in June 1940 they performed at Trentham Military Camp. The final concert in November 1940 opened with 'God Defend New Zealand' and ended with 'Land of Hope and Glory', 'There'll Always Be an England' and 'God Save the King'.

After serving with the Second New Zealand Expeditionary Force in Egypt and Europe during the war, Sergeant Fernie remained in London to study at the Royal Academy of Music, coming back to New Zealand for a few years before taking up an appointment at Westminster Cathedral.

In 1958, now an authority on Gregorian chant and sixteenth-century polyphony, Maxwell Fernie returned to his native New Zealand, wanting to escape from London's climate and a relentless five-year regime of organ playing and choir instruction at Westminster. He took up the directorship of the St Mary of the Angels Choir, a position he was to maintain until his death in 1999.

According to friend and former organ student Alan Simpson, by the mid-1960s Fernie had set new standards in choral music through St Mary of the Angels, establishing it as the leading church choir in the country. Simpson's judgement might be disputed by some, but at the very least it draws attention to Fernie's expertise and uncompromising faithfulness in unearthing the vitality and simplicity in masterpieces by Tomás Luis de Victoria and Giovanni Pierluigi da Palestrina. Fernie had dynamic and unorthodox ways of working with a choir and he influenced many notable choral conductors. The choir's electrifying singing of chant and polyphony and his organ playing helped form a new generation of musicians — Anthony Jennings, Peter Walls, Denis Smalley, Geoffrey Coker, Roy Tankersley, Christopher Hainsworth and Robert Oliver — the latter is the current director of music at the church, a former singing student of Fernie and one of the first conductors of the Wellington choir Cantoris. St Mary of the Angels was the place to be for these and other young musicians.[37]

A likely factor in Fernie's success was that he was as serious about the choir having fun socially as he was about the spiritual aims for St Mary's Choir. In addition to the choir parties, featuring sophisticated impromptu items and his own piano extemporisations, there were end-of-concert celebrations held regularly at the Wellington Railway Station, where 'startled commuters were treated to the full sonority of five to eight-part carols in the foyer, where the stone and marble and the loft dimensions created perfect acoustics'.

At the same time, a sign in the choir room in the church's crypt read *Ars nostra pro Deo* (Our art for God), and before every rehearsal a prayer to the Holy Spirit was sung. Greta Fernie, Maxwell's widow, confirms that his sincerity was as exuberant and deeply rooted as his high-spirited piano and organ improvisations.

Fernie's first singing student was Margaret Hunt, soon to become a well-known Wellington soloist and long-time member of St John's Church Choir. Other voice students included future singer/conductors Rosemary Turnbull and Ellen Barrett, along with Rosemary Quinn and two star students, Patricia Lawrey and Barry Mora. Wellington Teachers' College Head of Music, Laughton Pattrick, enticed the maestro to tutor at the college in Karori. In these ways Fernie reopened the eyes of singers and future conductors to what could be vocally possible in the choral medium.

An LP recording, *Sacred Polyphony of the XVI Century*, was made in 1963 in the resounding acoustic of the St Mary's Gothic-style building. It won an excellent review in the English music magazine *Gramophone*, bringing the choir an international reputation.[38] By this time the tone of the 50-voice choir had a Continental character — no doubt in part deriving from the cosmopolitan membership (hailing from Lebanon, Italy, Poland, the Netherlands and Vietnam, as well as many parts of the British Isles — this at a time when New Zealand's population was hardly cosmopolitan). The energetic, expressive sound, founded on singing with an open throat and deep diaphragmatic breathing, was a revelation to many connoisseurs of the art form. The choir's soprano tone has been described as reedy and bright, the tenors as brilliant, and the altos and basses as vigorous. All the service music was edited and handwritten by Fernie himself; copies with his spidery manuscript are still in use.

In 1967, Fernie was encouraged by Wellington musicians Judith White, Dorothy Freed, Penny Pruden and others to set up a secular choir. About 20 people were gathered together by word of mouth, and after a trial period the Schola Polyphonica Choir was founded, finally arriving at a membership of 40.[39] It was never intended to be a performance choir; members met simply to enjoy rehearsing some of the world's finest music.

> The Schola members found Maxwell's methods revolutionary and exciting. . . . He did not impose his stamp on [the music] so much as to allow it to take control of himself and his choir. A musical director who coached his singers in voice production, who made them stand [and] walked around poking their midriffs, saying 'marshmallow tummies' and 'no muscle', had to be special.[40]

After three years and some discreet auditioning, the choir began presenting public concerts. Initially they sang Palestrina and Victoria (including some chant), but later

LEFT Maxwell Fernie at St Mary of the Angels, Boulcott Street, Wellington, 1982. PHOTOGRAPHER SIMON TOWNSLEY, *THE DOMINION*

BELOW Maxwell Fernie and some members of the Schola Polyphonica in November 1975. Front row, from left: M. Coleman, Margaret Hunt, Ann Aitken, Penny Pruden, Jenny Pattrick, Yvonne James, John McMillan, P. Burnett, Michael Lawrence. Back row: Gillian Wilde, Jill Brewerton, Elizabeth Kerr, Judith White, Pam Gray, Diane Barnes, Penny Reeves. COURTESY OF C. H. PARKS, LOWER HUTT

drew on a wider range of styles than is now commonly remembered: the Monteverdi *Vespers*, Bach's *Mass in B Minor*, Haydn masses, Hector Berlioz's *Roméo et Juliette* (with Brian Priestman and the New Zealand Symphony Orchestra), Leoš Janáček's *Glagolitic Mass* and Britten's *Cantata Misericordium*.

Much talked about was the performance of an a cappella work that Fernie had taken a year to bring as close as possible to perfection. The Rachmaninov *Vespers*, said to be 'the last great crowning achievement of Russian Orthodox choral music', was presented in 1987 in the Wellington Town Hall.[41] It made enormous demands on the singers: 'passages of sustained high register fortissimo followed by long sections of pianissimo, requiring as a result of Maxwell's exacting standards, more control and support than the louder sections . . . many of the choristers were exhausted. . . . Maxwell's stamina and unflagging concentration carried them through'.[42]

Only one recording of the Schola was made — probably a gauge of Fernie's perfectionism. It comprised Victoria's *Tenebrae Responsories*, which are 18 a cappella motets for Holy Week, and it was released in 1983. The *New Zealand Listener* reviewer, Arthur Everard, proclaimed it to be 'a superb interpretation . . . the sound is bold and noble'.[43] It was remastered as a CD in 2008, with reviewer Lindis Taylor saying that it had stood the test of time: 'its reissue offers a new generation evidence of a unique choir working under a great choral conductor in music in which they were perhaps equalled but not excelled anywhere in the world'.[44]

Although Fernie added a new depth and variety to what the region's music lovers could enjoy, national recognition lagged well behind his local reputation. After he returned to New Zealand in 1958 it took about six years before his work at St Mary of the Angels began to be at all widely recognised. Typically, Fernie wasn't fussed about being acknowledged. Some recognition did come, however, when in 1969 the St Mary's Choir was invited to present a concert of sacred music at Holy Trinity Cathedral in Auckland. The timing of that invitation is interesting because in 1969 Auckland was beginning to take centre stage in New Zealand's choral life.[45]

Another Wellington leading light was Anthony Jennings. In his school years, Jennings had been regarded as something of a prodigy, accompanying church services as an organist at eight and forming his own parish choir at the age of 13, when attending Rongotai College. While still a student at Victoria University (he was in the first intake of performance music students studying organ with Max Fernie), Jennings was appointed organist and choirmaster at St Peter's Church, Willis Street, and also became conductor of the University Choir.

Immediately upon graduation in 1967, Jennings founded the Wellington Bach

Choir, taking on some extraordinarily ambitious projects. The youthful choir's presentations of the *Mass in B Minor* and the *St John Passion* and *St Matthew Passion* were said to be 'refreshing — a radical departure stylistically from the performances of the more established choirs'.[46]

In 1971, Jennings left Wellington to study at the Brussels Conservatoire and the Guildhall in London. A notable harpsichordist, he was to become one of New Zealand's leaders in the revival of interest in historical performances of baroque and early music. When he returned to New Zealand, he figured prominently with the Auckland Cathedral Choir and at the University of Auckland, and it would later be said that he opened up the sound of choral singers that he worked with. Terence Maskell, long-time colleague of both Peter Godfrey and Jennings, now says, 'Peter's *fortes* weren't especially robust. Tony's *fortes* were spine-tingling.'

Choral music was entering a new phase in Auckland after the war. At the university, Professor Horace Hollinrake had developed a large Music Club Choir, which, according to his son, Roger, was 'the prototype of numerous university choral groups that have flourished since'.[47] The repertoire in 1954 included English part-songs and Charles Parry's *Blest Pair of Sirens* (with orchestra and a choir numbering 78). Fellow staff member Thomas Rive directed a madrigal group in the same year, singing works by Jacques Arcadelt, Victoria, John Wilbye and other Tudor composers.

Hollinrake's influence was also felt on other university campuses. It was largely as a result of his efforts that advanced training in musical performance, including solo voice, was established in universities. Later, his successor, Charles Nalden, correctly credited him with the necessary far-sightedness, vision and patience to found such practical courses.

Unfortunately, Nalden then exaggeratedly stated that this founding step was the most profound 'ever to have been taken in the story of our country's musical development'.[48] Still, Hollinrake's work was highly significant. An 'Executant Music Diploma' was introduced in 1956 at the University of Auckland — a first for New Zealand universities. It came a year after Hollinrake's early and unexpected death at the age of 51.

The historical detail of how university performance courses were approved and introduced is less important than assessing their benefits since 1956. The training given by voice lecturers at the major institutions to aspiring soloists in opera, music theatre, lieder or oratorio foreshadowed the training of future conductors, choral coaches and elite choral singers that followed. Vocal training, whether at tertiary level or in schools or the community, was to play a key role in the blossoming of New Zealand's choral culture later in the century.

Meanwhile, in 1946, the fortunes of the Auckland Choral Society (ACS) were attracting the public's attention for a less than admirable reason. Colin Muston's conservative, even dull, 30-year tenure of the ACS was coming to an end. And the rumour mill was correct; there was a successor waiting in the wings, an Austrian émigré who had arrived in New Zealand in 1940, Georg Tintner.

Tintner won the position over dozens of other applicants — all of whom were in England — and he soon transformed the choir. The news travelled fast. Aucklanders were discovering that they had a Georg Tintner goldmine in their midst.

Within the choir, there were some who tormented Tintner because of his German heritage, but musically, he made a great start, even with *Hiawatha* — a work he regarded as a second-rate English pot-boiler. The following year, he conducted the *Peasant Cantata* — the first time in its 92 years that the ACS had sung Bach. While rehearsing his first *Messiah*, he was invited to take over the Auckland String Players, a group of 13 players founded by Owen Jensen. Reviewer Lin Saunders noted Tintner's 'painstaking preparation and a sincerity that puts the music before all else'. In August 1949, he directed the orchestra in Lilburn's *Diversions* and thereafter promoted Lilburn's music, considering him the best composer in Australasia.

The way Tintner transformed the ACS was by auditioning every member meticulously. This was the first time that voice tests had been permitted by an ACS committee, and evidently not before time: a 92-year-old bass who had been in the choir since 1879 had just retired. Choristers were 'upset when he outlawed knitting, reading, gossiping and arriving late'.[49]

Tintner's complete *Messiah* performances with the renovated choir, as well as his *Elijah* and Brahms' *Requiem*, were all acclaimed. After five years of rebuilding, he mounted the first New Zealand performance of Beethoven's *Missa Solemnis*. Around the same time, he presented a 10-night season of Bedřich Smetana's *Bartered Bride* opera that included tenor Ramon Opie, a young soprano, Heather Begg, and a highly trained chorus. Professionally, Georg Tintner had 'arrived' in Auckland.

But Wellington and the National Orchestra were a closed book for him. Partly because of his very demanding standards, he was regarded as difficult to work with, and as a foreigner he didn't stand a chance when seeking employment by comparison with Englishmen Michael Bowles, James Robertson and John Hopkins, or English-trained New Zealander Warwick Braithwaite, all of whom were appointed

ABOVE Georg Tintner conducting his last concert, *Messiah*, with the Auckland Choral Society in 1953.
AUCKLAND WAR MEMORIAL MUSEUM TĀMAKI PAENGA HIRA, MS-13-15

LEFT Georg Tintner conducting members of the Auckland Choral Society in 1953.
COURTESY OF TANYA BUCHDAHL TINTNER

to the National Orchestra over him. Respected observers such as Alfred Hill and Antony Alpers, a choral bass in the ACS, spoke publicly of him as the finest musician in New Zealand, a genius and a person with the ability to inspire a high degree of loyalty in amateur musicians, but all to no avail. Although arrogant and somewhat eccentric, Tintner was probably unfairly treated by the Broadcasting Service heads in Wellington. Rewa Bissett, a violinist in the String Players, thought that he was ostracised by 'the bigwigs in Wellington. They treated him a bit as if he was lucky to be here.'[50]

Elsewhere in the country, Tintner was held in greater regard. At the 1953 Cambridge Summer School in the Waikato, he gave Anton Bruckner's *Mass in F Minor* its first New Zealand outing. Not unusually, he conducted it from memory. Later in the year, he conducted the ACS in another work that he loved and promoted: Beethoven's oratorio *Christ on the Mount of Olives*. Added to the twice-weekly ACS rehearsals, he took on a Māori choir and drove fortnightly to Katikati to assist a friend with his choir: all this in addition to Orchestral Society and String Players rehearsals and free private harmony and theory classes. He led a busy life.

However, at age 36 Georg Tintner was frustrated and annoyed that he wasn't making greater strides in the conducting world. So when a job as resident conductor of the National Opera of Australia was offered, he faced a very difficult challenge. He would have liked to have stayed in New Zealand, attached to the place where he had felt 'for the first time in practice, the equality of man'. He knew that he would miss his sister, his wife and his farm, but he was persuaded by others to take the opportunity presented to him.

Before he left in 1953, Auckland audiences gave him warm ovations; they knew what they would be missing. Lin Saunders wrote of the choir's performance of the Bruckner *Mass in F Minor*: 'But for one man's fervent enthusiasm for one of the 19th century's most neglected great composers, Auckland would have missed a choral performance that for an hour touched off a mood of spiritual feeling rarely created in the concert hall. It was not surprising that in every way this was Mr Tintner's night.'[51]

Tintner's departure dealt a body blow to Auckland choral music. In retrospect one wonders why there was no serious attempt to create an attractive position for him that would have allowed him to stay in the city and take guest appointments overseas. Financially it may have been feasible. The pre-war 'bootstraps' no longer applied in a now booming economy; by the early 1950s, the Labour Government's social welfare schemes had helped give New Zealand the world's highest standard of living. And there was a new hunger for culture. However, the innovative thinking required to keep Tintner in Auckland was not yet common. He had been a life-saving bonanza to the Auckland Choral Society, but his time there — six and a half years — was relatively short. The city had been temporary guardians of a goldmine but now the mine had been closed down.

When Auckland choral musicians were left reeling from Georg Tintner's departure, they knew the crisis they faced. There was no obvious successor for the key position of conductor.[52]

Eventually, Ray Wilson, formerly organist and choirmaster of Auckland Baptist Tabernacle, agreed to take up the position. Astutely, he appointed as his deputy the fine accompanist and organist William (Bill) Power. In 1957, Wilson conducted his favourite work, the *St Matthew Passion*, for the first time in the history of the choir, and many times thereafter. He would exhort the choir: 'It's the greatest opera ever written. Even if you don't believe it, you've got to admit it's a helluva good story.' Society members found him a gifted, if slightly unorthodox, musician. 'He could be eccentric. On one occasion they arrived at rehearsal to find him busily sawing the legs off the Choral Society's grand piano. A set of new castors had made the instrument taller. So he had decided on instant surgery to restore it to a more comfortable height.'[53] In later years, National Orchestra conductor John Hopkins judged Wilson to be 'a very good chorus master'. Wilson held the position for 25 years.[54]

The other musical enterprise that had attracted public attention as Tintner was leaving the ACS was the growth of the Dorian Singers. Since the war, Harry Luscombe, a conductor and popular teachers' college senior lecturer, had been introducing the choir to a great deal of English music. He was said to be 'responsible for popularising the works of Vaughan Williams and contemporaries in New Zealand'.[55]

The greatest achievement of the Dorian Singers at this time was thought to be the 1957 performance (assisted by other groups) of Bach's *Mass in B Minor*.[56] 'Gussy', as he was commonly known, also generously gave his time to schools' festivals as conductor and pianist, and to the musical programmes of the university and other groups. He retired from the Dorian Singers in late 1960, after 20 years, and died less than a year later. The *Auckland Star*'s obituary referred to his work as 'keeping the flame of music alive' during the years: 'It was on the work of Mr Luscombe and a number of other dedicated musicians like him that the present flowering of music in New Zealand was founded.'[57] But he never implemented a succession plan and for several years a leadership vacuum had been looming.

Choral singing wasn't flowering so well in some other Auckland fields. At St Mary's Anglican Church in Parnell, the late 1940s and 1950s witnessed an unremarkable choir singing unremarkable music. Other church choirs were functioning faithfully, but often failed to provide an inspirational spark because they lacked a solid vocal grounding and confident leadership. At St Patrick's Cathedral it would be 1970 before Douglas Mews, organist, composer, teacher and musicologist, arrived from London to raise standards markedly.

Then Peter Godfrey arrived in Auckland with his wife Sheila and their four girls in November 1958.

Like many earlier British immigrants to New Zealand in search of a warmer climate, Godfrey had been looking for a long time to move away from the icy conditions that afflicted England every winter. In Marlborough, Wiltshire, Godfrey had been director of music at Marlborough College and conductor of three other choirs in the area. He was a former chorister and choral scholar of King's College Chapel, Cambridge, had studied music at Cambridge and the Royal College of Music,[58] and now was regarded as an outstanding organist, sought-after teacher and a choral trainer with a fine tenor voice. But he was restless.

The big chance came when Godfrey attended the Three Choirs Festival in Gloucester in 1957. He heard that a New Zealander, Malcolm Rickard, was attending the festival and he made it his business to have talks with Rickard about employment prospects in the land to which he wished to immigrate. All this led, finally, to the University of Auckland Head of Music, Charles Nalden, offering a lecturer's position, and Dean Monteith at St Mary's Anglican Cathedral offering the job of director of music.

St Mary's was an ageing parish choir and no attempt had been made to make it a cathedral choir; St Matthew-in-the-City had a choir of that calibre but was shut down around 1958. Dean Monteith's initiative to get Godfrey out from England and build a cathedral choir bore fruit almost immediately. Godfrey transformed the sound of the choir within a matter of months.

Music administrator Peter Averi records how he heard, in early 1959, a live church broadcast of matins and being 'bowled over by the sound of the choir without knowing which one it was'.[59] The electrifying effect on Averi made him aware of the change that this Englishman had brought about in the St Mary's Choir.

Godfrey set about trying to establish a choir like that at King's College, Cambridge, except that instead of having boy trebles he invited very good young female students from the university to join the choir. With a constant stream of excellent voices, his preference for a pure, straight sound in the soprano line could be satisfied. And with intelligent, committed members, his insistence on intonational perfection

ABOVE Peter Godfrey conducting in Auckland, 1970s. FROM *PETER GODFREY: FATHER OF NEW ZEALAND CHORAL MUSIC*, BY ELIZABETH SALMON, MĀKARO PRESS, 2015

LEFT Harry Luscombe, conductor of the Dorian Singers, 1940–60, photographed in 1949.
ALEXANDER TURNBULL LIBRARY, EPH-A-MUSIC-1949-001

became increasingly possible — even in the unrewarding acoustic of the timber-built cathedral. Possibly the dry acoustics were invaluable in seeking this perfection.

Within a short three years the choir's LP recording *Music for the Church's Year* was being talked of in England as 'better than many English cathedral choirs'. Further LPs followed, including *Devotions in Music for the Holy Communion* (featuring the music of Tallis, Gibbons and Purcell to Stanford and Vaughan Williams). *The Way of the Cross*, issued in 1969, was a 'Procession for Good Friday' and included portions of the Psalms partly based on plainsong and partly newly composed by Godfrey. Gillian Lander, who for a time played the organ for Godfrey at the 9.30 a.m. Parish Eucharist, and who joined St Mary's Choir in the late 1960s, was impressed by Godfrey's spiritual commitment. His habit of spending time in prayer and reflection in the side chapel before services seemed to indicate his purpose for devoting so much time to music at the church. In preparations for worship, he showed a depth of understanding that would go back to his early days at King's College, Cambridge, with fabled music director Boris Ord.

With the help of thorough, probing auditions, the setting of a membership age limit and focused hard work, Godfrey and the choir gained a reputation for consistency of tone, beauty of intonation and a substantial, fresh-sounding repertoire. Several members of the choir were to become well-known New Zealand musicians; they included Gillian Whitehead, Jack Body and Allan Thomas.

In 1968, Godfrey began an active interest in choir singing at the university and he formed an all-comers choir. Shortly afterwards, that interest was to be heightened when the University of Auckland was invited to represent New Zealand Universities at the Third International University Choral Festival in New York in 1972. It was clear that if a specially auditioned choir were to travel, programmes of mainly secular music would be needed for American campuses, and sacred music for the tour extension to King's College, Cambridge, Westminster Abbey and European centres. Additionally, Māori music arrangements and New Zealand compositions would be expected from a Kiwi choir. This tour would be a turning point in New Zealand choral music.

9

The worth of investing in young people, 1966–86

A crisp August morning in New Plymouth in 1966. Spotswood College's Music Room, with its stunning view of Mount Taranaki to the west. Fifty secondary students from around New Zealand looking at each other uncertainly. The National Adviser on School Music, William Walden-Mills, is about to explain what this 'Madrigal Course' is all about. Walden-Mills himself could not have foreseen how significant that first course would be.

The introductory session was the start of a concentrated week of six hours' singing every day, from 'warm-ups' to miniature classics by Arcadelt, Orlande de Lassus and Rachmaninoff, choruses from Haydn's *Creation* and madrigals of the sixteenth and seventeenth centuries. No one had ever seen anything like this before — no one in the educational establishment nor anyone in New Zealand's choral community.

In 1966, young people had plenty to occupy their time without going to a course in choral singing. There were the few who had managed to see The Beatles during their New Zealand tour two years earlier, and the many who hadn't, but were still in the grip of Beatlemania. Many were listening to other songs hitting number one in 1966: The Monkees, Rolling Stones, Bob Dylan, Nancy Sinatra and Stevie Wonder. Many were fans of homegrown pop stars Maria Dallas, Mr Lee Grant, and Ray Columbus and the Invaders. Added to this, the pirate radio station Radio Hauraki had made its first transmission and the popular television music show *C'mon,* hosted by Peter Sinclair, had begun. The 'mod' look was becoming fashionable, and opposition to the Vietnam War had started.

Future international opera star Kiri Te Kanawa had recently won the Mobil Song Quest, and symphony and chamber music concerts were within reach of most citizens if they wished to attend. Igor Stravinsky had conducted his own works with the National Orchestra in the Wellington Town Hall in 1961, and jazz great Thelonious Monk had toured the country for the Music Federation in 1965. Television was in its sixth year and films such as *A Man for All Seasons* and *Alfie* were showing in the theatres.

School teenagers could also find plenty of part-time work in the strong economy, and some of those who had travelled to New Plymouth for the madrigal course had probably worked to cover their expenses.

Within New Zealand's increasingly dynamic society, there was plenty of choice for secondary school pupils in their holidays. There was no tradition of singing in choirs during vacations, and no one would have recommended going to a madrigal course. There are several clues as to why 50 school students would opt to spend a precious holiday week with strangers in a school they probably hadn't heard of, singing mostly unknown classical music, and much of it in a demanding a cappella style. One is the calibre of the singers who participated, such as Bruce Greenfield, who later became one of the country's finest accompanists. Two others, also from Hutt Valley High School, were Judith Grant and Beverley Enting, named as outstanding singers by Walden-Mills, who had them sing 'O Had I Jubal's Lyre' as a duet. Another clue is the quality of the music teachers and singing traditions (even if recently established) in the 15 participating schools — schools where group singing, including assembly singing, was prized. These included Queen's High School (Dunedin), Pukekohe High School, Matamata College, Westlake Boys' High School (Auckland) and Wellington Girls' College. Naenae College from Lower Hutt had appointed Grahame Lilly as music master in 1954, and annual music festivals, which involved a massed choir, and smaller choirs soon appeared.

Of course, one or two pupils may have registered for the event out of frustration with what was *not* happening in their school. Then there was the attraction of socialising with like-minded young people.

In the months prior to the course, Walden-Mills had contacted school music teachers to stimulate registrations, and inserted notices in the *Education Gazette*. The host school had agreed to provide a group of sopranos, altos, tenors and basses to assist balance between the parts. The aim was to mount a vocal equivalent to the successful instrumental courses offered over the past seven years. With a reasonably balanced mixed-voice group in front of him, at 9 a.m. on Monday, 29 August 1966, Walden-Mills gave a downbeat to begin the week's rehearsals, and the course was under way.

Walden-Mills had invested his time, energy and expertise into the first New Zealand-wide choral singing event of its kind for young people of any age. A recording of the final demonstration concert of that madrigal course shows how much was accomplished in just five days.[1] Walden-Mills prepared the massed repertoire while sets of madrigals were rehearsed by the two course tutors, Ian Menzies (Taranaki District Music Adviser), me as Head of Music at Spotswood College, as well as by Walden-Mills himself.[2] Brigid McLafferty, 20-year-old assistant music teacher at Spotswood College, assisted with one of the small groups and sang with the choir.

At the time, only the participants knew about the initiative, but eventually big things grew out of that small beginning, including freely available group vocal tuition, The Big Sing (later involving a third of the secondary schools in the country), national choirs of international standard, training for student-age conductors, and more. These outcomes would become widely known and applauded, and thousands of dollars would be invested in choral music for young people. However, it is Walden-Mills who is the hero of the story. He must be saluted for his intuitively correct decision to mount the course and then develop the idea further.

News of the success of the first madrigal course quickly spread. Enthusiasm from it rubbed off onto the following year's 'National Holiday Choral Course

Madrigal Course Choir outside Whiteley Memorial Methodist Church, New Plymouth, August 1966. William Walden-Mills is centre front. ALEXANDER TURNBULL LIBRARY, PACOLL-5771-001

for Secondary Schools' (the new name) held at Wellington Girls' College. The demonstration concert at Wesley Church in Taranaki Street was enterprising.[3] Wesley choirmaster Malcolm Rickard had kindly agreed to stage the concert in association with his Chapel Choir, and Walden-Mills had advertised the concert under the name of 'The New Zealand Secondary Schools Choir'. This was partly, he said, to let the public know what high standards could be achieved by school students after rehearsing for only a week, and partly because the name 'demonstration concert' would not have drawn a crowd in the capital city. A rather grander name was needed. As it was, the event managed to attract a reasonable audience.[4]

But there was no intention of carrying over students from 1966 to the following year, and there was no structure set up to keep in touch with the students involved. Occasionally, in subsequent years, final concerts were advertised as the New Zealand Secondary Schools Choir, but courses were always publicised as Holiday Choral Courses.

Subsequent courses were held at Epsom Girls' Grammar (1969), Cashmere High School (1970) and Otumoetai College, Tauranga (1971). Walden-Mills continued to lead similar courses in various parts of the country until 1973. These seven years of national courses were influential in helping to identify untapped interests in choral singing among adolescents, and each reinforced how much progress could be made in six days of hard work under committed, musically astute leadership in an atmosphere of encouragement and respect.

After 1973, the holiday choral courses lapsed for two years. When I became the national music officer in the Department of Education's Head Office in 1975, one of my first decisions was to seek renewed funding to revive them. I obtained funds from within the Department to re-establish the annual national course and also to add up to three courses a year in the regions. Offering North Island and South Island events was the next logical step.[5] The courses, which were designed to be both fun (as befitting a holiday) and suitably serious, had already earned a good reputation. Parents and the public expected the demonstration concerts to confirm the high standards previously set, and to reveal new strengths and directions.

A joint event called the 'New Zealand Secondary Schools Choir and Orchestra' held at Epsom Girls' Grammar School in Auckland in December 1975 was the first holiday choral course in the new era. The orchestra of 94 was conducted by Walden-Mills (invited out of retirement to assist), while I led the choir, whose 52 members had come from 15 centres across the country. Course tutors and conductors of madrigal groups included Elizabeth Mintz (Kerr), Laughton Pattrick and Phillip Bird. The one week of rehearsals included choral music by Vaughan Williams, André Kopolyoff and Malcolm Williamson, along with four madrigals and a spiritual. The demonstration concert was very well reviewed.

O'Rorke Hall at the University of Auckland was the venue for another combined course in August 1977. Two works were prepared for the 150 musicians. The first was directed by John Emeleus, a Royal Academy of Music-trained conductor lecturing at Palmerston North Teachers' College. It was *The Rio Grande* with jazz syncopations and influences from ragtime and Duke Ellington, all within an English choral idiom that composer Constant Lambert knew so well. I conducted the second work, the festive Haydn *Te Deum*, which also featured syncopated rhythms and powerful unison singing. There was no air of condescension in putting these adult works in front of secondary students; it was felt that the performers would rise to the challenge. Choir member Nicola Jansen recalls 'the vibrancy and excitement of the final performance as well as challenging and rewarding rehearsals where all the young musicians came together with focus and determination to master the sophisticated repertoire'.

Interestingly, there were several participants who could have been accepted as either a player or a singer, and future members of the first National Youth Choir were to be found in this course.

In August 1978, half a dozen frustrated choristers in Palmerston North had a dilemma. They had been in rehearsals with 60 others at a secondary schools holiday choral course and applause at the end of the final concert in All Saints Church had just died away. They had sung together for three successive years. But they weren't eligible to attend any further courses. They were leaving school. Very, very politely, they asked the course director to make an exception to the attendance rule for the following year — just in *their* case, of course.

As course director, I was unexpectedly face to face with something totally admirable and not uncommon: barefaced enthusiasm for serious music-making. Their request was gratifying; the music that course members had been singing — Gabriel Fauré's *Requiem*, for example — was the kind of music they delighted in and could handle well. But where could they find more of the same? Opportunities in many towns and cities were limited. Socially, the six students would fit in well with the following year's course, and some valuable, experienced voices would be a bonus.

The choristers' requests confirmed the need for more choir openings for high school students, and the desirability of a choral track for school leavers similar to the orchestral pathway leading to the National Youth Orchestra. Agreeing to six school leavers returning in 1979 (to any course organised) put constructive pressure on me to do something about the wider problem. Clearly, a *post*-secondary school choir was desirable. The notion of such a choir had appealed to me in England two years earlier when hearing the County Durham Youth Choir perform in Durham Cathedral. The thought arose that we didn't have a choir like this at home, but if we did, we could do as well — or maybe better.[6]

I set about devising a national choir proposal to put to Director-General of Education William (Bill) Renwick and was somewhat unprepared for the level of encouragement that he immediately showed. When he was first approached with the youth choir idea his riposte was, 'There's only one thing wrong with that idea, Guy — you had it first!'[7]

It was fortunate to have Renwick's support. An unsympathetic departmental head could have made the birth of a national choir difficult. He was the right person in the right place at the right time.

The initial proposal put to Renwick needed to be based on developing a known growing point — an educational administration strategy widely adopted at the time. It also had to suceed because no one wanted to be involved with a highly publicised venture that went off half-cocked. If the concept were to become a reality, advertising and image would be crucial.

The concept needed to be attractive to discerning young enthusiasts from across the social spectrum and, if possible, appeal to all ages from 13 to 24. In addition, it had to be affordable and feasible for singers from Invercargill to Kaitāia. Just as importantly, it needed the best possible direction if it were to succeed. It appeared that having an internationally known conductor associated with the project would be an advantage. British choirmaster David Willcocks had been knighted just the previous year; having a knight of the realm directing the choir in its second year could attract many curious singers.

Peter Godfrey, widely regarded as New Zealand's leading choral director, was very encouraging and willing to be involved. Then, in order to get the best advice, in November 1978, a conference of youth choir experts, and others who would later be involved with the choir in some way, was held. Renwick opened that conference and continued, unfailingly, to support the project at every turn.

Sir John Marshall had a key role in establishing the status and financial viability of the proposed youth choir. Sir John was general manager of the National Bank and a former prime minister. He agreed to $10,000 as the amount initially needed by the

William (Bill) Renwick, Director-General of Education, 1975–88. Photographed circa 1978.
COURTESY OF MARGERY RENWICK

William Renwick

Bill Renwick grew up in financial poverty in the Great Depression. In his earliest years his father was unemployed and was away a lot, working in a road gang, but Bill had a warm, affectionate relationship with his mother. Later, he discovered the joys of music, particularly choral singing, when he was a primary school pupil and sang in the annual Primary Schools' Music Festivals in the Auckland Town Hall.

In an unfinished memoir he wrote: 'Singing with Professor Hollinrake was a thrilling experience. Songs we sang in those festivals, especially Handel's "Where'er you walk" and Schubert's "Hark! Hark! the Lark" remain among the loveliest songs I know.' Singing in the Friendly Road Children's Choir in the 1ZB studios in the centre of Auckland was also a source of pleasure to him.

After secondary education at Seddon Memorial Technical College, he completed a Bachelor of Arts degree while attending Auckland Teachers' College. During his first year of teaching, Head of Music Harry Luscombe 'encouraged student groups to perform choral and operatic pieces'. Renwick was impressed by Luscombe's two years of music appreciation in the college hall, 'making full use of the indispensable Carnegie collection of recordings'.

As a young teacher at Eastbourne's Muritai School he passed his musical enthusiasm on to the children he taught. One of the many who remember the experiences 50 years on, Jill Bagnall (taught by him in an 'experimental composite class' of 40 children), says 'he had a lovely singing voice'. After a day's teaching he would travel into Victoria University to take Master of Arts classes.

After five years' teaching, Renwick was appointed as a lecturer in education at Wellington Teachers' College, where he sang in Tom Young's Choral Club with other staff members and music students. Six years later he was involved in writing the influential report of Sir George Currie's Commission on Education. Staying in the Department of Education, he worked particularly on curriculum development and Māori education, rising to become director-general in late 1975.

Singing in the Phoenix Choir under Simon Tipping was about the only recreational pleasure he allowed time for when in charge of a state department. His wife, Margery, remembers an occasion when he cut an overseas trip a day short so that he would be back in time for the weekly choir rehearsal. Upon retirement, he took up a leadership role at Victoria University's Stout Research Centre as well as being a senior research fellow there. Renwick received an honorary doctorate from Deakin University at Geelong in recognition of his work for education in Australia and New Zealand. After retirement from the director-general's position, Renwick was awarded a CBE.

proposed choir. 'Gentleman Jack', as Sir John was affectionately known, became the first patron of the eventual youth choir and was very supportive in that role, including persuading Kiri Te Kanawa to continue to be involved. Other groups agreeing to lend assistance included Radio New Zealand (advertising and audition studios), Air New Zealand, Newmans Coach Lines, Wellington Central Rotary Club (arranging homestays) and Wellington Polytechnic to cover the fees of conductors and tutors by running each set of rehearsals as a polytechnic short course.

A National Youth Choir wasn't far off.

However, challenges had to be faced. The biggest hurdle was a political one. In early 1979, the new, young Minister of Education, Merv Wellington, had almost derailed the whole project. He'd had papers to comment on or sign for many weeks but hadn't responded.

Russell Marshall, the previous Minister of Education, had been keen, Director-General Renwick was enthusiastic, there was sufficient sponsorship funding, and apart from a few naysayers, most people with whom I had discussed the concept briefly were encouragingly supportive. But it had to have the approval of the Minister of Education because the initiative came from within his department. If there was no response from the Minister's office by the end of February 1979, plans would have to be cancelled. It would be impossible to make the venture work in the two years ahead.

The end of February came and went. A new submission was made to the Minister and he approved it two weeks later.[8] Now, there was pressure to make the project work within the time frame set. An already-prepared, bold A4 brochure was printed urgently. Five thousand of these brochures, 1000 posters and covering letters had to be posted to all known community, chamber and church choirs, all 450 secondary schools (both principals and music staff), to universities, teachers' colleges and polytechnics, public libraries, radio stations, Rotary clubs, the 20 district music advisers, singing teachers and others who would pass on the information. But in these very early days, there was little organisational infrastructure to take care of basic arrangements, and because of lack of time, relying upon volunteers wasn't an option. A solution was found in the typically laid-back Kiwi way of using resources right at hand. The Jansen family got on with the job — Judy, Guy, Nicola, Michael and Gregory spending a weekend stuffing envelopes in the large wooden building on Lambton Quay, home of the Department of Education's Head Office.

A short television announcement reported the formation of a national choir; Radio New Zealand news releases and *Listener* advertisements confirmed it.[9] The message was obviously widely heard, because in May and June more than 350 auditions needed to be organised throughout the country. Anthea Moller, Simon Tipping and I held the auditions in 12 radio stations, with recordings made for later comparison and ranking. Applicants were notified in late June, and a news release provided details about the number accepted and towns and cities represented.

Of just over 100 who were successful, one-third had never received vocal tuition. They were told to begin voice lessons immediately. Twenty successful applicants had been on a holiday choral course, some were as young as 13 years old, 33 schools were represented, others were tertiary students or had finished formal education, and many of the older applicants sang in the best-known adult choirs around the country.

Rural centres had not been disadvantaged; smaller towns like Balclutha, Rangiora, Greytown, Eltham and Cambridge were represented, and being in the choir became a talking point; understandably, winning a place in the only national singing team elicited respect. New Zealanders had long understood the prestige of being selected for a national sports team, and now choral music had identified some of its elite. The talents of those accepted had already been recognised in local communities because many of the successful applicants played instruments well enough to be in

LEFT Brochure advertising the National Youth Choir, 1979. AUTHOR'S COLLECTION

BELOW Guy Jansen conducting the first rehearsal of the National Youth Choir, 1979. FROM *CHOIR OF THE WORLD* BY SIMON TIPPING. DUNMORE PRESS, 2002, P. 18

an orchestra or perform in public.[10] Slowly, increasingly positive attitudes to singing in choirs were bedded down.

The small group of Wellington administrators was besieged with urgent questions about the choir's first meeting in mid-August, about travel subsidies (based on distance from Wellington), accommodation, music copies with practice tapes and pronunciation guides, and instructions on the new concert outfits.[11]

On 20 August 1979, on a sunny Monday morning in Lower Hutt, the first rehearsal began. One person dazzled everyone by arriving in what appeared to be a shining silver space suit. Another, Delyse Nottle, from Tauranga, had recently become Miss New Zealand and was later to be placed third in the Miss Universe Contest. Another, Martin Snell, from Dunedin, was later to become an international bass-baritone based in Europe. In all, 104 singers turned up, amid newspaper reporters, a television news cameraman, curious parents, tutors, accompanists and volunteers.

The new choir members — from the youngest, Anna van der Oest (13) from Blue Mountain College in Tapanui, Otago, to the oldest, David Hamilton (24) from the University of Auckland — soon got down to the work at hand.[12]

At the first rehearsal, leading voice teacher and soloist Anthea Moller led the group through warm-ups (a new and surprising activity for some). I took them through parts of the impressive *Psalm 100* by seventeenth-century composer Heinrich Schütz, followed by a cappella choral writing of prominent American choral composer Randall Thompson, and Simon Tipping began rehearsing three motets by Bruckner. In a subsequent rehearsal, Roy Tankersley introduced Johann Pachelbel's *Magnificat in D*, and Peter Godfrey gave them a taste of *Children's Voices* commissioned for the choir by Christopher Norton.[13] For some, the first rehearsal experience was a challenge; they had never experienced this new world where demanding music was sung virtually at sight at a high level. Some had to learn to follow a conductor properly. For others, the technical and artistic level of the first rehearsal was familiar territory; they had done this kind of thing before — many times. Gradually, the group began to coalesce into a unified vocal instrument.

By Friday evening, the conductors were more or less ready to pour the week's work into a preliminary concert, a kind of dummy run. This was played out at the Upper Hutt Civic Hall.

The official inaugural concert was held the following night at St Peter's Church on Willis Street, Wellington. Because of lack of changing rooms at St Peter's, choir members used the Red Cross facilities across the road. The long procession across the intersection a few minutes before 8 p.m., with green scarves fluttering in the not-too-warm August evening air, and with police holding back the traffic, was something to behold.

The audience, with many special guests, seemed to enjoy the eclectic and, now, rather odd-looking combination of items: Pachelbel's *Magnificat* with the Schola Musica strings, brass and timpani; *Children's Voices*; the three Bruckner motets — *Locus Iste, Virga Jesse* and *Ave Maria* — all conducted by Godfrey as principal guest conductor; along with Schütz's *Psalm 150* (with the New Zealand Symphony Orchestra brass); and I conducted three movements of Randall Thompson's (a cappella) *Peaceable Kingdom* as director of the choir.

Dominion critic Owen Jensen was generally impressed but correctly noted the lack of balance between voice-parts and added that 'immature voices pushed too far . . . can sound unpleasant'. At the post-event function in St John's Hall a few metres down Willis Street, Godfrey and I congratulated the choir on an excellent week and an inspiring concert, Godfrey adding, accurately enough, that the sopranos had sung 'bloody flat'.

Things weren't even approaching perfection in that first hectic week of the choir's life. There had been concentration on the techniques, demands and beauties of five differing repertoire styles, but within all of that, notes had to be correct, and even though music copies had been sent out long enough in advance, the sectional tutors still had work to do. Good relationships with and between choir members were a priority, but the group had to be pushed; there was a deadline ahead. Everyone was desperately making sure that the whole tricky, audacious enterprise was seen to be competent at least. Through all of this, a glimmer of a vision was beginning to grow about how good the choir could become, and how it might influence choir singing around the country.

After all the tumult and the shouting of a mostly successful choir inauguration had died down and choristers had departed for home, there was business to attend to. Auditions needed to be held to augment the choir for its August 1980 concert, and the search began in earnest for tenor 1s and bass 2s. These voice types were not naturally prolific in the choir's age range, but they were needed for better balance and a more resonant sound. Thirty-three new members made their debut at the May 1980 rehearsal and concert. This included finding funding for a much-needed administrator; a $20,000 grant from the National Bank covered that.

A further item of business was to reinforce the vocal tuition requirement. Members, even in rural areas, were expected to receive regular lessons and do home practice over the whole year. The gradual development of the choir's vocal flexibility and choral maturity over 1980 is evidence of the success of that voice-training policy.

Peter Godfrey practising with singers. CHOIRS AOTEAROA NZ

The choir that returned to sing in Wellington in August 1980 was a new, improved version: more members — especially in key male voice sections — better singers because of the tuition requirement, and a better-organised group with comprehensive administrative back-up. The choir was now ready to host one of choral music's international giants.

Sir David Willcocks, former director of music at King's College Chapel, Cambridge, and the best-known of British choral conductors, had already agreed to work with the Youth Choir in August 1980; so inaugural choir members had accordingly been selected for a two-year period, 1979–80. The opportunity to sing with Willcocks had been one of the incentives to join the choir. John Knox, Wellington choral aficionado and personal friend of Willcocks, had brokered the deal. Successfully combining a career in railways with a passion for choral singing, Knox had been a member of Willcocks' celebrated Bach Choir in London for three years, while overseeing the building of New Zealand Railways ferries.

Willcocks' guest conducting of the National Youth Choir in August 1980 was the icing on the cake in firmly establishing the one-year-old venture. What he brought to the choir was a deeper awareness of essentials; excellent tuning, blend and balance, rhythmic sense and the pacing of the flow of a piece were all crucial if the choir were ever to make its way in the wider world. But these were not to be at the expense of the soul of the music.

With 'musical ears like nobody else's', he was obsessive about tuning; he asked for sharp major thirds, believing that 'there's only one place a major third can be, and it can't vibrate'.[14] Choral composer John Rutter thinks that Willcocks' apparent love of 'terribly sharp thirds' was probably a reaction to a prevailing flatness among choirs, and if this is so, it marks out Willcocks as a pioneer warrior against the bane of amateur choirs — flat singing. He always seemed able to spot what was going on (incorrect notes or poor intonation), even in a large ensemble of voices.

The blend and balance of the large group probably mattered to him even more than the perfection and unanimity of tuning. His enthusiasm in working with amateur singers, who followed him carefully and entered into his love for the music, meant that each section would enthusiastically respond to him by modifying their volume and quality of tone. He watched singers' eyes, looking for intensity; the singers, in turn, absorbed what they needed from his restrained gestures, being confident in his knowledge of the score and the vibrancy of his direction.

It has been said that clear beat patterns were not important to Willcocks, but, in fact, there was a physical clarity to his beat that transmitted a rhythmic sense and flow

TOP Sir David Willcocks. AUTHOR'S COLLECTION

BELOW Willcocks has the full attention of the tenor section, 1980. CHOIRS AOTEAROA NZ

to choir members who were watching. At play there was a disciplined energy possibly fed by a lifelong involvement in jazz. This showed itself particularly in his treatment of the music of Schütz, Bach and Handel. In an early rehearsal he demonstrated the inherent dance-rhythms of the great Bach double motet *Singet dem Herrn* by dancing around the rehearsal piano.[15]

His sense of humour and personal charm were key ingredients in his success with young people.[16] He looked for opportunities to lighten rehearsals. When the choir gave him a thank-you gift of the finest Scotch whisky during a final rehearsal in the Wellington Town Hall, he responded immediately by popping the cork and taking a huge swig — more than a few drams! His willingness to talk at length with choir members after rehearsals had been apparent at a weekend choral workshop in Somerset, Devon, in 1976, and he showed the same willingness in Wellington. For him, it was one step towards developing a good rapport with his singers and it showed something of the humanity of the man.

In three Romantic-era Bruckner motets he asked the singers to create gentle pianissimos and follow his rubato treatment. He called for a work by the great early baroque composer Heinrich Schütz to be given as historically authentic a performance as possible: *Jauchzet dem Herrn, alle welt* ('Sing to the Lord, all ye lands') was sung

The National Youth Choir perform Michael Tippett's *A Child of Our Time*, Wellington Town Hall, August 1980, accompanied by the New Zealand Symphony Orchestra. In front, from left: Guy Jansen, Sir John Marshall, Sir David Willcocks, Peter Godfrey. CHOIRS AOTEAROA NZ

dramatically by separated double choir, a cappella, with crisp articulation, emphasising the German speech rhythms as the composer intended.[17] Professor Fred Page commented in his *Listener* review: 'One never hears enough of Schuetz and when one does . . . the work turns out to be a winner. The choir immediately showed the standard of their singing, direct and fresh. "Obviously," said a friend, "no one over the age of 25 should be allowed to sing in a choir." One could hear what he meant.'

Michael Tippett's secular oratorio *A Child of Our Time* demonstrated Willcocks' skilful handling of choral and orchestral forces. Many in the choir had not sung with the New Zealand Symphony Orchestra or any other professional orchestra before, and they were struck by the apparent ease with which Willcocks could seamlessly transfer his attention from one group to another. The orchestra players were not enthusiastic about Willcocks as an orchestral conductor, but the performance of the oratorio was a success. Page, writing warmly of it in the *Listener*, commented: 'Sir Michael Tippett's "Child of Our Time" made a stunning choice. . . . The only point I would query in the performance is that the chorus "Burn, Kill, Smash" wasn't harsh enough. But then do these youngsters know what the phrase "Crystal Night" meant?'

A Child of Our Time was sparked by *Kristallnacht* (the 'Night of Broken Glass') on 9 November 1938 in Nazi Germany, when Jewish homes and businesses were destroyed and some 30,000 men sent to concentration camps. The Youth Choir understood it as a strong social statement, its message extending to all human oppression and any unjust conditions that made persecution possible.

As this Tippett work was the means through which the Youth Choir made its entrée into the serious music world, it is worth dwelling briefly on the oratorio's engaging qualities. The composer's text is anguished and complex, and his music is equally challenging; sometimes quite painful to those used to more traditional choral/orchestral works. A powerful intensity comes through in the orchestral writing in direct ways, including tightly knotted chromatic shapes and spiky counterpoint, creating a palpable tension touching singer and listener alike. Within an eclectic choral style — at times radically chunky and awkward and at times simple and conservative — are two special features: demanding choral fugues, and spirituals harmonised simply and sung a cappella.[18]

This compelling and original work was the highlight of the Youth Choir's work in its first two years. Under Willcocks' superb leadership it brought heartfelt responses from choir and audience alike, even if the earnestness of the young singers didn't quite portray the horror of the murders, rioting and burning of over 250 synagogues 42 years earlier.

Through his preparation and conducting of a single, inspiring concert that included a major twentieth-century work, Willcocks had instilled a feeling of quiet pride in the achievements of the choir — a remarkable feat in just a week of rehearsals. At an after-event function in the Banquet Hall of the James Cook Hotel, Willcocks was farewelled with poignant displays of emotion, but not before he had entertained with some fine jazz playing on the hotel's grand piano. Choir members had found the 61-year-old living legend lovely to work with; everyone was grateful for his generous gift of time and reluctant to let him go. But he had positions with the Royal College of Music and the London Bach Choir to get back to. He had to return to his hemisphere and the choir needed to make their own way in theirs.[19]

It was decided by the choir's management committee that a re-auditioned group of 91 members should assemble in Auckland in May 1981, and that I would conduct the performances planned for St Patrick's Cathedral in Auckland, All Saints Church, Howick, and St Peter's Cathedral in Hamilton.

ABOVE Auckland concert of the National Youth Choir, St Patrick's Cathedral, May 1981. CHOIRS AOTEAROA NZ

LEFT National Youth Choir recording the 'Muppet Song' and other music at Auckland TV studios, May 1981. CHOIRS AOTEAROA NZ

For the three May concerts some repertoire from previous years were chosen, and to this was added the four *Christmas Motets* by Francis Poulenc, and *O Magnum Mysterium* and *O Domine Jesu Christe* by Giovanni Gabrieli. I also prepared and conducted a work commissioned from New Zealander Jack Body, *Vox Populi* (with tape), about expressions of mass hysteria. In the first rehearsals, choir members found the piece highly amusing. They weren't used to barking like dogs and screaming out top notes, as well as singing like angels. It wasn't long before the music's extremely heavy vocal demands meant that rehearsal time had to be limited. But with the composer at rehearsals, the choir's commitment remained and they conquered the new idiom. It was given a lively performance, Body was delighted, and the choir's repertoire world had been enlarged.[20]

Lin Saunders, in his review of the Auckland concert, thought that the choir 'revealed an astonishingly high standard . . . capable of both brilliance and extreme delicacy', while *Auckland Star* critic John Parker wrote that the 'spontaneous, ardent sound . . . excellent intonation and testing programme all added up to a triumph of a concert'.

However, a minor controversy arose. Three lighter songs had been programmed to conclude the concert: my choral arrangement of 'If' (Bread), Matthew Raymond's setting of 'The Fool on the Hill' (The Beatles) and 'The Rainbow Connection' from the popular television programme *The Muppet Show*. Some Auckland members of the choir were not happy about the choir singing such songs. But radio stations playing the 'Muppet Song' greatly increased public awareness of the choir and provided welcome exposure before necessary fundraising began. Partly for this reason, Colin Brown, administrator of the Youth Choir from May 1980, thought that lighter music should be featured much more. Brown was aware of the subtle financial implications of programming because of the choir's looming decision to undertake a major overseas tour in mid-1982. Organising two full-week national rehearsals and four regional rehearsals in 1981 was going to be a small task compared with the massive fundraising challenge ahead.

By late 1980, there was a serious proposal that in 1982 the National Youth Choir would travel for five weeks through Los Angeles to England, Holland, Belgium and Germany, and return through Singapore. It was an audacious proposition. By the time they began the tour, the choir would have been together for a maximum of five rehearsal weeks and seven concerts spread over three years. Hundreds of thousands of dollars would be needed for the tour. The catalyst had been an invitation from the organisers of an International Society for Music Education Conference in Bristol for the choir to represent New Zealand at the event in late July 1982. The invitation had been accepted without anyone knowing exactly how much work would be involved. This might have been seen as a foolhardy, risk-taking move, or as more evidence of a positive can-do attitude.

Arrangements were strengthened by Peter Godfrey visiting conductors and institutions when he was in Europe in mid-1981, and Colin Brown travelling there in May 1982. Successfully organising a long tour on the other side of the world for 86 singers, seven management staff and a supporters' group of 20 made huge demands on everyone involved. While details of the preparation have been well documented elsewhere,[21] the issue of the quantity of repertoire for the tour — 34 pieces rising to 46 by the end of the tour — needs closer examination. Along with conductor expertise and quality of voices, music (the choice and amount) is a crucial factor in the formation of a great choral tradition. It is relevant to ask whether useful guidelines were being laid down, perhaps unconsciously, at this formative stage of New Zealand's tradition.

There were many criteria that Godfrey and I simply took for granted when choosing the repertoire for the tour. The selection was to be: comprehensive, containing music for every occasion; representative of the choir's home country, with waiata, works by New Zealand composers Body, Norton and Ritchie, and two pieces by choir member David Hamilton;[22] substantial, with a combination of classics and new material from the sixteenth to twentieth centuries; and varied, including 20 folk songs, spirituals and arrangements.

Nevertheless, there was too much material to be assimilated in the time available. A dozen weekly rehearsals in the main centres before leaving would have helped enormously, partly to memorise more of the music and partly to obviate extra on-tour rehearsals to polish up new items. Future choir tours would learn from this problem, and more would fully realise the potential of the singers involved. However, the first Youth Choir was sufficiently prepared to present exciting, quality concerts. And so began a belief, perhaps a little cocky to start with, that a bunch of committed young Kiwis, representing their country, could sing as well as anyone else in the world.

On 18 July 1982, the choir was farewelled from the Auckland Town Hall. The tour was a remarkably optimistic venture. Among its ambitious plans was a concert in London with newly appointed Dame of the British Empire, 38-year-old Kiri Te Kanawa. The concert, in the prestigious Wembley Concert Hall, couldn't have been grander. It was sold out weeks in advance and the choir lifted their performance for the royal occasion, singing with a confident, unified tone after their several weeks of appearances in England. Three newly arranged waiata were in the programme,

ABOVE The National Youth Choir outside Wells Cathedral, 1982. Peter Godfrey (left) and Guy Jansen (right) are in the front row. CHOIRS AOTEAROA NZ

LEFT The National Youth Choir with Dame Kiri Te Kanawa at Wembley Concert Hall, 1982. CHOIRS AOTEAROA NZ

Te Kanawa joined with the choir five times and, along with Prince Charles, was a popular guest of the choir after the concert. Godfrey's conducting of *Singet dem Herrn* was warmly applauded by the *Music and Musicians* critic who said that it was 'as moving as any perfection could have been'.

A second highlight of the tour was a concert in King's College Chapel, Cambridge, a magnificent building in late Gothic architecture style and an acoustic 'extremely resonant but with a softness that makes it extraordinary'.[23] For Peter Godfrey it was like a homecoming, as he had sung there as a chorister and choral scholar, and had been acting director of music there, four years prior to the tour[24] (the six-month appointment in 1978 involving an exchange of positions with Sir Philip Ledger).[25] With the Youth Choir, Godfrey astutely chose to conduct Irish composer Charles Villiers Stanford's *Magnificat* for double choir. At the time the work was little known, so he was virtually reintroducing it to Stanford's adopted England.

The choir also sang in St Paul's Cathedral, York Minster and four other cathedrals, including Wells Cathedral, joining in its 800th-year celebrations.[26] The local paper praised the whole choir for their superb singing, and the sopranos for their 'elegant dynamic and tonal control' in the Poulenc *Christmas Motets*. 'Great heights' came later in the programme, and the article praised the wealth of expression in Lotti's 'Crucifixus', and re-emphasised the choir's youthful freshness in 'Lord, When the Sense' by John Ritchie.[27]

The influence of the tour was felt in two particular ways: first, on the New Zealand public, who from then on tended to hold choirs in higher esteem because a national choir of young singers had achieved notable results, especially by singing with Te Kanawa. The one or two reviews that surfaced back in New Zealand aided this perception. What experts overseas thought of our musical artists was still very important.

The second effect of the tour was on the choir members themselves. About half the group remained in Europe for some time at the end of the tour, but finally all returned, with renewed confidence in themselves, understanding that they could hold their own in the international choral scene, and that they were ready to repay to the New Zealand choral world some of the benefits that they had received. Very soon, this impact was felt in New Zealand through conducting, singing in elite choirs, taking musical leadership positions and building solo careers. As William Renwick once said, in a different context, 'National feeling feeds on itself.'[28]

While I was undertaking study at the University of Southern California (1982–84), my colleague David Wood supervised the National Holiday Choral Courses for Secondary Schools. By August 1984, I was once again available to conduct a course and very much looked forward to the opportunity. On the final day of the August course in Christchurch Cathedral, voting papers were given to all 60 choir members for them to indicate their favourite pieces from the week's schedule. Top of the pops were *See the Gypsies* (Zoltán Kodály), 'Kommt dir manchmal' from *Zigeunerlieder* (Brahms) and 'Hallelujah, Amen' from *Judas Maccabaeus* (Handel). Their preferences were used to shape the repertoire the following year when it was held at Havelock North High School. A popular song from the charts was also added.[29]

The course led to the consideration that another development, on top of the National Youth Choir, could grow from these national courses initiated by Walden-Mills almost 20 years ago. Having two holiday courses per year for secondary school students was fine, but there was little continuity between them, and the high levels of performance deserved greater public recognition. Without a clear, continuing structure, a secondary students' combined choir would never be invited to represent the sector. So a 'New Zealand Secondary Students Choir' was planned for 1986. The advertising through print media, radio, the *Education Gazette* and former participants publicised it under that name.

The name was carefully chosen. To retain political and artistic autonomy and put the focus on individuals rather than schools, the term Students Choir was chosen. Furthermore, the name had to be as different as possible from existing choir names. To reduce confusion with the 'National Youth Choir', and the 'National Holiday Choral Courses for Secondary Schools', a fresh-sounding title was necessary. The name appeared to work well enough — even if some folks still overlook the difference between 'Schools' and 'Students'.

In August 1986, at Wellington College, Roger Stevenson directed a week's rehearsals of 92 secondary students. They had passed simple auditions by tape for the New Zealand Secondary Students Choir (NZSSC). Many had been to holiday courses since 1983, which, now, would be seen as leading to this new national group. But the NZSSC was a different animal to the National Youth Choir; more like an all-comers choir with those who couldn't match pitch auditioned out at an early stage.[30] Hard work and enthusiasm generated excellent results, participants recalling how quickly they had to pick up vocal basics and even learn how to hold up their music high enough to see the conductor. Fortunately, sufficient members had looked over their music before they arrived and there were quite a few exceptional musicians who took a confident lead at rehearsal time.[31] The choir list includes family names well known for their interest in community and professional music. On such home influences and support does a strong choral tradition grow.

The climax to a week of rehearsals was a surprisingly good concert staged in the generous acoustics of Wellington Cathedral on Molesworth Street. Stevenson, Nicola Jansen and Igelese Ete conducted the first half of the concert, while I conducted the Fauré *Requiem*. The string players were the NZSO's Schola Musica, and Janet Gibbs was the organist.

Because I was too busy to keep working with the new NZSSC, Roger Stevenson, who had been course director for the week, was invited to take over. Stevenson's contribution to the choral development, artistic status, discipline and good humour of NZSSC proved to be enormous.

These innovations in choral signing occurred over 20 years, from August 1966, when National Music Adviser Walden-Mills mounted a singing week in Taranaki, to August 1986, when the first national ensemble for secondary students sang in Wellington. It was a relatively short time for such significant progress.

But were these developments inevitable? Possibly, but unlikely, if this story is compared with other countries' stories, and especially unlikely because there was none of the necessary infrastructure. It all had to be developed.

The two key infrastructures basic to the needs of national choirs were: freely available vocal tuition — absolutely essential if the choirs were to gain credibility and competitive success; and constantly available administrative support and professional-level musical assistance. Both were in place in New Zealand in sufficient time to allow the national choirs to play a strategic role in the evolution of choral singing.

As regards freely available group vocal tuition, for some time I had had my sights set on correcting an inequality in group music tuition offered to secondary students. Thousands of students had received free lessons on orchestral and band instruments since 1945 (when orchestral tuition in school time had been introduced), but few students had learned to sing. The only way to gain tuition on the 'vocal instrument' had been through privately paid for, individual lessons outside of school hours or, much less effectively, as part of a choir. Some educators and administrators did not consider the voice a priority, perpetuating the half-truth that 'everyone can sing'. This inequality between instrumental and vocal tuition had existed for 30 years.

Upon joining the Department of Education in 1975, I thought that ministerial approval would be needed to establish voice tuition. But having to write and promote a new policy would have been fruitless — a couple of hundred other new policies would have got through departmental gatekeepers before this one. Peter Boag, Assistant Director-General of Education, came up with a clever solution. He simply asked, why couldn't the voice be called an instrument? No objection was raised.

Secondary schools were notified that small-group vocal tuition could now be offered within the same parameters as instrumental tuition. Several schools took advantage of the opportunity immediately, using unused hours, or cutting back on string, woodwind, brass or percussion teaching. Boag's astute question and implied approval had far-reaching consequences: vocal training started becoming widespread nationally. Choral singing stood at the threshold of a new period of growth.[32]

A 1977 conference of experts confirmed the direction of the new rules and a guideline was issued.[33] David Wood compiled a departmental booklet on vocal and choral education, encouraging music specialists and principals to give new emphasis to the 'other half' of music-making: vocal music. The first part-time vocal itinerant teacher was prominent Wellington contralto Flora Edwards, appointed to visit Wellington schools, beginning with Newlands College.[34] Soon, hundreds of secondary students were receiving systematic voice instruction and it became the norm for schools to make such teaching available.[35] By the time the NZSSC was formed in 1986, the group tuition scheme had been operating for over eight years.

In the wider community, more choirs, within their two-hour rehearsals, were employing singing teachers for sessions on vocal technique and vocal health, and some choirs offered group lessons before rehearsals. The Festival Singers of Wellington, for example, had half its members learning in this way from 1978 onwards.[36] It was no longer assumed that one didn't need singing tuition to sing in a good choir.

What was needed to make a national choir successful was also organisational support of all kinds and professional-level musical assistance. Organisational help included the booking of venues, communications with singers, locating music copies and effective concert publicity — all indispensable backroom services. Examples were the working committee for the National Youth Choir in early 1979,[37] and the assistants for the rehearsals and first concert of the Secondary Students Choir in mid-1986.[38] Complementing them were a raft of office staff, colleagues, friends, family, tutors and experienced advisers.

Professional-level musical assistance was also vital. Every conductor needs a team of musicians with whom to work — assistant conductors, accompanists and singing coaches.

The work of two people in particular should be mentioned in connection to the National Youth Choir: David Wood, choral singer and previously head of music at Selwyn College, Auckland, who had multiple roles including secretary of a high-powered fundraising committee, innovative stage manager and convivial choir marshal; and Colin Brown, formerly general manager of Commercial Union Insurance before being appointed National Youth Choir administrator, dealing increasingly with the regular correspondence from choir members and planning a choir management scenario. This included setting up a board of trustees that included former Governor of the Reserve Bank Sir Alan Low, well-known business leaders, and Dame Sister Mary Leo, who had trained several of the choir's female singers and internationally recognised sopranos.[39]

In 1986, another contributor to the country's growing awareness of choirs was beginning to appear. These were regional and national choir competitions, open to any secondary schools wishing to take part. In time they would become known as Secondary School Choir Festivals.

The catalyst was the Westpac School Music Contest, begun by the Music Federation of New Zealand in 1965.[40] It ran instrumental chamber music competitions in up to 15 centres throughout the country, adding a composition section in 1972.[41] By 1977, the contest had become a successful annual fixture, with dozens of groups taking part.

Though the title of the contest implied that it embraced the whole range of music media found in schools, in fact it included only instrumental music. However, that was to change from 1977. Elisabeth Airey, who had been appointed administrator of the Music Federation in 1971 (and, therefore, also of the Westpac School Music Contest), was open to the suggestion of including a vocal component.

After Airey had consulted with Arthur Hilton, visionary president of the Music Federation, a vocal section was added.[42] The 1978 schedule allowed for a group of three to 15 singers, with or without accompaniment or conductor. A section for original choral composition was introduced in the same year. In retrospect, the adding of these components was a generous gesture on the part of the Music Federation, especially given that for the next seven years the Federation organised all three sections: instrumental, composition *and* vocal.

It was fortunate that the group vocal tuition scheme in schools was implemented before the School Music Contest's vocal section came on stream. Before the scheme, schools would have had to pay local singing teachers to coach vocal groups; now

Dame Sister Mary Leo, a National Youth Choir trustee and former singing teacher who trained several internationally recognised sopranos. ALEXANDER TURNBULL LIBRARY, PACOLL-8018-1-21

Education Department discretionary hours could be used. Fifty small choirs entered in the first year, and the Minister of Education approved funding to support the work. Singing standards at the contests rose year by year. When a two-section vocal contest differentiating between smaller and larger ensembles (3–5 singers and 6–15 singers) was added, yet more growth was encouraged.

In time, the Westpac contest became too popular. The organisers signalled a change in 1984 because of the very large numbers of young people taking part in some district contests (for example, Auckland had 20 choirs and 58 instrumental groups that year). As a result of the heavy organisational load (volunteer-dependent), it was decided to alternate the large instrumental groups and vocal section year by year. Fortunately, the vocal section, rather than the large instrumental section, was included in 1985. It was clear to some choral educators that by this time the vocal/choral dimension of the Westpac contest had outstayed its friendly welcome.

There was always the possibility, too, that the vocal part of the contest would become submerged in the essentially instrumental environment of the Music Federation. J. M. Thomson's history of the period provides evidence of this. His only substantial mention of the existence of a vocal section in the schools contest is a reference to (several) Māori and Pacific Island performers in 'a moving performance of Palestrina', and a photograph of the 1981 Christ's College Madrigal Group.[43]

As to the question of who would take over the vocal/choral sections of this national contest, inevitably, attention turned to the new kid on the block — the New Zealand Choral Federation, formed in July 1985 and housed in temporary accommodation on the ground floor of the Department of Education. In August that year, I met informally with some of the Choral Federation committee, with the aim of encouraging the fledgling organisation to take over the vocal sections of the Westpac School Music Contest. Surprisingly, the younger committee members weren't at all captivated by the idea. In fact, they said, it wasn't what the Federation was about and that school-level projects were of little interest. Views had changed by December of the same year at an inaugural meeting of the Wellington Regional Association of the Choral Federation. It was attended by 28 choral leaders and chaired by Wellington lawyer Bruce Corkill, who brought his administrative mind and choral experience to the task. It was decided that the question of 'Westpac involvement was a high priority', with a group of the New Zealand Choral Federation National Executive to decide 'on the level of involvement within the next fortnight'.[44]

That was the high noon of this little drama. Decisive action was taken just prior to Christmas 1985, the Choral Federation agreeing to arrange local events in 1986.

A limited number of choirs would be channelled into district events of the Westpac Contest. The eight-year-old choral contests had been saved, even though there was to be no national choral gathering in that year.

By agreeing, back in 1977, to a vocal/choral section in its instrumental contests, the Music Federation had enabled secondary school choirs to take a big step forward, but now they had to give away that component. The Choral Federation's decision to take responsibility for the contests had major consequences. In time, the contests would morph, in several stages, into The Big Sing and become the Choral Federation's star event.

In shedding the choral sections, the Music Federation's representative, Beverley Jones, wrote:

> The Federation feels that its contribution . . . over [eventually] ten years has been a significant one. Choral activity in schools appears now to be on a strong footing with numerous opportunities for involvement . . . as well as incentives such as regional and national choirs and workshops being available.[45]

Massive amounts of time, money and energy were poured into choral music for young people over a 20-year period. Artistic achievements, social satisfaction and personal and spiritual benefits are valuable outcomes, but they are difficult to appraise. It's also easy to imagine positive influences on the nature and scope of later choral activity, but producing proof is another matter.

Somewhat easier to appraise is the value of financial investments made during the period. Hundreds of people and institutions provided many tens of thousands of dollars for a cause they thought worthy and exciting. These included individual donors and local fundraisers, corporate sponsors and banks, the Departments of Internal Affairs and Education, schools, parents and, not least, singers and conductors themselves. In addition and very importantly, between 1966 and 1986, dozens of people, within their paid, professional employment, were able to make choral music a priority. Without these hidden contributions, as well as widespread funding, the initiatives could not have happened.

What is remarkable about the sums raised for the National Youth Choir, and particularly for its European tour, is that it was happening against a backdrop of a declining New Zealand economy, especially from 1973. Oil shocks and soaring prices, New Zealand's major export market, Britain, entering the EEC in 1973, a worsening balance of payments, increases in unemployment and inflation — all meant that money, now in shorter supply, tended to be spent with great forethought and restraint. And yet the necessary funding *was* raised.

From the outset of the National Youth Choir, all members were required to sing in their school choir or in a local community choir. But the standards of the youth choir and community choirs were drawing further and further apart, and it wasn't long before murmurings were heard about local groups that weren't satisfying to sing in. The allegiance of Youth Choir members was being stretched by the requirement to sing in a local choir.

It became clear that a major factor in the unhappiness was the standard of conducting in the regions. This was the elephant in the room. Frustrated Youth Choir members wanted to maintain a professional attitude and not talk about individual conductors. However, they often accurately identified deficiencies in basic gesturing and rehearsal techniques, and their analyses of the difficulties were perceptive. Nevertheless, tact would be needed in any improvements suggested. Good relationships between the National Youth Choir and the choral fraternity would always be essential, especially when raising funds for the choir's activities.

The first step to upgrading the skills of the country's conductors would be to recognise the inadequacy of the trial-and-error, teach yourself, learn from a book approach to conductor training. The second would be to accept the overseas evidence that the craft could be *taught*, not merely *caught* from being in a good choir. And the third step would be for those who had seen the debilitating effects of ineffective rehearsal and conducting techniques — the two initial National Youth Choir conductors — to put acceptable rescue plans in place.

10

The perplexing question of conductor training

There is a general consensus today that conductors of choirs need to be trained, but this has come from an attitudinal sea change over the last forty or so years. In the past, new conductors were expected to already know the basics of conducting and then improve on the job. Now, initial and ongoing training is considered essential. In today's world, training is available for everything, and accepting help for conducting a choir appears important and reasonable — particularly since even beginner choral conductors are asked to grapple with many technical and artistic issues.

It is worth listing some of conducting's key topics and challenges, because it hasn't always been obvious that they deserve systematic and sustained study. They include: the selection of quality repertoire appropriate for the choir envisaged; 'score-based imagination' and other detailed preparation; enhanced aural perception training and musicianship skills; significant practical knowledge of the voice; understanding of how to modify voices of a choir to create an artistic instrument; polished conducting techniques applied consistently; supervised practice of gestures, including easy-to-follow beat patterns; research-based rehearsal methodologies; knowledge of how to foster good-humoured and disciplined director–choir relationships; motivation — a conductor's dreams, vision and aesthetic joy; programme-building, administration, budgeting, remuneration; and mentoring, partnership coaching, networking and other support.

It's an impressive list. So why was the introduction of conductor training so long delayed? Why, only 40 years ago, had the notion of practical study of conducting either not occurred to most in the choral community or been dismissed from their thinking?

During 1980, there were in New Zealand two Englishmen — Sir David Willcocks and Peter Godfrey — who had not been trained to be conductors but who demonstrated dramatically effective choral skills. Anyone had only to listen to their choirs to recognise that the two men were at the top of their game. In August 1980, they were involved in cementing the place of the National Youth Choir and leading it to new heights of artistic expression.

In a lunchtime break during rehearsals of the 1980 National Youth Choir in Wellington, choral conducting was the hot topic of conversation. The discussion began harmlessly enough with the speculation that offering teaching in the subject would increase the number of good conductors. The participants in the vigorous conversation that ensued were David Willcocks, Peter Godfrey and me.

In these circumstances, it might have been ungracious to raise a question about whether New Zealand would always be dependent on experts from the 'Old Country' to grow choral music here. A related question could have been: Where would our own inspiring leaders come from in the future — how would they be produced?

The genteel chat soon became a weighty debate on whether choral conducting should be taught or not. One side claimed strenuously that it could only be learnt by copying what one saw in a good conductor; the other side argued that conducting skills and understandings could be taught and needed to be revealed systematically, just as in learning the piano or violin.

Lunchtime discussion at National Youth Choir rehearsal, St Andrew's on The Terrace Hall, Wellington, August 1980. From left: Guy Jansen, Peter Godfrey, Sir David Willcocks. NEW ZEALAND CHORAL FEDERATION

At the time, the English school of thought (which has since changed substantially) was that conducting could not be taught, and Willcocks defended this position. Like Godfrey, he had picked up the physical gestures of conducting by being in a good choir and watching and absorbing what the conductor did. Obviously, the legendary Boris Ord at King's College Chapel, Cambridge, and Dr Ernest Bullock and Sir Malcolm Sargent earlier, had done a great job with a young Willcocks. He credits them with imparting to him important facets of the conductor's craft.[1]

Willcocks' point of view deserves respect, especially because of his worldwide reputation. Former choral scholar at King's College, Cambridge, Simon Carrington, says that Willcocks 'makes people aware that he's listening all the time, reacting to what they are doing . . . That's a hard one to teach.' Carrington adds that showing clear beat patterns has never been important to Willcocks. In talking about singing for the maestro, Carrington says, 'You observe and you absorb and you think about the music and what's required, and then you extract it.' In contrast, at Yale University, where Carrington teaches, he says that they're 'almost obliged to make sure that students come out with some kind of elegance of gesture'.[2]

In 1980, Willcocks had already been director of music at King's for 17 years, had served 19 years as musical director of the London Bach Choir, and was currently director of the Royal College of Music. In the lunchtime debate he was adamant: if you're good enough, you'll pick it up by being in an excellent choir led by a first-class musician. And if you're not a natural, teaching won't help much. Years later, he continued to maintain the stance: 'You cannot teach conducting,' he said. 'The best thing you can do is to create opportunities for people to learn for themselves.'[3] He said that he had learned nothing from books on the subject and pointed out 'some of the greatest people have never studied conducting. I don't suppose Toscanini had a lesson in his life.'[4]

Peter Godfrey, however, was coming to a different conclusion. Godfrey wasn't so sure that there was a cut-and-dried answer. He was 'curious' about the teaching of conducting. This difference of opinion between the two is interesting. They were of almost the same age, were choral scholars together at King's College, and had been good friends since that time. The big difference is that Godfrey immigrated to New Zealand in 1958, and perhaps became keenly aware of the lack of high-quality choirs here, and consequently the lack of expert leadership skills to be absorbed by potential conductors. After more than 20 years in the country he had a desire to know where a new generation of directors might come from. He was beginning to question the English laissez-faire attitude that resulted in only a few new conductors coming through and, especially, he was reflecting on his own experiences as a student in England.

At the age of 15, Godfrey was required to conduct a group of 40 teenage boys who formed a house choir for a school music competition. He didn't learn about 'beating four or three beats in a bar' until three years later, when he was about to conduct a university orchestra at Cambridge. He decided, in his own delightful words:

> I must find out about four and three beats in a bar. And so I bought one of the few books available at the time, *Handbook of Conducting* by Scherchen, and made full use of that. The only time I have ever been told I was doing something wrong was just before that first concert when a university lecturer told me how to beat 6/8. But my curiosity about choral conducting continued.[5]

Since the 1830s, the English choral tradition had dominated the development of choirs in New Zealand, so it is not surprising to find little teaching of the craft of choral conducting in New Zealand over its first 150 years. English repertoire predominated, and some musicians who knew the repertoire well would have been pushed to the front of a rehearsal by fellow choristers, to face the singers and lead by waving their hands as best they knew. Virtually everyone involved in choral music in this new nation was just seeking to replicate choral life as they remembered it in their home country. So New Zealand continued the practice of thrusting into conductorships those people suitable by virtue of superior musicianship or singing ability, or even longevity of experience and charming personality.

Leaders of choirs were sometimes specialists who had learned their techniques in another country, often Scotland, Wales, other European countries or Canada. Upon arrival in the new colony, such musicians were soon identified and they gravitated towards directing local community or church choirs. Thus the fund of conducting expertise was increased — thanks to chorally minded immigrants.

So there is scant mention in New Zealand's recorded music histories of the teaching of conducting in pioneering days, nor even in the first half of the twentieth century. There were probably private lessons given, individual help generously offered and handy hints shared. And, no doubt, encouraging comments were proffered (or even dire warnings made) by choir members in the midst of rehearsals. Conductors of visiting choirs would have been of some help on a very short-term basis. But there is no evidence of any systematic, long-term teaching of the conducting craft.

What is intriguing is that this lack of conductor preparation persisted for so long. It was no one's responsibility, and although there was awareness of choral conducting training in some other countries, there was, in New Zealand, no institution or professional group offering to help the hundreds of choir directors in schools, churches and communities.

The exception to this pattern was in the educational field. District music advisers, beginning with the appointment of Geoff Wilson in the Wellington Education Board District in 1961, were given instruction on music leadership as part of their preparatory training. William Walden-Mills had been recently appointed National Music Adviser in the Department of Education, and his previous extensive experience included learning conducting at Kneller Hall, the Royal Military School of Music training institution in London.

In short induction courses for successive groups of music advisers, Walden-Mills passed on music-directing skills that were essentially military band-like in orientation. In addition to these elementary lessons, some district advisers incorporated short periods of conducting study into their extended overseas sojourns; for example, David Sell studied with Sir Thomas Beecham.

Walden-Mills was more than an army bandmaster. He was also a professional violinist and horn player, and he had sung with a semi-professional madrigal group in England, sparking an interest in a cappella singing that was to become his first love. Whether conducting Victoria, Britten and Edwin Carr or rehearsing secondary students in the delicate intricacies of a Byrd motet, Lassus madrigal or Seiber folk song, Walden-Mills was an effective conductor. In rehearsals with both his adult evening choir and at national school courses, he was personally encouraging and knowledgeable, and insisted on high standards of discipline.

Groups of government-employed district music advisers were thus given elementary conducting training, and in this they were a privileged group. However, what they could do was limited. Other music educators, even if they had senior positions in teacher training institutions or prominent schools, did not have even this incomplete training. They had *no* assistance. Within programmes such as teachers' refresher courses, Education Department courses and university programmes, there was nothing that recognised the vulnerabilities and responsibilities of choral directors and attempted to give them guidance.

In the 1960s and 1970s, budding conductors at every level still had to work out their own salvation while in front of a choral group. They learned as they rehearsed. That applied whether at universities, primary schools, advanced community choirs or volunteer church choirs. This trial-and-error method was not an obvious strategy. Often it was hidden because most eyes were on music or words, with few people watching the conductor.

In addition to this common learn-as-you-go approach, the personalities of conductors and their audition strategies resulted in a two-fold division of directors and choirs. On the one hand, there were some very good choirs usually led by dedicated, strong-minded directors working with committed and very musical choir members chosen through tough auditioning. On the other hand, there were choirs led by directors each assiduously reinventing a conducting wheel of their own. This latter group produced an understandable but bizarre spectacle with two striking features. First, the rather haphazard bringing together of a smorgasbord of skills, understandings and priorities picked up from other conductors (of varying abilities), and, second, each individual's wheel of concepts and actions came together without the filtering of coaching, mentoring, planning, focused analysis or informed guidance.

Now and again, conductors would have the good fortune of obtaining access to specialist assistance. This was generally from a dedicated individual offering a class or school to whoever would like to come. A good example of this is when eminent musician Ronald Dellow announced in June 1962 that he would take two separate choral conductors' schools in Hamilton and at Auckland University.[6]

Like most other New Zealanders beginning to conduct, I was moulded by the default trial-and-error, do-it-yourself training style as described, and it was sometimes very frustrating. Expert tuition was available in many other spheres of life; why not in the choral field? While it was apparent that there also wasn't training for coaches of rugby and other sports, there was a difference. Choral leadership, especially in schools, was intimately work-related; the 'choral coach', highly visible at every 'game', was expected to be a winner at each outing. The sense of vulnerability could be intense.

While teaching in New Plymouth in the mid-1960s, I gleaned technical aspects of conducting by reading Scherchen's *Handbook of Conducting* and other books. This was followed by gaining LTCL and FTCL diplomas in 'Choral Conducting, Organisation and Training'. The discipline and stimulus of the Trinity College work — even though it came from a culture a world away — provided confidence to meet musical challenges while 'conducting'. In my first teaching position I had formed a select choir (including some staff members) to sing Handel's 'And the Glory of the Lord', a massed choir to sing a Vernon Griffiths arrangement of the 'Hallelujah Chorus', and an evening choir to perform a range of repertoire. With all the groups, it was a lonely task trying to fathom how to help singers without having an established, confident gestural technique.

It was a boon for choral leaders to locate nearby expertise in order to lift skills to a new level. In my case this happened in the months prior to conducting Brahms' *German Requiem*, with the Palmerston North Choral Society in 1967. The high cost of frequent air travel would have ruled out regular professional-level study with anyone not accessible by car. Fortunately, Dobbs Franks in Wellington helped me prepare and integrate choral and orchestral aspects of the score. At the time, Franks, a former student at the Juilliard School in New York, was directing the Wellington Harmonic Society choir and Alex Lindsay Orchestra, and with his wife, Ruth Pearl, was also involved in playing for the New Zealand Broadcasting Corporation. Franks had been brought to New Zealand in 1965 to conduct *Porgy and Bess*, starring international opera singer Inia Te Wiata, for the New Zealand Opera Company.

My university and teachers' college music courses, while wonderful in so many ways, had not provided preparation for directing any substantial music, let alone a demanding classical masterpiece combining choir, orchestra and soloists. The benefits of study with Dobbs Franks became apparent in later years when I mounted New Zealand premieres of two operettas by Kurt Weill and directed major choral/orchestral works.

Reflecting on the conducting knowledge, confidence and skills I have since gained, an astounding thought has now arisen: I applied none of what I had received to teaching the future teachers of music for whom I had responsibility at Christchurch Teachers' College from 1968 to 1974. While six orchestral workshops were organised for former NZSO conductor Juan Matteucci to impart orchestral technique, nothing was offered to those who would soon be managing rehearsals for choirs, operetta choruses, assembly singing and other performance aspects of secondary school musical life. One reason for this oversight was that I didn't know how to teach conducting. No one ever questioned the gap in my teacher-training courses and, more importantly, neither was anyone questioning choral gaps in other tertiary courses around the country.

The absence of any contractual obligation for teachers' colleges to prepare future conductors for their very public appearances in schools and communities was allied to another deficiency. Nationally, there was no heritage at all of choral conducting education, no understanding or accepted models of choral conducting excellence — not even a rudimentary, flexible system of training. There was probably occasional coaching or the passing on of tips in college classrooms. Friendly help would have been at hand at meetings of continuing education agencies, Workers' Educational Associations and music societies, or from interested private music teachers. But most of this assistance would have been intuition-based, idiosyncratic, fragmented and limited.

In fact, in those years there was no worldwide agreement on even elementary principles of choral conducting. Even a little basic tuition would have been useful. While differing, confusing points of view would have been expressed, at least the real and ever-present needs of key musical leaders in the choral world would have been considered.

Sometimes it takes an extraordinarily moving experience to open one's eyes to new possibilities. This happened when about 30 New Zealanders observed Rodney Eichenberger presenting sessions at the 1974 Perth Conference of the International Society for Music Education. Hearing the University of Washington, Seattle, Chamber Singers (which contained several students studying conducting with Eichenberger), we were astonished by their lively and stylish interpretations of spirituals and gospel. The vibrancy of vocal sound emanating from the choir with its warm and enticing range of colours was etched on our minds. The primary reason for the success of the Chamber Singers' performances was located in the choral expertise of their director, Professor Eichenberger. He was a graduate of St Olaf College, Minnesota — a university renowned for its choral tradition — and had undertaken advanced conducting study at the universities of Denver, Washington and Iowa. The difference that could be made through systematic and thoughtful conducting education was suddenly obvious.

Constraints on the development of New Zealand's choral life were becoming apparent. There were problems with the ways choirs were rehearsed. There were severe doubts about the democracy-in-action kind of rehearsal where discerning choristers confidently articulated their opinions while the authority of embarrassed conductors ebbed away, as they didn't know how to respond. While a few outstanding leaders obtained excellent results in this cooperative, 'democratic' way, New Zealand choral music in general was never going to grow significantly under these circumstances.

My experience of the Eichenberger phenomenon in Perth in 1974 had begun to crystallise my thinking about aspiring conductors needing tuition. Talking with and observing many leading overseas choral practitioners while on a Churchill Travelling Fellowship in 1976 further convinced me. The final straw was being confronted by the hugely variable choral backgrounds of successful National Youth Choir auditionees in early 1979. The lack of thorough conducting training seemed unfair, confusing and needlessly discouraging. Little wonder that the topic was aired at that 1980 lunchtime

Rodney Eichenberger, a professor at the University of Southern California, and regular tutor at the summer schools. RODNEY EICHENBERGER COLLECTION

discussion in St Andrew's on The Terrace. But who was I to question the Willcocks' judgement about how the fine art of choral directing should be absorbed? What did I, the youngest at that occasion, with the trendy beard and comparatively little high-level experience, know about the best ways of picking up conducting techniques and wisdom? How sure was I that the English tradition of not teaching the subject needed to be challenged and reformed?

Into this choral leadership vacuum stepped Peter Godfrey, now becoming more aware that countries overseas were producing well-prepared conductors. In August 1979, Godfrey had attended the final weekend of one of Rodney Eichenberger's conducting courses in Melbourne. Eichenberger had become known within Australia as a dynamic, creative and personable teacher of conducting and Godfrey had met him at the earlier Perth conference. Godfrey was inspired to consider the viability of establishing a degree course in choral conducting at the University of Auckland, where he was Head of the Conservatorium of Music.

Godfrey used his 1981 sabbatical leave to investigate what courses other universities were offering. He visited Westminster Choir College in Princeton, and the University of Southern California in downtown Los Angeles, where Eichenberger was now Chair of the Choral and Church Music Department. Returning to Auckland, and in the midst of a busy schedule, Godfrey ran a conducting class. The content of that first class consisted of technical aspects of choral direction with members conducting other class participants under Godfrey's supervision. He concentrated on such things as momentum in the beat (one of his strengths), attacks and releases, and subdivision of the beat.[7]

Tecwyn Evans, 2018.
PHOTOGRAPHER KAARE VIEMOSE
FOR DANISH NATIONAL OPERA

Tecwyn Evans

Tecwyn Evans studied at the University of Otago with Jack Speirs, obtaining a first-class honours degree and a master's degree with distinction (both in composition), and he also helped develop the Southern Youth Choir. Following study on a Fulbright Scholarship with Brian Priestman and Simon Carrington in Kansas, Evans was appointed by Sir Andrew Davis as chorus master to Glyndebourne Festival Opera in 1999. This was followed by opera and orchestral work in Austria and many other countries.

He is now Director of Music at the Danish National Opera. Recently he has conducted the BBC Singers, *Messiah* with the Huddersfield Choral Society and the Royal Northern Sinfonia, and performances of Gershwin's *Crazy For You* musical with Gothenburg Opera. He lives in Sweden with his wife, Swedish soprano Susanna Andersson.

In addition to a repertoire ranging from Bach to Sir John Tavener and Sir James MacMillan, he champions New Zealand composers such as John Psathas, Anthony Ritchie and Ross Harris. In 2017, he was contracted to the University of Auckland as part-time lecturer in ensemble conducting. He says that his seven years in the New Zealand Youth Choir under Karen Grylls were hugely motivating for him once he knew he wanted to conduct.

Peter Godfrey taking a choral conducting course. FROM *IN TUNE: THE FIRST 10 YEARS OF THE NEW ZEALAND CHORAL FEDERATION 1985–1995*, P. 12. NZCF, 1995.

With this class, choral conducting education in New Zealand had been legitimised and welcomed, and a modest, disciplined beginning had been made in formal conducting training. Finally, the New Zealand choral community could look forward to the regular and approved transmission of best practice from successful local and international choral practitioners to young and not-so-young conducting students.

Within a year of the class being introduced, Godfrey had taken up an appointment as director of music at the Wellington Cathedral of St Paul and was unable to continue the work he had begun. Other degree subjects in conducting and choral music were added after Karen Grylls had returned from overseas graduate study and obtained a part-time lecturing position at the University of Auckland. Later, Associate Professor Grylls was to engineer a useful choral music 'pathway' through Auckland's Bachelor of Music degree. She was also to win recognition for choral studies offered through a postgraduate diploma and master's degree as well as provision for the award of a Doctor of Musical Arts in Choral Music. Senior students in these programmes undertake practical work with university and other choirs, and observe the work of Morag Atchison, Swedish voice specialist and soloist Catrin Johnsson, Robert Wiremu and other vocal coaches.[8]

Some other universities and polytechnic institutions began to teach conducting. Martin Setchell at the University of Canterbury, Simon Tipping at Wellington Polytechnic and Jack Speirs at the University of Otago were others who taught the subject. However, Auckland remained the front-runner, being best known and the most influential. Attempts to set up substantial courses at other universities have proved unsuccessful. It could be that New Zealand is not large enough to support more than one fully functioning teaching programme in choral music. And because of Auckland's choral culture, where students of conducting know each other and to a large extent support each other year round, it is no accident that so many Big Sing Finale choirs come from the City of Sails, and receive the top awards. The result of the concentration of intensive training in one city has meant that other centres can feel deprived of regular stimulation to achieve higher and higher standards. While replication of the Auckland system is not necessary, there will likely come a point when Christchurch or Wellington will feel compelled to provide a thorough programme in all aspects of choral music.

The story of how Jack Speirs came to have an impact on conducting education is particularly interesting. Peter Platt, Blair Professor of Music at the University of Otago from 1957 to 1975 and himself a skilled choir trainer, appointed Speirs from Yorkshire in 1965. Speirs had studied at Edinburgh University and at the Hochschule für Musik in Berlin, and officially his specialities in teaching were composition, instrumentation, analysis and twentieth-century music studies. However, he also became principal conductor of the Dunedin Sinfonia for 13 years and musical director of the Southern Consort of Voices for about 20 years. Speirs gave the small number of orchestral and choral conducting students (the class was deliberately a combined one) experience with his own performing groups and, today, he is primarily remembered as a teacher and mentor of conducting students.

They speak of his uncompromising desire for thorough musicianship and a clear choral sound, and they remember the new music that he presented. For example, he performed music by Arvo Pärt and Henryk Górecki before others introduced those composers to New Zealand. Three protégés in particular represent his impact: Holly

Holly Mathieson.
PHOTOGRAPHER IAN WATSON, COURTESY OF NYOS

Holly Mathieson

Holly Mathieson started studying composition with Jack Speirs at the age of 14, before embarking on her formal university studies with him at the University of Otago two years later. After completing a first-class honours degree in composition, analysis and conducting, Mathieson was awarded the Speirs Memorial Prize for Most Promising Conducting Student in 2000. She gained a master's degree in orchestral conducting at Melbourne University (2003) and then returned to Otago to do a PhD.

In 2014–15, she held one of the world's most prestigious fellowships for young conductors, the Leverhulme Fellowship at the Royal Conservatoire of Scotland. In 2016, Zonta New Zealand listed her in their Top 50 New Zealand Women of Achievement.

While choral conducting featured strongly in her New Zealand/Australian years, it is operatic and orchestral work that has involved her full-time in England and Scotland. Reported to be a passionate communicator, combined with crystalline technique and a collaborative approach, she has just finished a two-year post as assistant conductor at the Royal Scottish National Orchestra. She also has ongoing projects with the London Symphony and other British orchestras and is currently expanding her work into North America. Mathieson also works with Scottish Ballet.

She has recently led an inaugural tour around Scotland, where she now lives, of the innovative Nevis Ensemble, which aims to take music out of the concert hall and into isolated communities.

Michael Joel.
PHOTOGRAPHER
PETER GARRITY

Michael Joel

In 1992 Michael Joel completed a first-class honours degree in music at the University of Otago, majoring in conducting. He then studied with various overseas conductors. He became equally at home in the choral, orchestral and operatic repertoire, conducting the City of Dunedin Choir and other choral organisations, working at Canterbury Opera from 2003 until 2006, and conducting many New Zealand orchestras. These have included St Matthew's Chamber Orchestra, and principals and members of the New Zeland Symphony Orchestra and New Zealand String Quartet in a critically acclaimed performance of Mahler's 4th Symphony.

Joel has premiered works by New Zealand composers Gillian Whitehead, John Drummond, Jonathan Besser and Louise Webster. In 2014, he relocated to London to assist Plácido Domingo, Alexander Joel, Dan Ettinger and other conductors at the Royal Opera House. He is also a distinguished violist and teacher, and he shares the parenting of two daughters with Kiwi opera star wife Madeleine Pierard.

Mathieson, Tecwyn Evans and Michael Joel. Others who were influenced by him include Matthew Leese, Andrew Crooks and Peter Adams. A former member of the National Youth Choir and now associate professor of music, Adams continued Speirs' work at the University of Otago after Speirs died in 2000.

Soon after Peter Godfrey began his University of Auckland conducting class, he introduced conducting sessions into National Youth Choir rehearsals for members who were likely to conduct in their future careers. These sessions continued for many years. At Godfrey's suggestion, and with a grant from the Queen Elizabeth II Arts Council, conductors' workshops especially for teachers were set up in nine regions, from Invercargill to Auckland. Godfrey took most of them; Peter Watts or Karen Grylls led some.

In addition, a series of nationwide conducting workshops was led by prominent conductors under the auspices of the New Zealand Choral Federation (NZCF), formed in 1985. An NZCF Practical Training for Young Choral Conductors scheme was established in 1992, and another NZCF project, a 'guide for the enthusiastic choral director', *Absolutely Basic Choral Directing*, written by Shona McIntyre, Allan Purdy and Stephen Rowe, was released in 1995.

Taking the long view, maybe Peter Godfrey and I won that 1980 lunchtime debate. Certainly, Godfrey's long-running curiosity about the value of conducting training, and his decision to start a class at the University of Auckland less than two years later, can be seen as crucial to a renewal of choral activity in this country. Another indirect result of the lunchtime debate — also less than two years later — was that I had enrolled in a three-year graduate conducting programme in Southern California, not only to gain skills and knowledge for my own conducting but also to understand better what other countries thought was important about the art, craft, discipline and professional vocation of choral directing.

The unseemly spectacle of conductors having to work out their own professional development in full public view surely had to end. That it happened as late as 1982 is surprising from an internationalist's perspective. However, a stage had now been set for the standard of many choirs to improve dramatically: 'The quality of singing from any ensemble is only as good as the ears, ideas and musical knowledge of its conductor. This is true of all stages of choral expertise. . . . To be a conductor may seem a daunting occupation and, in many respects, it is; yet there are identifiable and necessary tools that can be learned.'[9]

11

We're all going on a summer holiday: Conductor training in action

In 1982, Peter Godfrey's University of Auckland class in choral conducting revealed a strong interest in the subject among students. But the vast majority of New Zealand's choir directors had never had a conducting lesson. How could help be offered to the hundreds of leaders of community, church, school, university and other choirs? The challenge was to teach these conductors 'identifiable and necessary tools', as Karen Grylls described them.

In 1985, a National Summer School in Choral Conducting was advertised for the following summer, marking the beginning of summer training opportunities. Over the next 25 years, 14 summer schools, two clinics and a retreat were attended by a total of more than 1300 conductors, singers and administrators. Most directors of choral societies, chamber choirs and other well-known choral groups in the country went to at least one event.

Cliff Richard's famous song 'We're All Going on a Summer Holiday' was about a summer trip to a place of fun, laughter and no more worries, where work would be left behind for a week or two. The only catch in the 1986 choral conducting version was that some intense, artistic hard work would be expected.

What was going to persuade musicians, young and old, proficient and inexperienced, to sacrifice up to eight days of their summer holidays to study the arcane subject of choral conducting? The best selling point turned out to be also the most practicable place to begin: a vocabulary of conducting gestures. These gestures were the 'conducting moves' used for sculpting music as well as beating time.

In a sense, gestural technique was the wrong place to start because composers' musical wishes had always been more important than a conductor's wishes or abilities, but for these schools the musical score would have to wait. The first step was to understand how the waving of hands and arms in front of a choir made a difference to how a group sounds. After this, the student conductor would prepare a score thoroughly and imaginatively and, being armed with a vocabulary of already-practised gestures, they could live the music, *be the music* for the choir, and draw out a good performance.[1]

In the late 1970s and early 1980s, the crucial role of communicating effectively through movements of the hands, arms, head or other parts of the body wasn't well understood by most conductors. Many hadn't considered whether their public image on the podium was appropriate or even helpful.

In my own case, I had directed various choirs reasonably successfully, including the National Youth Choir tour in 1982, but often this success had come with too little preparation and a conducting technique said to resemble a 'whirling windmill'. Geoff Newson, an experienced orchestral player and administrator, had seen this ungainly phenomenon in others, and he became concerned and brave enough to approach me about it. I had noted this as a matter to sort out during a period of graduate study at the University of Southern California (USC).

At USC I soon learned a more disciplined and effective style under the guidance of Rodney Eichenberger, one of the most highly regarded in this field in the United

States.[2] In my very first class, Eichenberger stepped forward, stopped the 30 or so master's and doctoral conducting students who were singing for me, took my hands, which were at a height of over six feet, and lowered them to a more useful level in front of my body. As a mature-age student it was an embarrassingly vulnerable moment for me, but the class applauded the greater musical focus that resulted. Improvement in the quality of the singing was the result, and I also felt more comfortable. I learned what it was like to be subjected to intense conducting instruction. Eichenberger's contributions to my own skill-set were many, but it was his coaching on how to teach conducting that was particularly illuminating. Besides identifying the craft's basic principles, it showed how an encouraging, empathetic approach could reap huge rewards.

Many of the USC conducting students were excellent music readers and therefore able to follow a conductor carefully. This meant that classes on gestural skills and interpretation could produce rapid improvement.[3] In four hours per week one could observe how others progressed, and how some were militantly unwilling to change their styles. Eichenberger's practical course (which centred on choir development) was built on principles of problem-solving and gentle persuasion rather than coercion. Less became more: the very focused, non-verbal miming art became a powerful tool. What the singers saw in each person's conducting was the musical response they gave.

I became very keen to share these discoveries with choir directors in New Zealand as soon as possible. Gestural fluency stood out as a top priority for any workshops that might be organised.

By early 1985, after I had returned home, further priorities for a first national conductors' gathering had become clear. First, the tone of the event — 'an accepting, caring atmosphere which fosters personal and professional growth' (as the 1985 publicity brochure would say). Giving this advance notice about an accepting attitude was essential, because even experienced conductors typically feel very vulnerable when others are watching their every movement.

Next, videotaping of each student's conducting — daily tutor groups, with members singing for each other's conducting, would (as at USC) involve videotaping of the hands-on, individualised tuition. Tapes would be analysed by the student over the following two days — a proven method of personal critique leading to better preparation.

Masterclasses were required — for all participants, where students could observe other tutors and see how different musical styles were treated. A forum and Q&A sessions would also be key ingredients.

The best-laid plans of a student conductor can come crashing down if their accompanist is not able to play the right notes at the right time and follow nuances closely. Experienced and accomplished accompanists were essential.

Consistent content among tutors was also necessary — to avoid student confusion, tutors needed to agree on the basic principles of choral direction, and to demonstrate a similar approach. There could be problems if students observed disparities between masterclasses and tutor group teaching, or between one summer school and the next.

It was easy to select Nelson as the centre for a summer school in January 1986. It was a popular choice as a holiday spot, with fabulous beaches nearby and fine weather almost guaranteed. The arts-minded population of about 33,000 were supportive of choral concerts and there were fine facilities at the Nelson Polytechnic and the nearby Nelson School of Music.

In early 1985, I travelled to Nelson as part of my national position in the Department of Education and made contacts crucial to establishing a credible national event. Nelson Polytechnic Department of Community Studies was willing to be involved, and Frank Stephens, head of the department (whom I had known previously), agreed to provide rooms for daily tutor groups and to print the publicity brochure. I negotiated within the Nelson School of Music the use of the acoustically friendly auditorium for plenary sessions and concerts.

Another stroke of good fortune was the Department of Internal Affairs Youth Services Committee's agreement to award scholarships to 24 young people attending the summer school. Recipients included many future choral leaders.[4] The awarding of these scholarships would give a youthful look to the first summer school.

The look could have been even more youthful if Godfrey and I had not made the mistake of setting the minimum age for participants at 16 years. We turned away 15-year-old David Childs, now a successful director of professional and church choirs in the United States and a distinguished choral composer. We didn't realise that there is no optimal age for good musicians to try their hand at conducting. Childs was right to be disappointed.

A comprehensive publicity brochure assured potential registrants that all kinds of music would be included: contemporary, popular, jazz and traditional art music; and it mentioned conducting points that would be covered: from preparation beat, the pacing of rehearsals and voice training, to the weight and colour of choral sound. The programme for the first summer school remained the basis for subsequent ones.

Brochures were issued at the Inaugural Conference of the New Zealand Choral Federation in July 1985, and advertising went out to choirs, music shops, libraries, tertiary institutions, secondary and intermediate schools, large primary schools and some churches. A unique musical event was promised and drew 100 participants from all walks of life and from all parts of the country, beginners and advanced. Several came from Australia.

Once teaching content priorities were established, there was no problem finding sufficient consistency of approach between the three tutors at the first summer school: Faye Dumont of Melbourne, Peter Godfrey and me. Dumont, a leading figure in Australia's choral life, had overlapped with me at USC for a semester, so I knew how she would teach.[5]

Godfrey was becoming known as a teacher of conducting, especially through his short courses during National Youth Choir rehearsal weeks.[6] I had worked with him at some of those courses and knew that he would go very quickly to musical interpretation rather than build and consolidate gestures. But somehow the three of us made the teaching work fluently. In addition, we knew the contexts of most of the 30 in each of our groups because we had all taught in schools and led community and church choirs. Also, we had excellent service from our accompanists.

There were professional and organisational challenges to be faced, however, as the first school began. Some participants felt awkward about being videotaped. They deliberately came without a tape and weren't about to purchase one from the school. From personal experience I understood their reluctance to make themselves vulnerable. Some self-conscious newcomers were successfully encouraged to get 'up front' after seeing others take the plunge. Others avoided the challenge by becoming part of a small army of 'assistants' needed for many tasks vital to the smooth running of such a school, such as setting up and operating videotape recorders and locking them away securely, setting up tutorial rooms, distributing and collecting music copies and assisting office staff with outside phone calls.

Group singing was absent from the priorities of that first summer school. Godfrey had suggested that the event should be called a singing school, but I believed that title would distract from its core intention to provide an opportunity for choir directors to learn the art and craft of conducting. So, the title had become National Summer School in Choral Conducting.

But there was plenty of opportunity to sing. Every tutor group, as well as the morning warm-ups and concerts, involved singing. The rehearsals and performance of Anthony Ritchie's commissioned work *Le vierge, le vivace et le bel aujourd'hui* added to the vocal activity.

Evaluation sheets filled in on the last day showed great satisfaction with and enthusiasm for the experience. It had not only been unique and exciting, but unexpectedly enlightening for some, a networking opportunity for others, and, for most, an eye-opener about how much there was to learn about choral conducting.

However, a problem loomed. It would be a full year before another school could be given. The rate of forgetting of skills and understandings would be high. Godfrey and I were committed to building on the groundwork laid in Nelson.

Godfrey led some regional two-day courses similar to the one he had run after National Youth Choir rehearsals in August 1985. A Christchurch course was originally intended for local music teachers as well, 'but the number of choir members applying was so great that no one else could be included'.[7] In spite of the satisfaction of running these events, Godfrey felt the frustration of short courses. It was like 'trying to teach the piano in two days', he said. Nevertheless, his courses continued, and many regular participants later became effective school and community choir directors.

For my part, I continued to hold conducting workshops around the country, including in Southland, Taupō and a series at Wellington Polytechnic. Like Godfrey, I baulked at the prospect of short, flash-in-the-pan workshops. I also looked for a way whereby students could monitor their own progress. The answer was an evening series of two-hour meetings spread over 10 weeks, allowing for members to practise between sessions.[8]

The summer school in 1986 was the first of 14 such events between 1986 and 2011. They came to be seen as a time of refreshment, new repertoire and networking for busy conductors, the go-to place for beginners to learn conducting (they appreciated the step-by-step induction process) or a professional top-up for those who knew they had yet more to learn. Many choirs would enable their conductor to attend by paying their fees.[9]

The Nelson summer school of 1987 was the first at which Karen Grylls was a tutor. In late 1985, she had returned from studying at the University of Washington, Seattle, to teach at the University of Auckland, and to take up the directorship of the Auckland Dorian Choir. In Seattle she had been working with John Rahn, Abraham Kaplan and Joan Catoni-Conlon, professors in music theory and conducting.[10] Grylls had not taught a lot of conducting, but postgraduate study with Kaplan and Catoni-Conlon, and occasionally conducting choirs at Washington, stood her in excellent stead. She had become a very skilled music analyst, and an emphasis on score preparation would be likely for future summer schools.

Another tutor appeared out of the blue. Young Finnish conductor Eric-Olof Söderström paid his own way from the other side of the world. He clearly knew a

Karen Grylls, a tutor at the summer schools from 1987. AUTHOR'S COLLECTION

Faye Dumont, founder of the Melbourne Youth Choir and one of the tutors for the first National Summer School in Choral Conducting. JAMES BYRON PHOTOGRAPHY

lot about choral music and had sung in excellent choirs, but as a tutor he tended to demonstrate his idiosyncratic style of conducting rather than emphasise broad principles. This conflicted with the school's priorities, but it could not be dealt with it as it was happening. Interestingly, although with four tutors more time could be given to each student conductor, there were several less than satisfied customers at the school. This may have foreshadowed the problem of lower registrations for the next school.

In 1989 there were only 45 registrations. Maybe this was because three of the tutors were the same as in previous years, or because of other factors such as the Lange Government's widespread restructuring creating a feeling of instability in the community. I downsized the event to a 'course' by asking Godfrey not to come and shifting to less expensive premises. All registrants except one still attended. Fortunately, Dumont, and Andrew Maries from York, England, were coming with expenses paid by other funders. Maries, an organist, oboist, clarinettist and choral conductor, led an innovative and well-received daily option on church music.

Undeterred by the drop in registrations, the organisers booked the world's leading choral specialist, Eric Ericson, to headline the next school in 1990. Ericson had become known in these terms after the Americans had 'discovered' him around 1971 when his three-LP set *Europäische Chormusik* (European Choral Music) was released. Through appearances of the Swedish Radio Choir at national conventions in the United States and many personal visits, he had become the favourite of a new generation of conductors there. He had visited New Zealand in 1988 with the Choir of the Stockholm Musikhögskolan (Royal University College of Music), which had been described by Lin Saunders as the best choir ever to have visited New Zealand,[11] and I was gratified that my invitation to, and hosting of, that choir had been a success. Ericson was fully intending to come to New Zealand for the summer school until he received an invitation from South America, which he felt he had to accept. This was enormously disappointing and also meant that the proposed school was doomed. The event had to be cancelled. It was the right decision.

The 1991 summer school in Nelson featured three talented new lecturers, each with their own distinctive merits. One was Rodney Eichenberger, who lectured on the effects of basic hand, arm and body positions, outlined attractive rehearsal methodologies, and (as on many future occasions) led reading sessions of unfamiliar classical and contemporary-style repertoire. Another was Marvin Keenze, from the Westminster Choir College, Princeton, New Jersey, who brought a gravitas and expertise to the study of vocal pedagogy not seen in New Zealand before, and pointed up the close connections between high-quality choral singing and singers' personal vocal abilities and training, as well as a conductor's necessary knowledge of the voice and a capacity to demonstrate that same pedagogical understanding. The third lecturer was Finnish conductor Seppo Murto. He had contacted me about coming to the school. It made me wonder whether Eric-Olof Söderström had talked to him enthusiastically about his experience at the summer school. This time we were offered an award-winning choir as well, Dominante, which was our first choir-in-residence. Besides demonstrating choral techniques with this 35-voice ensemble, Murto brought a practical understanding of joy in choir relationships. One of his tenors said to me that Dominante was a 'fellowship that . . . sings together, talks together, laughs together, cries together'.

It was helpful for New Zealanders to become acquainted at first hand with the choral tradition of another smallish country. Finland had become a foremost choral nation after several decades of painstaking work with children's and youth choirs, voice production teachers[12] and instrumental instruction.[13]

Peter Godfrey conducting an outdoor performance. AUTHOR'S COLLECTION

The summer schools were being seen as an opportunity to encourage grassroots development of singing among teenagers. Hence, in 1991, for the first time, an eight-day National Secondary Schools Choral Course, directed by Roger Stevenson and based at nearby Nelson College, ran concurrently with the conducting summer school. School pupils were accepted after minimal auditioning, and for many it initiated a lifetime of singing in choirs. At this particular school, they attended concerts, observed the visiting choir, Dominante, in rehearsal, trained with Eichenberger for four days, and spent several sessions with Keenze sharpening up basics of voice production. The flow-on effect was the building of expertise in the New Zealand Secondary Students Choir (which Stevenson also directed).

Godfrey, Grylls and I, now more and more involved in the general direction of the schools, became their informal artistic committee for the next 20 years.

The 1992 summer school in Wellington covered choral genres in an unusual way. A Ngāti Pōneke cultural group led the opening pōwhiri,[14] followed by an option in Māori choral music. This was significant for 1992 because from the early 1980s a Māori cultural renaissance had been under way. Issues such as sovereignty, tikanga (customs/protocol)[15] and the survival of te reo Māori became prominent, and they stimulated a sense of identity among Māori musicians.[16] Te Roopu Waiata Māori (New Zealand Māori Choir) was founded in 1989, while kapa haka competitions featured choral singing.

An option in Samoan choral music was also offered. The Samoan population in New Zealand had increased markedly in the 1980s, and had brought a unique Pacific influence to the country's music including jazz and opera. Pacific Island communities established church choirs, especially in Presbyterian and Congregational churches.

The jazz genre was accommodated by a Jazz Choir performance from students of Linfield College, Oregon, United States — the summer school's second choir-in-residence. The conductor, Vijay Singh, was a specialist in jazz styles and vocal improvisation. Everyone could see what depth a college group could achieve with daily rehearsals.

Linfield College Professor Gwen Leonard outlined a topic that was new to many attendees: the International Phonetic Alphabet. The choral conductor, Marvin Keenze, followed up his talk from the previous year with an illustrated lecture on the vocal instrument. Accurate knowledge of the voice and how best to use it in a choral context had already become an unavoidable factor for conductors determined to produce a great choir.

A National Choral Course for Secondary Students was also associated with this

LEFT Seppo Murto, director of Dominante and lecturer of the 1991 summer school. PHOTOGRAPHER TIITUS VERHE. DOMINANTE CHOIR ARCHIVES

BELOW Dominante, the Chamber Choir of the Helsinki University of Technology, Finland, and choir-in-residence at the 1991 summer school. PHOTOGRAPHER TIITUS VERHE. DOMINANTE CHOIR ARCHIVES

summer school. It was directed by Terence Maskell, head of music at Aorere College, Auckland, and it again involved Eichenberger.

Associate Professor Jack Speirs from the University of Otago, one of the country's most exciting conductors and conducting teachers, brought a different style of conducting to the 1993 summer school in Wellington. His presence represented a move away from the American-influenced conducting curriculum dominant in the first seven years of the school. He brought a very perceptive eye to his tutor group's efforts. This was the only summer school that he attended, but one of Speirs' legacies was his bringing to New Zealand audiences the music of twentieth-century European composers, in particular the deeply spiritual Estonian composer Arvo Pärt. Speirs was an award-winning composer himself, and as a conductor he knew what pieces would work with his ensembles.

Speirs also conducted the largest commissioned work seen at a summer school, David Hamilton's multi-choir *Dance-Song to the Creator* that incorporated the school's third choir-in-residence — the National Youth Choir of New Zealand, directed by Karen Grylls.[17]

A large number of other New Zealand compositions were sung, including works by prominent composers David Farquhar, Anthony Ritchie, Leonie Holmes and Helen Fisher. Following up the 1991 and 1992 programmes, a Samoan Choral Concert was presented by young Samoan leader Igelese Ete, a former member of the two national choirs.

The summer school programme was especially arranged to enable all conductors at the school to watch Eichenberger rehearse the Course for Secondary Students. With funding from the Health Sponsorship Council, it was now called the Smokefree National Choral Course. Adults were being gradually persuaded that high school pupils could attain great choral heights.

From 1993 onwards summer schools were held biennially. At Upper Hutt in 1995 the intention was to improve the standard of choral music in schools even further. Secondary students linked with this summer school were guaranteed a live audition for the next cycle of the New Zealand Secondary Students Choir; daily instruction from Eichenberger; and participation in rehearsals and performances with the fourth choir-in-residence, Brisbane's St Peter's Chorale — one of Australia's leading youth choirs.

The 1997 summer school was held at Karori in Wellington, with a focus on primary school choral teaching. 'So you've been landed with the choir?' This was the situation for many primary school teachers, and they had no experience to bring to their new responsibility. A two-day workshop, opening just before other school participants arrived, attracted 70 primary and intermediate school teachers, 30 from the Auckland region and 40 from 13 other centres. Some stayed on for the whole summer school. In this way, support could be given to the (sometimes reluctant) conductors of children's choirs.

The range of sessions shows how far the summer school programming had come. At the first school in 1986 we would never have imagined highlights such as Igelese Ete's evening session on 'Music of the Pacific Basin',[18] or Mike Brewer's entertaining 'Warm-up Riff — body, mind, spirit', or Karen Grylls' demonstration, based on evidential research from around the world, of the effective placement of singers in choirs. Nor would we have imagined appointing three assistant tutors: Julie Jackson, David Childs and Christopher Kiver,[19] with the aim of encouraging more conductors to be coaches in their communities.

Again, a secondary course ran parallel with the summer school.

Two short courses in the largest cities that had not hosted a full summer school provided an opportunity to focus on good long-term resources for conductors. Karen Grylls and Roy Tankersley, who directed and administered the clinics in Auckland and Christchurch, produced 118 pages of *Course Notes* in book form, which included Jenny McLeod's *Nau te Hau Kia Puawai te Aroha* (Twelve Māori Songs) compiled with the help of Dr Tīmoti Kāretu.[20] Many participants had never been to a full summer school, and there was a great range of choirs represented. Names like Friendly Road Choir, University of Waikato Chamber Choir, Samoan Community Choir, Flaxmere Primary School (Hastings), and North Shore's 100 Voice Chorale illustrate that diversity.

There had always been Australians venturing across the Tasman to sample summer school fare. After four years working in Brisbane and visiting all the states' capital cities, I was aware that Australia's choral conducting needs were similar to New Zealand's. There was no good reason why a full summer school couldn't be presented in Australia, although the imagined prospect of the summer schools wandering off to Australia alarmed some members of the Choral Society's executive in New Zealand, and they were right to be protective of a valuable asset that they had helped to build. There were also tax, legal and logistical questions to be answered. But the likelihood that the English-speaking world's best-known choral composer, John Rutter, would be available for Brisbane in January 1999 was the catalyst for an Australian-based summer school; it was too good an opportunity to pass up.

ABOVE Christopher Kiver, director of choral activities at Penn State University, and summer school tutor. PHOTOGRAPHER ANNEMARIE MOUNTZ

LEFT Igelese Ete, lecturer on music of the Pacific Basin and conductor of the Samoan Choral Concert, at the 1992 summer school. PHOTOGRAPHER UNKNOWN

Registrations for the school at the University of Queensland School of Music, St Lucia, had been closed at 200, with over 30 from New Zealand and four from Singapore. Additional tutors had hurriedly been persuaded to attend to cope with the record numbers, and a special conducting tutor group for secondary students was created.

Considered by Sir David Willcocks to be 'the most gifted composer of his generation', Rutter brought to the school a superb musicianship and musicological knowledge. He directed a large choir of participants and Brisbane choristers in a deeply felt performance of one of his most recent compositions, 'A Clare Benediction'. Some were taken aback by his exuberant and, arguably, unhelpful conducting of Stanford's *I Was Glad*, but all were delighted to meet the man, who was known to choir members all around the world, and who had perfected the art of Christmas carol arrangements.[21]

There were also other attractions. One was the choir-in-residence, a youth chamber choir, Candomino, from Helsinki, winner of the BBC Let the Peoples Sing competition in 1980. Directed by Tauno Satomaa, their distinctive repertoire (sometimes using techniques honouring ancient *runo* singing practices), and their cohesive sound based on the Finnish language's soft consonants and refined vowels, displayed a depth of tone regardless of whether they were singing quietly or loudly.

In addition, Candomino was pleased to help with launching something new in this part of the southern hemisphere: an inaugural Australasian Choral Conducting Competition. Competitors (maximum age 35) were required to learn some of the demanding Candomino repertoire for the semi-final and final stages. A panel of five judged Andrew Wailes, of Sydney, to be the winner.

Responses from the evaluation sheets, such as 'Perfect as it is' and 'A brilliant convention', suggested that this had been the most successful summer school ever held. At the same time, responses were not short on honest self-appraisal: 'The way I beat four has been corrected. . . . I wouldn't have taken it on board if I hadn't known why I needed to change.' One humble soul wrote, 'From knowing nothing I've advanced to knowing next to nothing.'

Alongside the expected and deserved praise for John Rutter were hundreds of other warm, appreciative remarks: the 'international calibre of tutors'; 'Candomino clarified what a choir responds to'; and 'Andrew Maries was an inspiration'. Delegates seemed to have had only two main problems: tiredness and the quality of biscuits at morning and afternoon teas.

However, there were signs of finer thinking and greater discernment in the

TOP LEFT Internationally renowned composer John Rutter, choir director of the 1999 summer school in Brisbane.

TOP RIGHT The cover design for the enrolment brochure and handbook, 1999. AUTHOR'S COLLECTION

BELOW Finnish choir Candomino, choir-in-residence at the 1999 Brisbane summer school, with director Tauno Satomaa. CANDOMINO CHOIR ARCHIVES school than preoccupation with the catering. The experiences of Rutter's 'A Clare Benediction', Candomino's unusually inspiring singing, originally created half a world away, the surprising performances in the finale of the conducting competition, and the powerful effect of the music in Sunday services, came together to mean more than the sum of their parts. To those delegates open to rich experiences there was the possibility that all this had an aesthetic value deeper than just the musical feelings and excitement — important as these responses were. The summer school was in the business of aesthetic enjoyment and growth. As an executive group interested in how participants might perceive and enjoy the impact of the summer school, the committee cared about aesthetic quality in as many aspects of the school as possible.[22]

Three events in three years — the 1997 school, the 1998 clinics and the sell-out 1999 Brisbane 'Spectacular' with John Rutter — all hinted at a thirst for more conducting education throughout Australasia. It was almost a given that the next summer school should be staged in both countries, running two events in quick succession, using the same lecturers and tutors. This buoyant market for conducting training in Australia and New Zealand would allow for the introduction of new approaches and new faces.

Tutors new to summer schools in New Zealand were Jo-Michael Scheibe, Bob Chilcott (member of the King's Singers for 12 years, conductor of the 200-voice chorus at the Royal College of Music in London and one of Britain's most accessible choral composers), Dave Jorlett (experienced teacher from Minnesota and a changing-voice specialist) and Ngāpō (Bub) Wehi (composer and leading Auckland exponent of Māori performing arts).

It was the beginning of a fruitful relationship between Bub Wehi, his whānau and Karen Grylls, who was beginning to introduce the singing of waiata and other Māori customs into the National Youth Choir. Kiwi choral singing was to gain a new resonance and colour at its leading edge, and this unique element would come to be recognised globally.

Based at the University of Auckland, the first 2001 school was notable for two other reasons. One was a second Australasian Conducting Competition with finalists fronting the choir-in-residence, Tower Voices New Zealand, directed by Karen Grylls.[23] Wendy Patston from Auckland emerged as winner. Another reason was an official farewell to Rodney Eichenberger, who had done so much to deepen the appeal and expand the horizons of choral singing in this country. Sustained applause and a standing ovation recognised his outstanding contributions over 16 years.

When a very large number of those enrolling for the second school at the University of Queensland in 2001 opted for a secondary school repertoire strand, it was clear that a majority of delegates had a school choir.[24] The popularity of that strand was in contrast to a plenary session on the penultimate evening, entitled 'The Internet for Choral Musicians'. This offering looked worthy enough on paper, but people didn't realise its significance; it was ahead of its time. A highlight of the school was a guest choir, the Brisbane Birralee Voices (founder/director: Julie Christiansen) working in an open rehearsal with Jo-Michael Scheibe and Bob Chilcott in the St John's Chapel.[25]

Back in New Zealand, a tricky situation was developing. At 70 years old one might have been forgiven for thinking that Rodney Eichenberger would not be available for any more night-long, economy fare flights across the Pacific. However, he still wanted to come. He offered to call into New Zealand on his way back from Australia to Florida in early January 2003. While, of course, everyone was keen to learn more from him, the timing was wrong for a summer school. To the rescue came Felicia Edgecombe, at the time head of music at Queen Margaret College, Thorndon. In one stroke she relocated the event, now a 'retreat' rather than a summer school, to the fine facilities at her college and set it on an upward trajectory.

It was a close call, but 80 delegates came from all over the country for the intensive three-day event held in Wellington in 2003. For the first time a composer-in-residence was appointed, Rosemary Russell, who set to music two Gerard Manley Hopkins poems: 'God's Grandeur', commissioned for the summer school and prepared by Eichenberger, and 'Pied Beauty', for a Wellington secondary schools' representative choir that Stevenson and Eichenberger trained over two days. Ten members of the Brisbane Birralee Voices joined in that group.

In its early stages, the 2005 school was in jeopardy for reasons similar to the 2003 retreat. Although the Victoria University Centre for Continuing Education in Wellington was contracted to provide most administrative services, and experienced arts administrator Jacqui Coats spearheaded arrangements, I was out of the country. In my role as (absent) director I distinctly remember calling Coats in 2004, from a highway phone on the road from Chicago to Indianapolis, to finalise an application for funding from Creative New Zealand to cover the travel of overseas guests and of myself from Chicago. This was the reality of how our organisation was working.

With the aim of promoting singing as a family-wide taonga, a holiday programme for families and a 'New Year's Eve Special' was envisaged. However, a qualified director to run children's activities at that time of year could not be found and the idea was dropped. All through the unstable planning period, the invited overseas guests remained confirmed. Three new conductors: Professor Jerry Blackstone — director of choirs at the University of Michigan, Dr David Childs from Vanderbilt University, Tennessee, and Dr Carl Crossin from the University of Adelaide — gave added spark to the programme.[26]

After a decade of innovations (Brisbane and Auckland twice and Christchurch once), we had resumed activities in the capital city and I had returned to live in New Zealand. A new 'normal' could be established after a turbulent period of growth; gone was the helter-skelter planning, constantly newly formed committees, and shaky communications with an absent director, even if those situations did sometimes produce fresh ideas. Creativity and newness are wonderful qualities but so are stability, a proven tradition and a sense of balanced repose. Everything needed to come back to Wellington for the organisation to find itself again.

In 2007, in Wellington, a new name promised a slightly new emphasis: A Summer School for Choral Leaders: Conductors, Administrators, Accompanists. It offered support for those people in the choral universe who were often forgotten: administrators and accompanists. The two new strands each only drew a group of seven, most probably because summer schools were now indelibly linked to conductors rather than to choral leaders in general.

Mary Hopper, professor of choral music at the Wheaton College Conservatory of Music, Illinois, offered sessions on 'Spirituals and Gospel' and 'Music for Women's Voices by African-American Composers'. In addition, Hopper, with Felicia Edgecombe, explored the topics of choir relationships, the benefits of choral singing to society, and singing groups and choirs in churches. During the school, special guest Peter Godfrey was formally recognised as one of New Zealand's icons, thanked for his enormous contribution to our country's choral development, and was asked to share memories of those summer schools which he had attended over the previous 21 years.

One of the advantages of employing Victoria Continuing Education again was the production of a 65-page handbook, compiled by Jacqui Coats, containing plenary notes, resources and extensive repertoire lists along with music for the pōwhiri and the grace before meals — Charles Wood's 'Oculi Omnium'.[27] Another first for this school was that delegates could work with (paid) mentors for half-hour periods during lunch hours or other convenient times. For this exercise we needed many new mentors for the 81 people registered. Delegates came from places as varied as Waitomo, Queenstown, Taumarunui, Greytown, Kaipara and New South Wales. In a report to Creative New Zealand, which had granted $10,000 towards the summer school, I quoted an evaluative comment from the Choral Federation publication *Breve*. The report of one attendee sums up how participants generally felt about their summer school experiences: 'A must place to be for all who are passionate about doing the best for their choir. It was exciting, stimulating, extending, informative, friendly, motivating and a place to learn, learn and learn some more.'

Two days after the conclusion of the 2007 school, members of International Summer Schools in Choral Conducting Incorporated (ISSCC) discussed at their AGM where the fourteenth school should be held in 2009. A Hamilton group of four was interested in organising the event in conjunction with a professional conference agency. Three had taken part in the administration strand of the just-concluded school and the fourth had attended the 2003 retreat, so they all knew what the schools were about. One reason for deciding on a one-off move to Hamilton was to give the Wellington ISSCC a break, but another was to serve the choral community who lived in the northern part of the country. We were also intrigued by a provocative question in one of the documents given to us: 'Is the WEL Energy Academy of Performing Arts at the University of Waikato [where the school would be held] the best choral and chamber music venue in New Zealand?' The prospect of rewarding acoustics is perennially interesting to choral buffs.

Dr Peggy Koopman-Boyden and her committee organised an excellent school for the 45 full-time attendees. Jerry Blackstone's imaginative and spectacularly energetic rehearsing of Mozart's *Coronation Mass* was a standout, with his effortless incorporation of local choristers into daily rehearsals. Another feature of the school was the work of Dr Debra Shearer-Dirié, a sessional lecturer in aural music and conducting at the University of Queensland.[28] Her relaxed conducting of ethnic music and traditional choral gems impressed.

Rachael Griffiths-Hughes, a member of the organising committee, and I agreed to be co-directors and we shared a tutor group — a new arrangement that worked well.

Once again, a great diversity of backgrounds was represented in those who attended. Various ethnic and Christian traditions were represented, from the Auckland Baptist Tabernacle Mandarin Congregation Choir, the Church College of New Zealand, Vision College (Hamilton), the Ruapehu Catholic Club Choir and Madrigal Companie (New Plymouth), to an independent boys' school, the Southern Youth Choir (Dunedin) and a young vocal collective from Hamilton.

Some regular attendees wanted to know if they could earn more than a mere 'Certificate of Participation' at the end of a summer school. It was true that these intensive January weeks deserved greater recognition, and in pointing to the need for professional accreditation they echoed a recommendation that I had made many years before to a tertiary institution. But in the absence of any academic accreditation,

ABOVE Felicia Edgecombe (left), tutor at the 2000 summer retreat, and Rosemary Russell, composer-in-residence at the 2000 summer retreat, photographed in 2002. PHOTOGRAPHER CATHY ANSLOW. QUEEN MARGARET COLLEGE, WELLINGTON

LEFT Mary Hopper, professor of choral music at the Wheaton College Conservatory of Music, Illinois, and tutor at the summer retreat in 2000. PHOTOGRAPHER JEFF NELSON the best that our schools could do was to continue to issue attendance certificates.

For a long time it had been apparent that the proper home for ISSCC Inc. was probably within the structure of the Choral Federation. When the summer schools began, the Federation was only six months old — still finding its feet — and conductor training wasn't a concern to the new movers and shakers. However, 25 years later, thinking had changed. The time had come for a united front on conductor training. New Zealand was too small to have two agencies attempting to do similar things. It was decided to gift ISSCC to the one professional body for choral music in the country — the Choral Federation.

In retrospect, the most significant session at the final summer school of 2010/11 in Wellington was entitled 'What makes a good Association of Choral Directors?' A new professional body was to rise out of the ashes of the ISSCC and we had advice of the highest international quality on hand; Jo-Michael Scheibe was, at the time, president-elect of the American Choral Directors Association, and Mary Hopper, already president of the Illinois state organisation, was to become president of the national association within a few years.[29]

The first two days of the Directors' Convention were vintage ISSCC in programming, while the final days were in the hands of a newly constituted New Zealand Choral Federation Association of Choral Directors (although the personnel were almost the same!). A formal dinner on 2 January 2011 in a transformed Queen Margaret College Hall marked both 25 years of summer school life and the seamless transition to a new brand. In formally launching the new association, the guest speaker, Chris Finlayson, Minister for Arts, Culture and Heritage, remarked that New Zealand's early choristers would

> marvel at the distinguished record of international success for our elite choirs — unsung heroes whose accomplishments should be more widely known. . . . I am doing my bit to spread that news. I enjoy reminding people rugby is not the only thing New Zealand excels in. Years ago, our great singers such as Kiri Te Kanawa and Donald McIntyre established a profile of excellence in singing for New Zealand in countries which have little or no interest in rugby. Our soloists, the Youth Choir and Voices NZ have all continued that fine tradition.

But, Finlayson concluded, 'The potential for great choral singing remains unfilled without the vision, musicality and dedication of great directors.'

TOP Debra Shearer-Dirié, musical director of the Brisbane Concert Choir, and tutor at the 2009 summer school. PHOTOGRAPHER RENE MARCEL

BELOW Association of Choral Directors convention participants at rehearsal in Sacred Heart Cathedral, January 2011. PHOTOGRAPHER ANN-MARIE STAPP

The five-day convention concluded with Hopper, Scheibe and Christopher Kiver conducting in the beautiful acoustics and surroundings of Sacred Heart Cathedral in Thorndon.

Thus ISSCC Inc. was wound up and Te Kotahitanga Manu Reo e Aotearoa (New Zealand Choral Federation) Association of Choral Directors soon won everyone's loyalty. More than a dozen people offered to help set up the fledgling organisation, and everyone present at the convention was made a foundation member of the new body. The dramatically successful final event of the summer schools, including the lavish evening of celebration, was an important springboard for the nurturing of future directors who had vision, proven musicality and dedication. Continuity of nurturing was assured by the agreed salute: 'The King is dead, long live the King!'

In 1908, one of the world's musical revolutionaries, Arnold Schönberg, wrote the last movement of his *String Quartet No 2* with no key signature.[30] This signified his transition to an atonal musical idiom in which traditional harmony is abandoned. In New Zealand, choral conducting education had entered a new era. Would its future be like that final movement of Schönberg's 2nd String Quartet — dissolution of familiar foundations, and assurances abandoned, an adventure to another universe? Hardly likely, because most of the same people were involved before and after 2011.

Within 18 months an Association of Choral Directors convention was held at Wellington College. Choral Connect was chosen as a title by Rosemary Russell and Christine Argyle because it suggested a new world of the internet and closer collaboration. There were facilitated sessions for conductors to network and share solutions to common problems. Several summer school features were retained: the one-on-one mentoring, repertoire sessions (with a music sampler beautifully produced by SOUNZ) and a choir-in-residence. Jo-Michael Scheibe's University of Southern California University Singers sang for a masterclass and presented open rehearsals and a delightful concert.

The convention also hosted a children's holiday course led by Christine Argyle and Megan Flint. A 'demonstration and performance' after two days' work was a telling foretaste of an impressive Wellington Young Voices children's choir created soon afterwards.

The 2014 Choral Connect was aimed at attracting delegates from one particular province, while still making it easy for anyone to attend. The venue, Lindisfarne College, Hastings, was excellent and the event was judged highly successful by those

TOP LEFT Jo-Michael Scheibe, conductor of the University of Southern California University Singers, choir-in-residence at the Association of Choral Directors convention 2011. USC THORNTON SCHOOL OF MUSIC. DEPARTMENT OF CHORAL AND SACRED MUSIC

TOP RIGHT Latvian composer Ēriks Ešenvalds, who presented a commissioned work at Choral Connect 2017. PHOTOGRAPHER AIVARS KRASTIŅŠ

BELOW Jerry Blackstone, emeritus professor of conducting at the University of Michigan, who presented works at Choral Connect 2014. PHOTOGRAPHER PETER SMITH who attended. But with 58 paying delegates and only six from the targeted province — Hawke's Bay — the well-intentioned venture ended in deficit. Musically, it was probably the best school of its kind thus far. This is not surprising considering the calibre of the guest artists from the University of Michigan, a large public university with a student population of 45,000.

The director of the University of Michigan's choral programme was Dr Jerry Blackstone, said to be the leading conductor of his generation, and his singers were graduate and undergraduate students majoring in vocal performance, music education or conducting. This premier choir from 11 choral ensembles on the Ann Arbor, Michigan, campus not only made themselves available for all the conducting masterclasses but also presented a solo voice recital.

A Convention Sing, in St Matthew's Church, Hastings, was Maurice Duruflé's *Requiem* led by Blackstone, with accompanist Scott Van Ornum, and the University of Michigan Chamber Choir.

A third Choral Connect was offered in Auckland's acoustically rich Holy Trinity Cathedral in 2017. This new-style affair was a gentle but powerful breath of fresh air coming, seemingly, from another planet: Latvian composer Ēriks Ešenvalds personally delivered a heart-warming commissioned work; workshops with choral composers showed how conductors could better prepare scores; seasoned conductor/humourist André Thomas revealed African-American music's integrity;[31] two national choirs did us all very proud (directed by David Squire and Andrew Withington); and an exquisitely sung pōwhiri, prepared with local kaumātua, was led by the organising team.[32]

An Auckland team, headed by Karen Grylls, Jono Palmer, Rowan Johnston and administrator Cathryn Wyllie, had sailed in a new direction, finding that they could further expand and enhance the world of conducting education.

MasterCard
BlackBerry

12

A world in union: The New Zealand Choral Federation

Over 21,000 members from 230 chamber and community choirs, over 280 school choirs and 400 individual memberships: that's the New Zealand Choral Federation (NZCF) in 2019. It organises events in its 10 regions as well as national events, including The Big Sing for secondary school choirs, which involves some 10,000 singers annually, and Sing Aotearoa, a national choral festival. Without doubt NZCF's many activities have led to greater numbers being involved in choirs, increased public awareness of choral singing, and higher standards in choral performances. The driving force behind it was Peter Godfrey. But a federation like this had been a long time coming.

The notion of a nationwide association of choirs had been floated several times before, but the people promoting the idea hadn't had Godfrey's mana or his supporting cast.[1]

In 1965, Stanley Jackson, conductor of the Phoenix Choir in Wellington, had proposed a Federation of Choral Societies, and later the same year William Hawkey, conductor of the Christchurch Harmonic Society, urged committees of large choirs to send delegates to an inaugural meeting of the proposed federation. That meeting happened, but nothing came from it. Then, in 1980, representatives of the country's five symphonic choirs met.[2] Money provided the catalyst — they met to dispute changes in Radio New Zealand's broadcast fees, which had helped choirs over the previous 40 years.[3]

All through this period, Malcolm Rickard, the Orpheus Choir conductor, was against the formation of a federation of choirs. He appeared to be unwilling to support anything for the 'have-nots' that might jeopardise his choir's favoured status as one of the 'haves'. His insider position in the New Zealand Broadcasting Service and close association with the National Orchestra had often led to preferential treatment for the Orpheus Choir; for example, in 1968, the choir had been used for six Symphony Orchestra concerts. In a small country such apparent favouritism isn't constructive, and in this case it was holding back bigger picture progress.

Hawkey's *New Zealand Choral News*, which appeared in Christchurch in 1970, had had the valiant aim to 'help build national choral morale'. If its national coverage had been wider during the three years of production, it may have prepared the ground for a national choral association. As it was, very few today can recall even hearing about it.

On a personal level, I was aware of the vacuum that existed because of the lack of a professional body for choirs and conductors. In an October 1981 letter to Peter Godfrey I expressed a wish for an agency 'through which choirs in New Zealand could keep in touch with each other. Interestingly, we have both been thinking lately about the need for some kind of federation of choirs. The following ideas might perhaps be useful to take such a project a stage further.'[4] I listed seven possible aims. Surprisingly, none of them mentioned conductor training, which only later came to be seen as important. I suggested that Godfrey be the president of such a federation, and work with a small Wellington-based organising committee.

Godfrey was just what was needed — someone with standing, drive and national recognition. His own interest in a federation had been stimulated by attending a Loughborough Singing Week in Leicestershire in 1982. As an observer at a planning meeting for an International Federation for Choral Music, he had been asked to report briefly on choral life in New Zealand, but he had found it difficult. There was no national professional body to provide relevant information, and he had to admit that choirs were one of the few musical groups without a national federation. At Loughborough he was encouraged to start a local federation when he returned to New Zealand, but it couldn't be a priority for him in 1982 because of his involvement in the National Youth Choir's first international tour, nor could it be in 1983 because of his new position at Wellington Cathedral.

Finally, early in 1984, he began moving on the idea of a national association of choirs. He quickly enlisted David Wood and Margery Charlton, formerly his assistant at the University of Auckland, who had had years of experience with the National Youth Choir and other groups and had become regarded as a choral organisation whiz. The three of them met in May. The venture was under way.

In June, an interim steering committee of Godfrey, Wood, Elizabeth Kerr and Simon Tipping was established in Wellington, followed by Christchurch and Auckland meetings. At the July 1984 meeting in Christchurch, long-time conductor Martin Setchell noted that the meeting was the first-ever official gathering of conductors of all the main city choirs.[5] At many further meetings in the historic Government Buildings on Lambton Quay in Wellington, Godfrey, Wood and a Wellington committee worked through the details.[6]

Decisions were made under the watchful eye of Godfrey. His measured, dignified authority allowed for issues to be vigorously contested, but congenial consensus was never far away. Everyone respected this elder statesman and we all wanted the project that he was spearheading to succeed. His unique position in the choral community made it inevitable that hundreds of choral musicians would fall in with his suggestions for a federation and support the project.

But sometimes, while always listening for an emerging majority view, Godfrey had to deal with conflicting opinions. Margery Charlton wrote to Wood and Godfrey: 'I have to confess to some dismay at the prospect of waiting until August 1985 to call an inaugural meeting, and I can't see that allying it with a *visiting* choir has much to commend it.'[7] Charlton had not been party to discussions on what enticements would be necessary to encourage participants to travel to a national conference. Choral icon Sir David Willcocks and a top overseas choir, in combination, seemed to some of us to be the ideal drawcards.

Although New Zealand had not heard of Rodney Eichenberger and his elite choir at that stage, Godfrey was happy to accept a recommendation that the Americans be

The poster for the inaugural conference of the New Zealand Choral Federation, 1985. COURTESY OF MRS L. CLAUSON invited. I remember taking a tape recorder to a meeting early on, to let those gathered hear an excerpt of the University of Southern California Chamber Singers before an official invitation was issued to the group.[8] They could see why I was confident that the Singers would be suitable for the occasion.

Finally, a date in July 1985, when Sir David Willcocks would be conducting in Wellington, was selected for the launch of the federation and its inaugural conference. Eichenberger and his Singers were confirmed, and a publicity campaign was begun. The launching of the New Zealand Choral Federation, Godfrey's special project, was a spectacular success, and it became part of his legacy.

The first conference, held in the Hugh Mackenzie Building at Victoria University, and accompanied by a bracing southerly, was attended by over 230 conductors, singers, accompanists and administrators from throughout New Zealand. From the beginning, it had a vision that was not limited to local resources. Eichenberger led a two-hour masterclass with four young conductors chosen by the organising committee.[9] His Chamber Singers presented a warmly received public concert at St Paul's Cathedral and a choral service at St John's Presbyterian Church. They also took part in 'Hymn for the Lady' by Jenny McLeod; with a determination to be musically innovative, this work had been commissioned for the conference.[10]

It was a busy weekend. Willcocks conducted McLeod's composition in the Michael Fowler Centre before directing Wellington choir Schola Polyphonica with the New Zealand Symphony Orchestra in Bach's *Mass in B Minor*.[11] An inaugural business meeting (masterminded by David Wood, lawyer-chorister Bruce Corkill and Godfrey), which centred on a draft constitution and tentative future activities, was chaired by Director-General of Education Bill Renwick.

The list of conference participants was almost a who's who of choral musicians, and a massive 156 offered to sing in the Eichenberger masterclass choir. It contained many who had already contributed a great deal to the advancement of choral singing in New Zealand, or who were soon to become influential.[12]

As the conference concluded, participant Gwenyth Logan spoke for many when she said, 'I feel a glow from having witnessed a musical milestone, significant for its birth amidst a wealth of stimulus in the conference events, and for the promise of increased and nationally integrated activity to strengthen choral music in so many spheres.'[13] Besides being inspirational and educative, the event was also organisationally timely because it challenged leaders in the field to bring greater coordination between regional and local activities. Enthusiastic volunteers arranged sponsorship funding, several regional committees were established, a national

John Rosser, founding chair of the NZCF Governance Board.
PHOTOGRAPHER LUKE PILKINTON-CHING

John Rosser

John Rosser has been a key figure in the professional choral union's work since 2006. In that time, he has been chair of the Governance Board for all but four years, taken responsibility for major NZCF events such as Sing Aotearoa, convened The Big Sing committee and, with Grant Hutchinson, has managed the Federation's day-to-day affairs.

An honours classics graduate, holder of a licentiate diploma in singing, foundation member of the National Youth Choir, and director of Viva Voce, which he formed in 1985, Rosser developed a fondness for massed-choir events during his work for Auckland's annual Symphony under the Stars from 1994 to 2009. This open-air spectacle involved an audience of around a quarter of a million, and a 'willing amateur' choir of up to 1000 members in the Auckland Domain.

Appointment as associate conductor and chorus director of New Zealand Opera gave Rosser freedom to give many hours of unpaid work to the Choral Federation. His credibility as a successful choral director was a big factor in the re-formed NZCF's acceptance by rank-and-file members of the Federation. With Karen Grylls he united the rather dispirited remnants of the pre-2006 national and regional set-up, and he ensured that the new body displayed a concern for elite chamber choirs as well as choral societies and other volunteer groups. His comfortable, professional approach has seen the NZCF grow numerically and in influence.

Rosser's latest major project has been to lead an NZCF team to win the bid for the 2020 World Symposium on Choral Music to be held in New Zealand (details in Chapter 15).

newsletter, *Quire*, began to circulate, and a national executive dealt with the large issues.[14] NZCF became one of the most active arts organisations in the nation.

A tradition of well-attended annual conferences for both singers and conductors was cemented in place in July 1986 with the Federation's conference in Wellington, featuring Richard Marlow and his Cambridge University Chamber Choir, Pacific leader Alf Hunkin and other musicians. Over the next 10 years, choral and vocal experts such as New Zealander Michael Leighton Jones (senior lecturer in singing at the University of Queensland), Sir David Willcocks, Honor McKellar and Jack Speirs of Dunedin, Timothy Brown (University of Cambridge), the Song Company (Australia), Marvin Keenze and Simon Halsey were invited to annual conference venues throughout the country. Through the NZCF, New Zealanders were becoming increasingly exposed to overseas and local leaders of this calibre.

By incorporating a vocal section into the Westpac School Music Contest, and fostering it for 10 years, the Chamber Music Federation of New Zealand had made a significant contribution to choral music. When in 1985 it announced that it was stepping away from the vocal section, NZCF agreed to arrange local schools' festival events the following year, thus averting the demise of the initiative. Two choirs selected from local festivals, the Havelock North High School First Fifteen and Epsom Girls' Grammar School's Opus 15, were invited to perform at the instrumental finals of the Westpac Contest. Havelock North were placed first for the third year in a row.

The process of saving the schools' festivals continued in 1987 when the Department of Education planned a national Choral Finale at St John's Presbyterian Church on Willis Street, Wellington. Choirs competed in sections such as Baroque, New Zealand and Gospel. If placings in the various sections had been aggregated, Opus 15 from Epsom Girls' Grammar School (directed by David Hamilton) would have been clear winners.

The Choral Federation became fully committed in 1988, organising the Finale in the Wellington Town Hall's Concert Chamber in association with the Department of Education. Nine choral groups had been selected from 117 choirs representing 90 schools. Sir David Willcocks, a special guest, was sure that the Governor-General and Lady Reeves who were present 'must have been proud of the boys and girls who performed'.[15] Earlier in the year, regional festivals had boosted the fortunes of the fledgling enterprise. As an example, 22 choirs, from Dargaville High School in the north to Aorere College in South Auckland, had competed in the Auckland festival in May.

It is instructive to note the names of the young choir trainers, conductors, accompanists and soloists in that Auckland Regional Festival.[16] They were virtually

TOP First Fifteen, Havelock North High School. Director: Roger Stevenson. *HAWKE'S BAY HERALD TRIBUNE*, 18 AUGUST 1986

BELOW LEFT Opus 15, Epsom Girls' Grammar School, Auckland, 1987. PHOTOGRAPH BY A PARENT, PRESENTED TO THE DIRECTOR, DAVID HAMILTON

BELOW RIGHT The programme cover for the Regional Festivals for the NZCF Secondary Schools' Choral Festival, 1988. AUTHOR'S COLLECTION unknown then but were already putting their heads above the parapet. From the earliest days of these festivals, musicians were taking the opportunity to expand personal musical skills in order to help young people develop their vocal talent and to 'experience the deep joys of choral singing'.[17]

The Choral Federation also took responsibility for the 1989 Festival Finale in association with the Hillary Commission for Recreation and Sport. It was staged in the Wellington Town Hall auditorium on a Sunday afternoon. In this event, and in succeeding years, the number of students taking part steadily increased.

As Megan Flint argues, the wider exposure provided by Smokefree sponsorship in 1992 led to a surge in the number of schools and choirs involved (from 110 choirs in 1991 to 161 in 1992).[18] Gold, Silver and Bronze awards continued to be made in each of eight categories, but later the categories were reduced to three: New Zealand Composition or Arrangement; European Composition up to 1930 (and later to the present day); and Other Styles, including popular songs and vocal jazz. All three were required to fit within a 10-minute time limit.

The Smokefree sponsorship also, fortuitously, enabled the schools' festival to be held out of Wellington.[19] The festival's organising committee had deliberated for some time on the wisdom of letting the festival loose on the rest of the country, spreading the benefits of a Finale experience further afield. More choirs and conductors, even if they were not selected to participate, might take the opportunity to attend their nearest Finale. Audiences, including many parents, in the four major centres would be able to see the rising standards of secondary school choirs; it was important that parents bought into the project and were incentivised to support their choirs. That was the hope. Now, with sufficient funding available, the hope could become reality.[20] As it turned out, the Dunedin Town Hall event in August 1993 was highly successful, even if the three-day festival had got off to an irregular start: snow was drifting down onto some choirs outside First Church as they lined up waiting for a pōwhiri, while other groups had their travel plans disrupted.

However, without doubt, the growth of choral education was furthered by staging Festival Finales in various parts of the country.

Also, in 1993, Lois Coplon was appointed national coordinator of the festivals, and the singers, in particular, recall not only her capable organisation but also her good humour and the wonderful rapport she had with them year after year.[21]

Student numbers continued to increase during the late 1990s, and musical standards kept rising.

In 1991 when the Department of Education's Head Office in Wellington could no longer provide office space for the New Zealand Choral Federation, and an Auckland-based secretariat was offered, the centre of energy shifted north. Aucklander Graham Hoffmann had been appointed general secretary of NZCF in 1989, and he became the organisation's front-runner for the next 18 years. Hoffman's credentials for the Choral Federation's secretarial role combined musical and business experience. Besides having been secretary of Auckland NZCF, he held a Master of Music degree, was tenor in the Auckland University Singers and Orlando Singers, had operated as a business contractor in London, and had worked at grassroots level to make sure that New Zealand's Year of Commemoration in 1990 (the 150th anniversary of the signing of the Treaty of Waitangi, New Zealand's founding document) was celebrated by the choral world.[22]

Hoffman took up a paid position as general manager of NZCF in the year of the shift to Auckland. For a number of years, he provided office premises in his home at no cost. Later, he leased an office in downtown Auckland.

Craig Pollock, who was experienced in funding and marketing operations, was appointed as a development consultant on a pro bono basis.[23] Among their achievements, Hoffmann and Pollock helped create three new NZCF regions, fostered cooperative ventures, and kept abreast of changes in the arts sector, such as the emergence of Creative New Zealand and its new policies. One of their initiatives was to institute a press clipping service. With over 2000 articles appearing nationwide in 1994 alone, they were astonished at the extent of choral activity in New Zealand.

Hoffman and Pollock's drive towards strategic planning and a more 'professional' approach after the Federation's initial 'five-year developmental stage' wasn't always understood or appreciated, however, and sometimes it was resisted.[24] Hoffman's insistence that the Secondary Schools' Festival always be held in Wellington rather than move around the four main centres was not widely supported. And, on occasion, Hoffmann's negotiations were not timely enough: the 1996 World Symposium on Choral Music (WSCM), which was to be shared between Australia and New Zealand, finally ended up being a wholly Sydney affair. He did employ John Rosser (gratis) to organise and run what was called the Auckland International Festival of Choirs as an offshoot of the Sydney Symposium, and they attracted six of the best choirs at the fourth WSCM to perform in New Zealand on their way home.

Garry Maher took up the position of NZCF general manager in August 2004. Part of his contribution to the organisation was to obtain a very good insurance package for choirs. Sometime after he had taken up the position, he was told by Creative New

Graham Hoffman, general secretary of NZCF 1989–2004. FROM *IN TUNE: THE FIRST 10 YEARS OF THE NEW ZEALAND CHORAL FEDERATION*. NZCF, 1995

Christine Argyle (NZCF chief executive and chair of the Governance Board 2012–14), Peter Godfrey (patron NZCF) and Grant Hutchinson (CEO NZCF), 2004. PHOTOGRAPHER JAY BERRYMAN

Zealand that NZCF would be funded on the existing basis (bulk funding) for one further year, but after that it would be on an event-by-event basis. It appears that Creative New Zealand was not happy that there had been funding for several years for initiatives that hadn't been put into operation and also that funds had been moved from one project to another.

The next year, 2005, was inevitably going to be a difficult one. When Maher threatened to sue the NZCF Executive for appointing him to a position they knew they couldn't afford, things began to fall apart.

Newly appointed staff members Shona McIntyre, events and membership services manager from February 2004, and Caroline Mumford, treasurer, did their best in applying for funds from Creative New Zealand. Working until December 2005, McIntyre set in place all the organisation and manuals of operation for 2006 events. She then handed on to executive member/conductor Leonie Lawson the computer, digital files and the like for Lawson to continue the work in the New Year. With two other unpaid NZCF National Executive members (Di Lenihan and Yvonne Hewitt), Lawson helped to save the organisation. In conjunction with treasurer Michael Littlewood (a member of the NZCF Auckland region's committee), they looked after the nuts and bolts of the organisation for two years. In particular, they ensured that the Secondary Schools' Festivals continued. They also began negotiations with Creative New Zealand to renew a funding commitment.

NZCF had been a hair's breadth away from disaster. The 22-year-old choral organisation, which had begun with so much promise, could have collapsed. The August 2007 edition of *Breve*, the NZCF newsletter, summarised the situation succinctly: 'Because of changes in the NZCF's funding arrangements, the physical premises of NZCF National's office had first to be given up and then we lost our three full-time employees.'

Sadly Graham Hoffman died in 2004. The following year Karen Grylls recognised his contribution and his 'passion for biculturalism and New Zealand's musical traditions', particularly in the context of Sing Aotearoa and in the building of relationships with kapa haka groups and national choirs. She said that he 'will be remembered as highly significant and immensely important in New Zealand's choral life'. Significantly, he helped to bring Māori music into the mainstream of the country's cultural activities.[25]

From November 2006, a new constitution, a freshly appointed Governance Board and, eventually, restored funding from Creative New Zealand gave the national 'union' a new start.[26] The Choral Federation regained momentum.

The Governance Board were soon seeking an executive officer. In 2008 they found one in Grant Hutchinson, who had immigrated to Hamilton from South Africa before moving to Christchurch in 1998, where he became director of music at St Michael's Church. Organist and master of the choristers at the historic St Mary's Cathedral in Port Elizabeth, he had been well known as a musical entrepreneur. Hutchinson had both choral experience (he had just taken over conductorship of the Christchurch Jubilate Singers) and business experience (coming from a sales and marketing management background). His appointment gave a new solidity to NZCF administration procedures.

Many NZCF initiatives have contributed a great deal to Kiwi choral activities: The Kid's Sing, The Classic Sing (for adults, which has become Singfest), Primary Gestures (with Megan Flint, children's choir pedagogue), Fine Tuning (for The Big Sing choirs and their conductors), and Giving Direction (for conductors in general).

All these innovations are strategically targeted and much appreciated. NZCF has bonded choral musicians together throughout the country, deliberately garnering support for the smaller choirs, and, for a relatively small subscription, gaining their loyalty to attend Federation activities.

Christine Argyle, NZCF chief executive, chair of the Governance Board 2012–14, and vice-chair 2010–12. PHOTOGRAPHER MICHAEL PARSONS, 2012

Christine Argyle

Christine Argyle's two-year stint singing in the semi-chorus (chamber choir) of the London Symphony Chorus gave her the opportunity to work with conductors Richard Hickox, Claudio Abbado, Lorin Maazel and Sir Colin Davis.

Besides singing in many concerts and recordings with the London Symphony Chorus, Argyle took the opportunity to hear celebrated groups such as the Monteverdi Choir (John Eliot Gardiner), and while working at the BBC she sang with Stephen Layton and the Holst Singers. Argyle's special interest and expertise in choral music was furthered by membership of the National Youth Choir and an LTCL in Singing.

Argyle became vice-chair of the Choral Federation in 2010 and chair two years later, liaising regularly with regional representatives, undertaking large editing tasks and helping to guide the formation of the Association of Choral Directors. She has been compère and adjudicator for The Big Sing, trained many conductors, established Wellington's Nota Bene chamber choir, and has sung for 20 years in the Voices New Zealand Chamber Choir. At the time when good children's choirs were in short supply, Argyle founded Wellington Young Voices and has shepherded them to the stage, where they now receive invitations to sing with the New Zealand Symphony Orchestra and Orchestra Wellington. Argyle's contributions to choral singing in New Zealand as a conductor, singer, advocate, entrepreneur, mentor and administrator have been extremely significant.

Seven of the most influential accomplishments of the Choral Federation are: choral workshops for singers; Sing Aotearoa; National Choral Clinics for conductors and singers; the Association of Choral Directors; Rugby World Cup Anthem choirs; international choral links; and Secondary School Choral Festivals/The Big Sing. This last accomplishment has been spectacularly successful. The details of their rebranding and continued growth are described in Chapter 14.

Ever since David Willcocks first visited New Zealand in 1978, when still director of the Royal College of Music, he had led choir workshops here. The weekend workshops attracted hundreds of choral singers whenever and wherever they were offered. There was no specific help given to conductors, but levels of expertise in choral technique were raised.

In the early days of the NZCF a series of choral workshops to assist teachers, particularly of school choirs, was set up at Peter Godfrey's suggestion.[27] A grant from the Queen Elizabeth II Arts Council provided funding for workshops to be held in centres from Invercargill to Auckland, led mainly by Godfrey himself, and occasionally by Karen Grylls and Peter Watts. As successful as it was, the scheme could not reach many of the teachers who needed the tuition most. At around the same time, three members of an NZCF Education Group — Shona McIntyre, Allan Purdy and Stephen Rowe — released a teaching aid, *ABCD (Absolutely Basic Choral Directing)*. As one of the two music advisers in the Auckland region, McIntyre lamented the lack of quality group singing in the schools she visited. Too often, she said, this consisted of:

> children sitting cross-legged and slumped on the mat area at the front of the class, or in a similar position on a cold wooden assembly hall floor, facing a large work chart or projected image, 'singing' to the accompaniment of a tape (often played on less than adequate equipment), guitar, or in a few cases, piano. The result? . . . a raucous, forced, untuned shouting match![28]

Further workshops for unskilled teachers were led by Roy Tankersley and others.

Workshops, organised independently of the NZCF, and catering for both conductors and singers, had been organised in 1981 for Frank Pooler, the California State University Long Beach maestro, in Havelock North and Wellington, and in 1988 in Christchurch, Wellington and Auckland for the legendary Swedish specialist Eric Ericson.[29]

Thus, when the NZCF was formed it was a given that choral workshops led by New Zealand and overseas conductors would continue to be offered. In its first 10 years these were often linked with NZCF annual conferences, but in any event an annual weekend workshop provided a specific opportunity to choristers from smaller choirs. They could join in performances of choral/orchestral works that were beyond the resources of their local group. An example of this was the workshopped performance of Handel's *Israel in Egypt* in 1995 in the Wellington Town Hall conducted by Peter Godfrey.[30] The Wellington region of the NZFC has, since the 1990s, continued the practice of workshopping a major choral work, generally using the Vivian Street Salvation Army Citadel, chosen for its rewarding acoustic for both rehearsal and performance. The 2018 event, featuring choruses and arias from Handel and Mozart, and Mozart's *Vesperae solennes de confessore*, was led by Tecwyn Evans, with Mark Dorrell as principal accompanist.

The concept of a singing weekend to commemorate the 150th anniversary of the signing of the Treaty of Waitangi developed in the minds of Graham Hoffman and music educator Greg Tata from an idea by their friend Paraire Huata. They wanted to give choral expression to the Māori renaissance that was occurring over the whole country. The result was Sing Aotearoa, a major festival at Ōhakune, near Mount Ruapehu, over Labour Weekend in 1990. Planned in conjunction with local kaumātua, it opened with a pōwhiri on Maungarongo Marae which 'enhanced the spiritual symbolism of the event and set the scene for a weekend of singing together'.[31] With crucial financial support from the 1990 Commission, and the patronage of Sir Edmund Hillary and Dame Kiri Te Kanawa, the festival drew over 450 from around the country.

Participants' comments encompassed the sheer joy of singing on the snowy slopes of Mount Ruapehu; the pleasure of hearing the Auckland Dorian Choir sing Chris Marshall's commissioned work *To the Horizon: Images of New Zealand*, based on New Zealand poems and prose readings; and 'the sadness that all New Zealanders couldn't feel the unanimity there was [at that event] between Māori and European'.[32] John Willmott, chair of the Auckland Choral Association, was particularly taken with Willi Gohl, the Swiss multilingual expert who, he said, inspired instant four-part harmony in the massed singing. Others recalled Te Roopu Waiata Māori (National Māori Choir), organised and conducted by Rim D. Paul, the wealth of workshops (including two by poet Hone Tuwhare and actor Beryl Te Wiata), or Craig Pollock's good-humoured banter as announcements were given, and the generous hospitality of Ōhakune residents.[33]

TOP Dame Kiri Te Kanawa and Sir Edmund Hillary, patrons of Sing Aotearoa, with organisers Graham Hoffman and Greg Tata, Ōhakune, 1990. NEW ZEALAND CHORAL FEDERATION ARCHIVES

BELOW Singing on Mount Ruapehu at the Sing Aotearoa Ōhakune festival, 19–22 October 1990. AUTHOR'S COLLECTION

For the next Sing Aotearoa (1993), composer Jenny McLeod wrote *He Iwi Kotahi Tatou — We Are One People*, for Māori choir, chamber choir and massed choir. Later that year, after the death of festival visionary Kelly Harris, Greg Tata paid tribute to Kelly with:

> He reo kāhore he tinana: Kāhore he waiata
> The voice without the body has no song
> Engari, ko te wairua ka rongo na tonu.
> However, with the spirit it lives on.

After 2000, the festivals lapsed for a number of years. A revamped Sing Aotearoa in Rotorua in 2009 featured a 'Geyser Sing' held at the New Zealand Māori Arts and Crafts Institute at Te Puia geothermal valley, as well as a pōwhiri and hāngi on a marae.[34]

Now Sing Aotearoa, with further appearances in 2013 and 2016, has evolved into a national choral fiesta, celebrating New Zealand's unique cultural heritage, drawing inspiration from its now permanent city venue — Rotorua. International guest performers lead most of the music-making, New Zealand's finest ensembles present evening concerts, and invited speakers lead dozens of masterclasses, workshops and demonstrations, with subjects ranging from Taonga Puoro (Māori musical instruments) and Singing for Well-Being, Interconnection and Illness Recovery, to a forum on Choral Futures.[35]

The idea of national choral clinics for conductors appealed when suggested in August 2007, and a preliminary flyer was distributed later in the year. Then came the news that 12 major choral clinics were to be held from Whangārei to Invercargill in August/September 2008. It was a long time since the whole country had been offered instruction like this. The clinics were to be especially for conductors ('from the elite to the novice'), but would also cater for singers, who were promised 'invigorating singing experiences', with the carefully selected new music suited to many ability levels.[36] Tone Bianca Dahl from Norway was to lead two clinics in Christchurch to cover Canterbury and Westland, and one in Nelson, which also catered for Marlborough; Debra Shearer-Dirié from Brisbane was to lead clinics in Invercargill and Dunedin; Christopher Kiver from Pennsylvania was to cover Wellington, Whanganui for Taranaki and Manawatū, and Hastings for the East Coast; Rodney Eichenberger, from Florida, was asked to go to Hamilton for Waikato, Bay of Plenty and Taupō, Whangārei for Northland, and to end with two clinics in Auckland. With thorough national advertising, nearly 250 conductors enrolled, along with several hundred singers, including senior high school students.

There were some organisational problems along the way, with music not always arriving on time from overseas, and frequent budget overruns causing costs to blow out dramatically in some regions. However, to the participants, the clinics were seen as a professional operation, and regional convenors reported warm comments from observers and participants.[37] By introducing this and other initiatives, it had shown the Choral Federation's membership that the new-look NZCF Governance Board was on track. For the first time for several years, members' attentions had been turned again to the necessity of having well-trained conductors. The national clinics were another step towards developing a more competent choral leadership.

Before the Association of Choral Directors (ACD) within NZCF was begun in 2011, there had been vigorous debate within the new Governance Board about the place that choral directors should have in NZCF — as distinct from the needs of (the far more numerous) singers. Karen Grylls and I argued that, while we had a healthy tradition of singing workshops with inspirational overseas and local conductors, there needed to be a much greater focus on choir leaders, such as there was in Finland, Sweden, the United States and other nations. The very name New Zealand Choral Federation probably suggested that it was primarily a federation of *choirs*, whereas many other countries had separated out conductors from singers by forming two different organisations. We had chosen not to do that, but it was now time to plan to more fully serve the needs of conductors at all levels. The new programmes of Giving Direction, Primary Gestures and Fine Tuning were all specifically ACD initiatives.

Another achievement of the Choral Federation was providing Rugby World Cup Anthem choirs. New Zealand has always been a sporting nation, with rugby taking a pre-eminent position. Many choral devotees have been avid followers of the national sport. Twenty nations were to compete at the Rugby World Cup, to be held in New Zealand in September and October 2011. Initially it had not been at all clear how the national anthems of those 20 nations would be delivered; soloists or recorded music had generally been used previously. The Sydney Olympic Games, 11 years earlier, had used leading local choral expert Lyn Williams to train choirs for medal ceremonies, and the artistic results generated widespread favourable comment. It was pointed out that this country could do the same. Finally, the NZCF won the contract to sing the anthems at the 48 matches, and 11 conductors were invited to conduct on three or four

TOP John Rosser, who led the 2011 Rugby World Cup choirs project. PHOTOGRAPHER LUKE PILKINTON-CHING

BELOW Norwegian conductor Tone Bianca Dahl, who presented national choral clinics in 2008. PHOTOGRAPHER ANNA JULIA GRANBERG occasions each. NZCF was going to be an integral part of the largest sporting event ever held in New Zealand.

NZCF workshops were held in several centres to teach the anthems to anyone who wished to attend. The workshop tutors tried to meet the challenges of each country's anthem, with the pronunciation difficulties of some of the languages. (New Zealand's mainly monolingual tradition wasn't particularly helpful at this time.) National auditions followed. There was a great variety of backgrounds among the successful applicants — including opera chorus members and soloists. Choral arrangements of all 20 anthems were made by New Zealand composer Anthony Ritchie and recorded in Auckland by a select NZCF choir — over the top of tracks already laid down by the New Zealand Symphony Orchestra. It was a major undertaking, but one that was needed to provide not only a back-up recording for the matches but also vital teaching aids. Local rehearsals were organised for learning and memorising the pieces. All this activity gave exposure within musical communities to a special, publicly recognised task for choral music-makers.

As happens with a lot of brilliant ideas, a number of people were responsible for the World Cup initiative, but it was Choral Federation Chair John Rosser who took leadership of it. He approached the Rugby Union and its agency and, despite all kinds of setbacks, he successfully won the confidence of officials. The result was that within New Zealand a huge number of people heard an NZCF Anthem choir singing live at one of the Cup matches. Over two million New Zealanders watched the final on television.

Turning to international viewings of the World Cup, it has been estimated that over the whole tournament potentially billions tuned in, if multiple viewings are counted. Rosser's work over more than a year, together with that of the national coordinator, Thérèse Kelly, was honoured in Auckland and by the Governance Board. There was a small surge in NZCF membership as participating singers were encouraged to take part in NZCF activities.

Through attendance at Rugby World Cup games, many New Zealanders became aware, at least fleetingly, of the Choral Federation and its high professional standards. The name of the organisation was mentioned as choirs were announced at the grounds, the singing of the anthems was of high quality and the effectiveness of the conductors was clear.[38]

New Zealand has suffered from isolation in the past, but the formation of the New Zealand Choral Federation has given an impetus to build and maintain links with other countries, especially with sister organisations. In recent years, NZCF Chief Executive Grant Hutchinson has been a member of the Asia Pacific Choral Working Committee, which undertakes regional initiatives of the International Federation for Choral Music (IFCM), and reciprocal associate membership of the Federation has been offered to Australia, Hong Kong, Japan, Malaysia, Myanmar and Vietnam for a number of years. Peter Godfrey was a special adviser to the Board of the IFCM for a time. Karen Grylls was an IFCM board member, and her choirs were selected for World Symposia in Vancouver, Sydney and Argentina. She also presented papers on several occasions. NZCF Chair John Rosser was sent as New Zealand representative to the Copenhagen World Symposium on Choral Music in 2008. There he made contact with leading administrators and conductors. He also attended the Barcelona Symposium in 2017.

But in addition to these formal relationships, individual Kiwi directors have, from the earliest days, taken it upon themselves to travel to various parts of the globe to discover what the rest of the world is doing with their choirs.

Don Whelan, director of music at the Cathedral of the Blessed Sacrament in Christchurch, was part of a small contingent who attended the first World Choral Symposium in Vienna, Austria, in 1987. His positive report, upon return, convinced me to attend the next symposium in Stockholm, Helsinki and Tallinn.[39] I was captivated, and so attended the following four symposia — in Vancouver, Sydney, Rotterdam and Minneapolis.[40] At these, I became increasingly confident that New Zealand was on track to produce superior outcomes in the choral field. I felt reassured that the people being invited to lead our conducting summer schools and workshops were well able to tutor conductors and singers towards excellence. I was not alone. Dozens of other directors travelling overseas were coming back similarly inspired. Some have been used by the Choral Federation to lead seminars and workshops, or to head up regional committees.

As would be true for every discipline, training, refreshment and work abroad has made a significant contribution to the rise of the choral art in this country.[41] It is inevitable that trips abroad affect conductors' attitudes to making music with their choirs at home. Sometimes they have learned what not to do or have become more discerning about repertoire that is meretricious, overly sentimental or just too cleverly promoted. A few have studied the distinctive choral styles of other countries. Sometimes New Zealanders develop a new pride in our indigenous music as their

An Anthem choir at the Rugby World Cup All Blacks vs Canada game in Wellington, 2 October 2011. PHOTOGRAPHER BEA SELWOOD choirs share waiata with new audiences. At other times, and perhaps most tellingly, they are simply helped to see what is needed in their personal conducting style to achieve new artistic levels.

Experienced choral musicians have populated the unpaid Governance Board of NZCF, just as they have the national advisory and regional representative committees. They meet together in the bonds of mutual respect, patience and robust discussion.

Peter Godfrey started a federation that would propel choral singing and conducting to greater heights in New Zealand. And it is one of Godfrey's disciples, John Rosser, who has not only made sure that Godfrey's vision was continued but burnished and reinvigorated.[42]

Rosser gave one of the eulogies at Godfrey's memorial service in St Paul's Cathedral, Wellington, in November 2017, and at the Auckland service in February 2018. He was a huge fan of the man with the urbane wit and the 'unerring ear', who insisted on 'accurate tuning and shapely phrasing'. He loved Godfrey's rehearsals because of the discipline rather than in spite of it.[43] Rosser's leadership has given NZCF stability and consistency of outlook, and he has been a key factor in NZCF's contributions to choral singing.

Appropriately, after stepping down as president, Godfrey was invited to be patron of the Federation. On 1 May 2012, an NZCF afternoon tea to celebrate his ninetieth birthday was held in the Mayoral Chambers of the Wellington Town Hall. It was an opportunity to briefly recall his stellar contributions to New Zealand over the previous 54 years. In an amusing reply, he explained his sorrow at being compelled to miss his usual Tuesday choir rehearsal in order to attend the birthday function. He had *never* missed a rehearsal before.[44] It is a fitting tribute to Godfrey and to the NZCF that Governor-General Dame Patsy Reddy, a well-known supporter of the arts, became the new patron of the organisation.

Through the platform of NZCF, Peter Godfrey inspired two generations of choral musicians. That he had come from England was a great advantage, such was New Zealand's English heritage, but he became deeply committed to this country, forgoing two enticing invitations to return to his English roots. Godfrey had seen the potential in New Zealand and had determinedly placed its choral singing on the world stage. It is no surprise that Kiwi conductors saw him as their exemplar. His presence encouraged them to never give up on attempting to foster a noble and compellingly rich field of endeavour in their native land.

Juliet Dreaver, chair of NZCF Governance Board 2019, and vice-chair 2016–18. PHOTOGRAPHER JOSEPH KELLY

Juliet Dreaver

Juliet Dreaver grew up hearing tales of her parents' years in St Mary's Cathedral Choir with a young Peter Godfrey. At 15 she was a foundation member of the National Youth Choir, remaining in the choir for nine years, during which time she sang in Auckland University Singers with Peter Godfrey, touring with the National Youth Choir in 1982 and 1988, and joining the newly formed Viva Voce with John Rosser.

A background in music and performance has been an advantage for her career in the world of advertising production 'where arts and commerce merge'. She spent 17 years at Saatchi and Saatchi Wellington, five of these as Head of Television, and since then has continued to create significant New Zealand and international campaigns in a freelance capacity.

The demands of a project-based career have made regular choir membership difficult, but along with some years with the Women of Note quintet she has moved over time into support and governance roles. She managed the Wellington appearances of the Rugby World Cup 2011 Anthem choirs and served on the inaugural board of Wellington's Orpheus Choir. She was elected to the NZCF board in 2013 and became chair on John Rosser's retirement in April 2018.

The board she leads encompasses a diverse range of skills — law, finance, teaching, change management, commercial production and HR — along with choral conducting expertise. She is a member of the core organising team for the World Symposium on Choral Music 2020, which she regards as both a privilege and her 'biggest production challenge yet!'

13

The flourishing of a rich choral culture, 1972–99

In 1972, Peter Godfrey took an Auckland choir to New York. On the face of it, this did not appear a remarkable event, because choirs had travelled before. But this tour was the catalyst for a significant shift in choral singing throughout New Zealand.

A combination of circumstances had conspired to push Godfrey in this crucial direction: University of Canterbury Professor John Ritchie had recommended to James Bjorge, a visiting choral festival director, that Auckland represent New Zealand at the 1972 Universities Choral Festival in New York; the University of Auckland insisted that Godfrey take up the opportunity and he auditioned for a new choir specifically with a tour in mind. He spread the auditioning net through the whole university, including recently graduated students. An astute auditioner, he selected people under the age of 25 who were not only good musicians but also mature enough to handle a rigorous tour schedule.

Between September 1970 and early April 1972, a 40-voice choir rehearsed twice a week, raised money, toured the North Island in a polishing-up concert series, and was fitted out and farewelled for an overseas tour. Margery Charlton, who had quickly become a cornerstone of Godfrey's organisational team, was tour administrator.[1] Ronald Dellow, one of New Zealand's first professionally trained church musicians, was assistant conductor.[2]

Life wasn't straightforward in the lead-up to the tour. Government support was lacking and fundraising by the students and supporters wasn't easy. There were many unknowns in the venture. Almost no members had previously travelled outside New Zealand, and it was also the first time that Godfrey had conducted a New Zealand choir outside this country. But the tour went ahead. Its success would be dependent on the conductor, the quality of the preparation and the choral abilities of those chosen.

It was predictable that the name of New Zealand and New Zealand choral singing would not draw great crowds. However, it was important that the concerts, including those at festivals in Washington and New York, be first class, as this was the first exposure of an elite New Zealand chamber choir to an international audience.

The New York appearance of the choir was at the Third International Universities Choral Festival. The words of the 'Cowboy Carol', 'There'll be a new world beginnin' from tonight', in the setting by Malcolm Sargent popularised in the 1950s and 1960s, would have been exactly right for the night of the 1972 Lincoln Center Gala Concert. The festival director later wrote to the University of Auckland, thanking the choir for their 'stunning concert performances' and also for being splendid representatives of New Zealand: 'If a vote had been taken among the choruses, I'm sure that you Kiwis would have been selected the most friendly and popular group.'[3]

The choir then toured within the United States and travelled on to England, Holland, West Germany and Singapore, and was well-reviewed everywhere. Earlier overseas visits by the Royal Christchurch Musical Society and the Christchurch

Harmonic Society, significant as they were, didn't have the cutting edge of Godfrey's tour de force. His choir's artistry, in particular, was much admired wherever they sang, and his Antipodean ensemble was compared favourably with similar northern hemisphere choirs. Their singing of many New Zealand compositions was especially applauded; the music of New Zealand's foremost choral composers had been given overseas exposure for the first time.

This tour put the country's choral music on the international map and set a high bar for future overseas tours by local choirs; it also convinced Godfrey that a New Zealand choir could match the best in the world. But disappointingly, at the end of it all, plaudits and recognition from the New Zealand public were almost non-existent.

News of the choir's achievements did filter back into local choral consciousness, but it took over a year, helped by the release of two LP recordings of music from the tour. Of course, those taking part hadn't done so to gain public approval; their motivation had been to take an opportunity to sing on the world stage with a proven conductor. In this, the singers felt no social or musical restraints, and their self-confidence engendered a similar confidence in later tours by other choirs. But they achieved all this with minimal public support. Theirs was a classic story of being good keen Kiwi pioneers.

Maybe even more significantly, the tour influenced the majority of the choir to continue with singing and also to give leadership in the choral field. More than four and a half decades later, many of the 'fortunate forty' are still active as choral singers, soloists, conductors, accompanists, administrators, entrepreneurs, discerning concert-goers and firm encouragers of other people. Some, such as Terence Maskell, are prominent leaders.

After it returned to New Zealand, the Festival Choir was re-formed and became the Auckland University Singers. They travelled to Perth in 1974 to sing at a conference of the International Society for Music Education, but on that tour the circumstances weren't kind to the choir. By the time they had coped with air and bus strikes and other challenges, they weren't at the top of their game.

During the 1970s, Peter Godfrey's influence was felt in another arena. In 1961, he had taken over Auckland choir the Dorian Singers, while still keeping his position as director of music at St Mary's Cathedral. After 1974, when he was appointed Professor of Music at the University of Auckland and gave up the Cathedral Choir, the Dorian Singers became his only conducting commitment outside of the university.

TOP A pre-tour rehearsal of the Auckland University Festival Choir in Albert Park near the University of Auckland, 1972.
MARGO KNIGHTBRIDGE/DORIAN CHOIR ARCHIVES

BELOW The Festival Choir in the Philharmonic Hall, Lincoln Center, New York, April 1972.
FROM *PETER GODFREY: FATHER OF NZ CHORAL MUSIC* BY ELIZABETH SALMON. MĀKARO PRESS, 2015, P. 108.

Terence Maskell with Amitai (left) and Pene Pati (centre), later of Sol3 Mio, who now also sing with the San Francisco Opera.
PHOTOGRAPHER UNKNOWN

Terence Maskell

One of the most well-known members of the original Auckland University Festival Choir is Terence Maskell. Mainly a self-taught musician, he sang in an intermediate school folk choir and as a treble in his local Methodist church choir, where he later played the organ. There was no choir at his secondary school, Otahuhu College, but as a teenager he learned the clarinet, playing for five years in the school orchestra and gaining some choral conducting experience at a neighbouring Methodist church. He had his first formal piano lesson at age 19 from a relative and taught himself sufficient music theory to be accepted into the University of Auckland, later completing a Diploma in Music in organ with Anthony Jennings. But it was being in Peter Godfrey's choir at St Mary's Cathedral for 15 years that mainly helped make Maskell so successful.

When Godfrey went to King's College, Cambridge, on an exchange position in 1978, Maskell was asked to take charge of another of Godfrey's choirs, the Auckland University Singers. Later, he became an assistant to Jennings at Holy Trinity Cathedral, singing, conducting and playing the organ. Then, during his nine years as director of the Auckland Youth Choir, he won numerous international awards.

In 2001, he formed a special kind of choir, The Graduate Choir New Zealand, which was a logical extension of his 20 years' work with young Māori and Polynesian singers at Aorere College in South Auckland. He says of Pasifika students that with sensitive teaching, they can blend their own and Western traditions. 'Singing is fundamental to their cultures, whilst boys in other cultures do not always see singing as a worthwhile pastime, preferring instead the sports field.'

Initially just for high school-leavers, The Graduate Choir has developed a unique cultural blend of voices, known for its precision, warmth, versatility of sound and appealing repertoire. It has appeared regularly on television and RNZ programmes, and it was invited to perform at the 2005 convention of the Association of British Choral Directors. Recordings of the choir include performances of Douglas Mews' 'A Sound Came from Heaven', David Hamilton's 'Karanga', which was written for the choir's 2005 tour to the United Kingdom, and John Rutter's setting for male voices of 'Down by the Sally Gardens'.

Maskell says of his singers that they bare their souls every time they stand to sing — 'it is one of the most exposed forms of musical expression'. He remembers when Samoan brothers Pene and Amitai Pati arrived at the college and he auditioned them for the choir. He was amazed by the beauty and potential of their young voices (not surprising; he was about to welcome two of the future Sol3 Mio opera and entertainment stars into his musical domain), but he had work to do to make sure that they turned up at all rehearsals, learned their music and developed healthy singing habits. He later took both boys to an advanced level on piano. He deserves some of the credit for the international success of Sol3 Mio.

Maskell has developed a strong, individualistic philosophy of choral education. This has arisen largely through observation and a reliance on the ear — rather than through any formal training. When visiting the United States on a 2001 Woolf Fisher Fellowship, he was surprised to observe graduate conducting classes focusing on repertoire and choral techniques that he had learned for himself and had been using for a long time in his own choirs.

The choir had had a proud history under conductors Albert Bryant and Harry Luscombe, including, in 1956, its first performance of Bach's *Mass in B Minor*; a soloist was young Donald McIntyre, later to become one of the world's famous Wagnerian basses. It was originally intended as a chamber choir, but its character changed when numbers dwindled and many Auckland Teachers' College students were invited to join.

Godfrey expanded the size and the repertoire of the choir, including contemporary works such as Penderecki's *Stabat Mater*. In 1972, it won the mixed-voice section of the BBC Let the Peoples Sing competition.

The Dorian Singers were encouraged to plan their own ambitious adventure abroad when they heard about the success of the University Festival Choir's tours. Nothing could hold them back from a 1975 tour of four countries in Europe and three weeks in England, where they travelled under the name New Zealand Dorian Choir to give them national identity. Reviews of their overseas concerts suggest that their ambitions were more than fulfilled and their lengthy fundraising efforts justified.

C. S. Cooper, the *New Zealand Herald* correspondent in London, reported that after the choir's prime European recital at Munster, West Germany, they were described as 'Fabulous. One of the great choirs of the world.'[4] They had put their ability on the line by including in the programme the formidable — and well-known to Germans — *Singet dem Herrn* by J. S. Bach. A Salisbury Cathedral concert provided the audience with 'a memory of musical perfection',[5] and an appearance at St John's, Smith Square, in London, moved Professor Christopher Grier of the Royal College of Music to say that the choir was of 'a calibre equal to the best of its British and Continental equivalents'.[6]

Godfrey said that this lengthy tour had broken new ground:

> The choir had to work hard to establish the fact that to listen to a New Zealand choir was indeed worthwhile. The work bore fruit, however, as the choir was subsequently invited back to Britain to sing as the representative of the Commonwealth at the 250th anniversary of the Three Choirs Festival, 1977, as well as to present a programme in the BBC Henry Wood Promenade Concerts.[7]

Hailed in Britain as a great choir, members arrived back in their home country demoralised because, as with the University Festival Choir, they had been, and continued to be, virtually ignored by the New Zealand media. Ian Kendall, chair of the choir's committee and a singing member, put the disregard for the brilliant overseas

The New Zealand Dorian Choir at Bonn University, 1975. MARGO KNIGHTBRIDGE/DORIAN CHOIR ARCHIVES

TOP Publicity shot for Dorian Choir farewell concert, 1977. Front row, from left: Nora Vine (Lewis), Lana Peat, Alison Yarnton (Glenny). Middle row: Margo Knightbridge, Chris Hubbert, David Griffiths. At rear: Terence Maskell. MARGO KNIGHTBRIDGE/DORIAN CHOIR ARCHIVES

BELOW New Zealand Dorian Choir at St Wilfred's Church, Harrogate, 1977. MARGO KNIGHTBRIDGE/DORIAN CHOIR ARCHIVES reviews down to the country's focus on sport. It wasn't the only time that rugby and sports generally were blamed for poor media coverage.

The choir accepted the invitation to return to Britain in 1977. As well as singing in a BBC Proms concert, at King's College Cambridge, at York Minster and at the Harrogate Festival, they performed at Gloucester Cathedral during the prestigious Three Choirs Festival (the oldest music festival in the world). In a review of its performance, the *Guardian* critic found the choir 'splendidly vital and resilient and the grading of tone and chording in the Palestrina "Gloria" near perfection'.[8]

The Times critic William Mann highlighted Jack Body's *Carol to St Stephen*: 'a spectacular piece using choirs in the aisles, soloists on stage and in the audience, all to dramatic effect; and finally a short "Beatus [*sic*] Virgo" by David Griffiths full of sumptuously curdled harmonies'.[9] Peter Stadlen of the *Daily Telegraph* thought that Godfrey was based at 'Oakland University'. It wasn't the only time Auckland was confused with Oakland, California. He said of *Beata Virgo*: 'a born encore . . . with gorgeous sound as it unfolded step by step like a diatonic fan and back again until it peters out on the unison. Church music can be fun.'[10]

On the morning that the choir went down to a summer festival at Dartington Hall in Devon, they entertained frustrated Londoners on the Underground when the tube system had been disrupted by rain and a violent thunderstorm. Over 1000 commuters on the District Line platforms suddenly heard the New Zealanders sing. After each verse of 'Early One Morning', applause rang out, so Godfrey added the bonus of 'Little David Play on Yo' Harp'.

Upon returning from the tour, Deputy Conductor Elizabeth Beverley talked of the 'electrifying' reception in Gloucester with its 'fantastic ovation from the beginning. . . . At the celebration dinner afterwards the choir was one excited family, just as if the All Blacks had won a test series.'

The momentum of choral excellence, which Godfrey had initiated with the University Festival Choir in 1972, had been carried forward with the Dorian Choir, and as the group gave concerts around New Zealand, more people became aware of its quality. Godfrey himself had given a new face to choral singing — one of excellence with a distinctive English elegance, featuring a straight-toned vocal style encapsulating impeccable intonation. Significantly, because he was becoming thought of in the public arena as the country's outstanding choral director, he was helping New Zealand become aware of its emerging high standing in the world of choirs.

All the Godfrey/University Festival Choir/Dorian Choir activities were centred in Auckland. And other developments were also occurring in that city; for example, a specialist group co-founded by Margo Knightbridge in 1972, the 11-voice Orlando Singers, which set their own high standards.[11]

But in the rest of the country during the 1970s, other factors were contributing to the development of a rich choral culture.

Community choirs continued to thrive through dedicated leadership and the programming of accessible music. Cathedral choirs were influential; they flourished by attracting excellent singers and providing musicianship training and the priceless advantage of weekly sight-reading experience. Peter Godfrey's heart was in cathedral choral music from the day he set foot in New Zealand in 1958. The doyen of cathedral directors of music, Godfrey continued to conduct and play at cathedral and church services until almost the end of his life.

Royal School of Church Music (RSCM) winter choir schools and Voice for Life programmes were of help to young choristers in cathedrals and larger churches, although generally church choirs continued to decline in numbers from the 1970s. The leaders of the five RSCM branches in 2019 are all well-known choral conductors: Reverend Alison Stewart (Wellington), Rachael Griffiths-Hughes (Waikato), Neil Shroff (Auckland), Bruce Aitken (Otago/Southland) and Paul Ellis (Canterbury, and national president). Michael Stewart, one of the country's leading organists, is director of music at the Wellington Cathedral of St Paul. He also directs the early music choir The Tudor Consort and is deputy conductor of the New Zealand Youth Choir.

Another church musician and conductor who has contributed greatly over more than 40 years is Roy Tankersley at St Mark's and St Andrew's, Palmerston North. Music educator, organist, harpsichordist and composer, Tankersley has led the Bach Choir in Wellington and Schola Sacra Choir in Whanganui with distinction, as well as choirs in Gisborne, Dunedin and Palmerston North.[12]

New choirs of a traditional hue sprouted up around New Zealand during the 1970s. In Christchurch, the women's choir Liederkränzchen was succeeded by Elizabeth Wemyss's Harmonic Singers (1973), and later, Nan Anderson's Cecilian Singers. Similar new groups around the country were partly influenced by the ready access to recordings of overseas choirs and songs suitable for arranging for choirs. A beginning conductor could become inspired to copy what they heard on an LP.

A sample of the choirs established in the 1970s shows the range of these initiatives: Cantoris (1970), Scuola di Chiesa (1972), Celebration Singers (1973), The

Emeritus Professor Peter Godfrey, former director of music at St Paul's Cathedral, Wellington, returns to the cathedral to conduct the choir at a service, February 2007.
PHOTOGRAPHER JAY BERRYMAN

Renaissance Singers (1975), Festival Singers of Wellington (1976), Jubilate Singers (1977), Auckland Bach Cantata Society (1977) and the National Youth Choir (1979).[13]

Membership of existing choirs didn't appear to be adversely affected by new groups coming into being; new choir members seemed to keep on appearing, and there were almost enough tenors to go around!

When it came to voice training and coaching, pupils of private voice teachers had typically been the comparative few who were seeking solo singing training. Tertiary vocal training, which had begun at the University of Auckland, enabled many more people to learn how to use their voice. It became so widespread that conductors, vocal coaches and serious choral singers across the country were able to receive substantial tuition. The Education Department's 1977 Small Group Vocal Tuition scheme, which offered free tuition to secondary students, was a crucial step towards later vocal coaching for choirs entering The Big Sing, and for national choirs.

The production of LP recordings of Māori choirs by Kiwi-Pacific Records and other agencies gave exposure to traditional chants, waiata aroha, poi and waiata-ā-ringa, as well as hymns, spirituals and new compositions. Inia Te Wiata and a Māori Opera Chorus produced a comprehensive collection, as did the Waihirere Māori Club, concert parties from St Stephen's and Queen Victoria Schools, and the Wellington Anglican Māori Club guided by Reverend Kingi Ihaka. This was also the time of the Howard Morrison Quartet and Māori showbands. Based on earlier festivals, a national biennial event, Te Matatini, was established in 1972 to nurture Māori performing arts.[14]

The cumulative benefits of vocal coaching, begun in the 1970s, became apparent in the succeeding decades. Jean Cumming was an itinerant voice teacher in Christchurch and vocal coach for several New Zealand Secondary Students Choirs conducted by Roger Stevenson. In the 1990s, Stevenson led three tours to the Hawai'i World Project Festivals (1990, 1992 and 1996), returning each time with Gold Awards. The choir's vocal quality, based on small-group tuition in the schools and carefully honed by Cumming and singer-conductor Stevenson in rehearsals, was a major element in their successes. Completing this 'dream team' were accompanist Shona Murray and section tutor Roy Tankersley.

As regards Māori music, the earlier interest in such music became, by the early 1980s, part of a Māori cultural revival, emphasising issues such as sovereignty, tikanga and the survival of te reo Māori.[15] Among the bands formed were Herbs and Dread Beat and Blood, with their Māori, Pacific and reggae rhythms, and in 1989 a national Māori choir: Te Roopu Waiata Māori. The Maori Catholic community has celebrated Easter each year for the last 73 years with the Hui Aranga, an Easter gathering which includes choir and kapa haka competitions.

Also in this period, singer-songwriter Hirini Melbourne notably composed songs for kōhanga reo (pre-school language-learning nests).

A key point in the Kiwi choral story was when, in July 1996, Karen Grylls, as director of the New Zealand Youth Choir, began to work with Māori performing arts leader Bub Wehi. Two years earlier, Grylls had arranged for leading Māori music educators Keri Kaa and Te Taite Cooper to tutor the choir in preparation for them to sing Wehi's 'Kua Rongo' as part of their repertoire, precipitated by Keri Kaa's work with Elise Bradley's Westlake Girls' High School's award-winning choir Key Cygnetures. Soon, Kaa's influence was seen in both national choirs: the New Zealand Secondary Students Choir, which Bradley was leading, and the National Youth Choir, which Grylls was leading.

Now, though, Grylls wanted to understand much more about Māori singing, including their powerful vocal energy. Within a few weeks of working with Wehi, the National Youth Choir and Te Waka Huia provided an electrifying opening to an

Roger Stevenson with opera singer Jonathon Lemalu.
CHOIRS AOTEAROA NZ

Auckland concert in a pōwhiri that reviewer Heath Lees said was 'by stages terrifying and thrilling, then hugely welcoming'.[16] Within a month this cross-cultural partnership led to a special moment when a Kiwi choir and a kapa haka group stood on the same stage for a first international performance together. It was on 8 August 1996, in the Sydney Opera House Concert Hall, as part of the Fourth World Symposium on Choral Music. For me, as an expatriate living in Australia at the time, the sound of Wehi's Te Waka Huia and the National Youth Choir singing the Wehi whānau's 'Tīmatanga' was unexpectedly riveting.[17] More than that, it was truly extraordinary. The singing not only had accuracy and stylistic precision but also what jazz aficionados call soul. The audience response was vociferous and choir members said it was spine-chilling.

Afterwards, when talking to members of the packed-out international audience, I found that they, too, had detected a new international sound: excellent Māori voices blended with excellent Pākehā voices in a sophisticated manner. Many couldn't believe that they had heard such new tonal beauty. The National Youth Choir had learned fresh, exciting choral colours from the vocal timbres of their Māori cousins. They would never sound the same again.

Ngāpō (Bub) Wehi, 2001. *GISBORNE HERALD*

Ngāpō (Bub) Wehi

Born in 1934, Bub Wehi was of Te Whakatōhea, Ngāi Tūhoe, Te Whānau-ā-Apanui, Ngāpuhi and Ngāti Kahu heritage. He was one of the most decorated exponents of Māori performing arts, and he held the record for the most national wins in the history of kapa haka. Those involved were his Gisborne-based group, Waihirere, and Te Waka Huia, a family-oriented kapa haka group which he and his wife, Pimia Wehi, started in West Auckland in 1981. Wehi is credited with bringing kapa haka into the mainstream arts.

Wehi led performances at Polynesian and Aotearoa Festivals and represented Aotearoa New Zealand at four South Pacific Arts Festivals: Suva (1972), Port Moresby (1980), Rarotonga (1992) and Townsville (1998). Te Waka Huia appeared at the opening of the Seoul Olympics in 1988 and at the closing of the Commonwealth Games in Victoria, Canada, in 1994. In the same year, Wehi was appointed chair of the Te Waka Toi Board of Creative New Zealand (QEII Arts Council of New Zealand). In 2011, he was awarded a QSM.

With community and chamber choirs, new groups kept appearing in the 1980s, especially classically oriented ones such as Jack Speirs' Southern Consort of Voices (1980), Pauline Fitchett's Northern Chorale, Johnsonville (1983), Lois McNeill's Waikanae Chorale (1983), which later became the Kapiti Chorale under Peter Godfrey, John Rosser's Viva Voce (1985), Simon Ravens' Tudor Consort (1986), my soloists' chamber choir Bel Canto (1987), and Anthony Jennings' Collegium Vocale (1988).

Groups established in the 1990s included the Kapiti Chamber Choir, formed by Paddy Nash and Peter Godfrey, Patricia Murray's Capital Choir (where else but in Wellington) and the Southern Youth Choir (Maureen Smith and Anthony Ritchie), all in 1992, and the Baroque Voices in 1994 (Pepe Becker).

Distinctly new kinds of choirs also appeared. For example, an Auckland group, GALS (the Gay and Lesbian Singers) was formed in 1992.[18] A Chinese Choir, established as part of the ministry of the Mandarin Congregation at the Auckland Baptist Tabernacle, was started in 1996.[19] The diversity of groups meant that there was a choral singing experience available for everyone. Community music and gospel music expert Tony Backhouse made the comment that 'it feels that there are just a lot more people singing in choirs'.[20]

Alongside traditional choirs, there had long been a Kiwi tradition of folk singing.[21] Revived in the 1950s and 1960s, it gained momentum in the 1970s and 1980s as part of a worldwide folk music movement. When New Zealand enthusiasts such as guitarist/folk singer Neil Colquhoun began moving through the country, reviving songs of the gold diggers, gum diggers and other colonists, folk singing changed from being a café culture to gaining a huge following in schools and in the community.[22] Classic and modern folk music was sung in groups large and small.

From about 1990, new modern styles and genres of group singing also appeared: barbershop, gospel, world music, ethnic music, a cappella (unaccompanied singing) and others. These new groups had 'alternate repertoires' (a term used by Tony Backhouse). Backhouse doesn't think there were close ties between these newcomers. There may have been refugees from the folk or barbershop worlds into gospel, but otherwise he doesn't see a direct line from one genre to another. Some community choirs sang a mix of world music and gospel, some a larger eclectic mix.

The barbershop chorus or quartet was a distinctively fresh genre based on close harmony singing that originated in the southern United States in the late nineteenth century. A Sweet Adelines chorus (women's barbershop group) began in New Zealand in 1985. The Sweet Adelines Faultline Chorus, which began in 1988 in Wellington, was placed fourth in the world when they competed in Seattle, Washington, and in

TOP Viva Voce, 1985; ten of the choir members were in the National Youth Choir. COURTESY OF JOHN ROSSER

BELOW The Tudor Consort at St Paul's Cathedral, Dunedin, 1987. PHOTOGRAPHER PEPE BECKER

2012 they were judged the best small chorus in New Zealand. A small barbershop association established itself in the 1980s, but the first New Zealand barbershop convention wasn't held until 1990, when three choruses made up Barbershop Harmony New Zealand.

Gospel singing was another popular genre from 1990 onwards. The African-American gospel music tradition, with stated values of social justice, spirituality, joy and respect, was being rediscovered.[23] Backhouse founded an a cappella gospel choir called the Café of the Gate of Salvation in Sydney in 1986. He then ran workshops in Auckland and Wellington from about 1992. He says that he began to pay serious attention to gospel music when he realised there was depth in it that he wasn't hearing anywhere else.

A seminal moment for gospel in this country was the formation of Heaven Bent in Auckland in 1995. Backhouse says that he didn't initiate the new group; rather, members of one of his workshops just got together to carry on singing his material. Choirs which evolved from Heaven Bent included Jubilation, which appears to be the only choir that had some repertoire of New Zealand-composed gospel, with songs written by members. Arrangements and adaptations of American gospel were the norm.

14

The new millennium

The 2000s have seen the creation of more opportunities for people to sing together. Traditional community and chamber choirs have continued to be established. Choirs have appeared in prisons, workplaces and retirement villages, and the remarkable The Big Sing has gone from strength to strength. But this growing choral activity hasn't encompassed all of the country equally.

In 2004, Christine Argyle founded Nota Bene with former members of the New Zealand Youth Choir (which the National Youth Choir was renamed in 2002); this was a strategy which Simon Ravens and John Rosser had followed earlier when forming their elite choirs. Bryan Crump floated Doubtful Sounds in 2005, and Isaac Stone launched his 56-voice Supertonic in 2014.[1] Arriving in New Zealand in 2015, Mark Stamper was imbued with the desire to create a select chamber ensemble, Inspirare, in which the 20 singers could be paid for each concert season.[2]

Increased opportunities for singing together have also arisen through the work of practical visionaries like John Knox, original conductor of the Wainuiomata Choir (eastern Lower Hutt), who would frequently initiate combined choirs' gatherings, or (almost casually) organise a group to travel to Verona, Italy, to sing with Pavarotti in the Verdi *Requiem*, or take a party to a choir festival in Australia or China.

The Grey Warblers in Rotorua is an example of a U3A (University of the Third Age) choir of seniors. The U3A Tauranga choral group describe themselves modestly as 'just a group blending in song', but sometimes avoiding the 'choir' word is part of a strategic policy. Such is the case with the seven unauditioned groups of Take Note Singers (David Dell and Felicia Edgecombe) in the Hutt Valley, Porirua and Kāpiti Coast; valuable choral experience and 'heaps of fun' have been hallmarks of their popularity since 2002.

Space prohibits listing all the new groups formed in the 2000s and, in any event, there is no way by which accurate information about this can be found. A substantial number of new choirs don't immediately link up with the Choral Federation, either nationally or regionally. While the online advertising of concerts by Federation regional branches can give a clue to the busyness of member choirs, other local groups can fly under the radar, maintaining contact with their audiences in their own ways.[3]

Chorus and ensemble work in opera and musicals has provided further openings for dedicated choralists across the country. Opportunities for advanced ensemble training have been provided by National Singing Schools in Hawke's Bay, the National Opera Schools in Whanganui and at similar events.

Singers with an unsatisfied appetite for higher-level repertoire have been grateful for the Teapot Valley choral summer schools, which Nelson musical entrepreneurs Carl and Inga Browning began in 2000. Around 1200 singers have participated in the nine-day events over the past 18 years. Two exceptional features have been vocal coaching for all 90 singers from Judy Bellingham, University of Otago voice specialist, and holiday concerts in the Nelson School of Music auditorium, Nelson Cathedral and other suitable venues.

TOP LEFT Christine Argyle, founder and director of chamber choir Nota Bene, 2019. PHOTOGRAPHER LUKE PILKINTON-CHING

TOP RIGHT Tony Backhouse, Australasia's foremost gospel exponent, 2017. PHOTOGRAPHER ALEX CRAIG

BELOW Take Note Singers, conducted by Felicia Edgecombe. PHOTOGRAPHER KAT LOVE

Some of the world's best choral musicians have been pleased to lend their support. Six of the schools have been directed by Sir David Willcocks, seven by Ebbe Munk, director of the Royal Chapel Choir of Copenhagen, and others by Brian Kay, former member of the King's Singers, and Ben Parry, director of the National Youth Choir of Great Britain.[4]

The Teapot Valley choral summer school gives scholarships to young singers to attend the British National Youth Choir. Some of those competing for scholarships have been members of the New Zealand Youth Choir as conductors or soloists.

Meanwhile the popularity of barbershop has exploded since the 1990s, especially at secondary school level, with around 1500 high school students now involved in six regional contests. Interestingly, students typically take part in both regular school choirs and barbershop groups when they have the interest and time to do so. A recent development is the emergence of mixed-voice quartets at school and adult levels, rather than the single-sex groupings of the past.

In 2002, the Musical Island Boys from Tawa College, Wellington, won the national barbershop quartet contest, then the New Zealand Secondary School Championship trophy. Concentrating on barbershop singing, they went on to win numerous international awards, and became the best in the world, being named International Quartet Champions at the Annual International Barbershop Singing Convention in Las Vegas in 2014.

Wellington-based Vocal FX, formed in 2003, was ranked sixth-best in the world at the Barbershop Harmony Society International Convention in Nashville, Tennessee, in 2016. Its director, Charlotte Murray, was the first woman to be named, internationally, as a Barbershop Harmony Society Master Director. The barbershop phenomenon again indicates the potency of New Zealanders seizing an opportunity with both hands, believing that they can do anything that they set their mind to.

Gospel singing has also continued to spread is wings. Apart from people singing in churches, more than 500 gospel singers are active in community groups. Some groups have adopted striking names: Sunny Side Up (Dunedin), Gale Force Gospel (Wellington), Mosaic (Nelson), Bright On Vibes and Global Voices (Christchurch). There are gospel choirs of varying sizes in Kāpiti, Riverside (Motueka), Akaroa, Coromandel, Napier and Martinborough (Wairarapa). Chasing Grace (Auckland) is one of the few gospel quartets.

Tony Backhouse has become Australasia's foremost gospel exponent, and has led over 2000 vocal workshops throughout the world. In a book on directing vocal groups, he outlines an approach influenced mainly by 'the tone, dynamics, devices

TOP Charlotte Murray conducting Vocal FX at the Barbershop Harmony Society International Competition, 2016. PHOTOGRAPHER SHONA MURRAY

BELOW Musical Island Boys, International Quartet Champions 2014. BARBERSHOP HARMONY SOCIETY 2014

and delivery of African American gospel choirs and quartets. . . . [Urban gospel star] Kirk Franklin's choirs and South African choir Barorisi Ba Morena inspire me.'[5]

New Zealand is a country of immigrants and is now one of the most ethnically diverse countries in the world. Ethnic choirs, therefore, have had a venerable heritage in New Zealand, beginning with the Dunedin Burns Club Choir, established in 1891 to spread the use of Scottish poetry and music.

A strong Welsh singing culture has persisted, with the Cambrian Society of Canterbury choir established in the early 1890s, to focus on *cymanfa ganu* — the singing of sacred songs in parts. The first Auckland Welsh Choir was formed in 1988 to boost the morale of the Welsh rugby team in its game against New Zealand at Eden Park, but despite an inspirational effort by the choir, including multiple renditions of their favourite hymn-chorus 'Bread of Heaven', Wales lost heavily to the All Blacks. The choir was later re-established independently.

Ethnic choirs have continued to be formed. Examples are the Wellington Filipino Community Choir, which first sang together in 1996 in a performance welcoming new immigrants from the Philippines to New Zealand; and Vox Serbicus, created in 2002 to sing both the inspirational sacred repertoire of the Serbian Orthodox Church, and the rhythmic and fiery folk tunes which are part of the vast tradition of Serbian choral music. The music is all sung a cappella in a traditional Slavic style. Vox Serbicus has chapters in Christchurch and Wellington. Other ethnic choirs include a Japanese choir and Dalmatian choir in Auckland.

A multi-ethnic choir was formed in Auckland in September 2015, bringing together more than 50 cultures from all over the Auckland region for a celebration of International Peace Day. Its aim was to present New Zealand to the world as a multicultural nation living in peace.

Workplace choirs, commonplace in Sweden for over 50 years, haven't become popular to the same extent in New Zealand. There have been some trade unionist choirs, one of which was called Choir, Choir Pants on Fire. Radio New Zealand had a high-profile chorale, which included Jim Mora, now Sunday morning host. In addition, The Treasury, New Zealand Government's lead economic and financial adviser, has boasted a choir for over 20 years. It has often taken part in an interdepartmental Christmas choir that serenades listeners with 'Rudolph the Red-nosed Reindeer' in Latin, and included a performance in the good acoustics of the Treasury foyer at No. 1 The Terrace, Wellington.

Wellington's Counsel in Concert has been running since 2009. It comprises a choir of lawyers and other legal professionals from the region and an orchestra from the New Zealand Symphony Orchestra and Orchestra Wellington. A Lawyers' Choir was also established in Christchurch in 2016. Made up of 'current and former judges, practising barristers and solicitors, legal secretaries and law clerks', it is co-conducted by choral specialist Helen Charlton and lawyer/musician Matthew Everingham.[6]

Another workplace choir sprang up in 2008 in the Maths and Computer Science building at the University of Canterbury. Its director was Professor Jan Evans-Freeman, pro vice chancellor of the College of Engineering, who formerly directed a university choir in Manchester, England.

World music has been another phenomenon. The terms 'non-Western music' and 'ethnomusicology' had been in use for a long time before the term 'world music' was popularised in the 1980s and evolved into a new choral form. A world music group is made up of singers regardless of the level of their musical knowledge, experience and music-reading skills. Songs, which include popular numbers from non-Western urban communities (such as South African 'township' music), are taught by ear and memorised in all-comers community groups. The social and personal benefits of singing are emphasised. The repertoire is seen as a vehicle to show joy and celebration, express grief, promote a sense of wellbeing, or accompany everyday work — all this without worrying about having a good enough voice or getting the notes right.

The world music movement, developed in the UK in the 1960s, was slow in arriving here. But it has been promoted very successfully in New Zealand since the early 2000s by New Zealander Julian Raphael, a highly qualified music educator, composer and performer, who had worked in England. In 2005, he began to build his Wellington Community Choir and it has become a vibrant and popular group. He was a guest conductor at Sing Aotearoa, the country's premier forum for choral music, in 2013 and 2016.

Raphael and composer/soloist/conductor Carol Shortis set up a community network, the Song Leaders' Network Aotearoa, in 2012 to help confident vocal leaders discover the pleasure of leading singing with others and to encourage more teachers to sing with their students at school. The network recommends the Natural Voice philosophy. This aims at a healthy use of the voice by connecting a free breathing technique to the whole body.

Tony Backhouse, patron of Song Leaders' Network Aotearoa, has commented: 'Over the last twenty years there has been a wonderful growth in group singing here, but few resources outside the prevailing choral tradition to train those who want to learn how to direct and guide singers in alternate repertoires. So it's time for community singing in New Zealand to take the next step.'[7]

Raphael and Shortis are two people taking that next step. Shortis arranges songs from around the world for her groups, being particularly drawn to English folk and Celtic-language music. She will be using such songs with a new Paraparaumu choir she has recently started, with an initial membership of 100. She explained who the choir was intended for: 'The choir is specially for shower divas, lonely crooners, people who "think they can't sing" (pah!), those who have never sung en masse, or certainly not since school . . . through to those of us who already know the deep pleasure of being part of a choir.'

Contemporary rock and pop have been the focus for other groups. The Young at Heart Chorus in Auckland grew partly from an award-winning documentary in 2007 about elderly citizens (average age 81) in Massachusetts who enjoyed songs by Jimi Hendrix, Coldplay and Sonic Youth. It developed further from a 2010 visit to New Zealand of the American Young at Heart Chorus.[8] In 2019, the Auckland group comprised about 30 men and women over the age of 70 meeting weekly to sing contemporary rock and pop music, including arrangements of songs by the Black Eyed Peas, Red Hot Chili Peppers and One Direction.

The Christchurch Pops Choir was created in 2011 after Christchurch's magnitude-6.3 earthquake caused widespread damage and deaths. One of the aims of the choir, which performs a wide range of music such as pop, rock, jazz, swing, soul and musical theatre, was to bring a sense of joy to the people of the stricken city. It was mainly the brainchild of young conductor and entrepreneur Luke Di Somma. The current director is Matthew Everingham.

Under the influence of the television show *Glee*, running from about 2009 to 2015, interest in modern a cappella increased greatly. In 2016, a new event, the Pan Pacific Harmony Festival for under-25-year-olds, drew a cappella singers from many countries to the Aotea Centre in Auckland. By mid-2017, one estimate was that New Zealand had more a cappella singers per capita than anywhere else in the world. In 2017, an Auckland choir opened a global broadcast for the United Nations 35th International Day of Peace.

Choral singing therapy has been developed by music therapists and speech therapists in New Zealand and internationally. Overseas groups tend to focus on a specific population, but in New Zealand the approach is more inclusive, catering for people with Parkinson's disease, for those with stroke, dementia and brain injury, as well as for partners and carers.

The CeleBRation Choir, based at the University of Auckland's Centre for Brain Research and led by music therapist Alison Talmage (and previously also Shari Storie),

TOP CeleBRation Choir performing at Brain Day, Centre for Brain Research, University of Auckland, 23 March 2019. PHOTOGRAPHER DAVID TALMAGE

BELOW Trade union singers Choir Choir Pants on Fire mark International Working Women's Day on 9 March 1999 at Wellington Railway Station. From left: Pinky Agnew, Hazel Armstrong, Viv Walker and Anna Kenny. ALEXANDER TURNBULL LIBRARY/*EVENING POST*, EP 1999/0701

was launched in 2009 with a focus on communication rehabilitation and wellbeing for adults living with a neurological condition. Weekly sessions enable singers to enjoy familiar songs as well as new repertoire, and participate in research led by Professor Suzanne Purdy. Similar groups have followed, notably the Brainwaves Singers (Tauranga), Cantabrainers Choir (Christchurch), SoundsWell Singers (Wellington) and Sing Up Rodney (Silverdale and Warkworth).

A number of conductors around the country have set up small choirs to sing at the bedside of palliative care patients. Wellingtonian Carol Shortis has such a group, called the Whakaahuru Singers.

In 2005, Dr Julie Jackson, a senior lecturer at the University of Waikato, was invited to Waikeria Prison (near Te Awamutu) to introduce a choir competition for the prisoners. The event was so successful that it was repeated in 2006. However, when the senior prison administrator, who had invited her, left, the competition was abandoned.

In 2010, though, a Pacific Choir, made up of prison inmates, was born in the Spring Hill Corrections Facility near Meremere. Today, 44 men from five Pacific Island cultures sing in the choir. Its repertoire, originally of hymns, has expanded to include traditional Pacific Island songs, and the choir has produced a CD. A special performance for community members, church leaders and media demonstrated their powerful voices, under the guidance of choirmaster Tagaloa Peter Su'a.

In 2015, Liana Stupples and Shona McNeil pioneered the first gospel choir in Arohata Women's Prison in Tawa, near Wellington. Since September 2017, singer Tina Cross has been running a 'Power of Song' workshop for inmates at Auckland Prison.

In February 2018, the New Zealand Youth Choir, under director David Squire, rehearsed with an informal singing group at the Auckland Women's Regional Correctional Facility and then presented a concert to all the women prisoners. The choir's operations manager Emma Billings, who had suggested the visit, was moved by the response from the women.

In addition to choirs for therapy, choirs for seniors aimed at healthy ageing have sprung up. In 2007, Julie Jackson approached Hilda Ross Retirement Village, sited a few minutes away from the University of Waikato campus, about starting a Glee Club for the villagers. This was the beginning of Jackson's pioneering work in choral singing with senior citizens. Choirs were also set up in several other retirement villages. Jackson received reports that physical and mental health had improved, with greater levels of energy and alertness, and a stronger sense of community.

In 2013, Jackson (under her married name, Jackson-Gough) organised a Retirement Villages Association Festival of Choirs at St Paul's Cathedral in Wellington. Sponsored by Bay Audiology, the festival was held over two days and attended by nearly 700 people. Competition between the best choirs was keen and participants took great pride in memorising their music and delivering best-ever performances.

No sooner had Jackson's resources company Harmonic Health, created to assist client choirs with quality music materials, got off to a good start than Jackson's health began to deteriorate. She passed away in 2015.

Today there are over 80 choirs in retirement villages throughout New Zealand.[9] And there are many other seniors' choirs such as those that musician and social worker Ann-Marie Stapp has built in Paraparaumu and Ōtaki, north of Wellington. These choirs can have a wide-ranging repertoire.[10]

The question of where conductors and advisers will come from isn't relevant only to seniors' choirs. An increased number of choirs, and more opportunities to sing, leads to more choir leaders being needed, particularly vocal coaches, directors and assistant conductors.

Two vocal pedagogues who have helped to define the vocal coach role in the 2000s are Morag Atchison and Rachel Alexander. Atchison, who studied at the University of Auckland and Royal Academy of Music (London), and established herself as one of New Zealand's leading sopranos, became a lecturer in voice at the University of Auckland. She was the vocal coach to the New Zealand Youth Choir, and tutor for both the University Chamber Choir and Choralation, from Westlake Girls' and Boys' High Schools, a choir that has won several platinum awards at The Big Sing. She was the first Doctor of Musical Arts in vocal studies from a New Zealand university.

Vocal pedagogue Rachel Alexander has worked as an assistant director and vocal consultant to the New Zealand Secondary Students Choir. She holds a Master of Music (Hons) in voice from the University of Auckland. Her comprehensive choral experience includes membership of the New Zealand Youth Choir, New Zealand Opera Chorus for nine years, Voices New Zealand Chamber Choir, and conducting at Diocesan School for Girls. A trained secondary teacher, Alexander is a singing tutor and classroom teacher, and is vocal coach to the school's top choir, the St Cecilia Singers, conducted by Shona McIntyre-Bull.

Atchison has been impressed with how Karen Grylls, in rehearsals, has taken on board what she calls 'the trade of the voice studio'.[11] The language about the voice used by the singing teacher is also used in choral rehearsals. The vocal values and technical ideas in voice studio and rehearsal room now match rather than clash — as was often the case in the past when some singing teachers would not allow their charges to sing in a choir and students didn't know who to follow. Now, collective knowledge is the

Isaac Stone, 2019.
PHOTOGRAPHER
BARRY PRESCOTT

Isaac Stone

Isaac Stone received substantial encouragement from participation in a school music programme at Tawa College, Wellington, from small-group vocal and instrumental tuition, and from five years of music study and private piano lessons. He holds a Bachelor of Music in classical voice and ACTL in piano.

He was a member of the New Zealand Secondary Students Choir (2005–6), the New Zealand Youth Choir (2008–16), and now Voices New Zealand Chamber Choir. Stone was a student in Ken Young's New Zealand School of Music conducting class and a participant in three national conductors' schools.

Stone has been an intentional observer of the directors he has sung with: Shona Murray, Roger Stevenson, Elise Bradley, David Squire and Karen Grylls. He is a former conductor of the Wellington Youth Choir and is currently conductor of Tawa College's Blue Notes, which has been invited five times to The Big Sing Finales. At Tawa College, he teaches classroom music and brass instruments, and leads the choral programme.

Stone founded a new chamber choir, Supertonic, which has already received critical acclaim. It covers a wide musical spectrum, from a pop spectacular celebrating Fleetwood Mac and David Bowie, through Vaughan Williams' *Mass in G Minor*, to the neglected music of Clara Schumann, Fanny Mendelssohn and Lili Boulanger, along with works written by composers suffering imprisonment. He has been innovative in the use of a new concert venue (Pipitea Marae) that provides a gratifying acoustic for his new choir and its projected audience.

Isaac Stone conducts Supertonic, 2019.
PHOTOGRAPHER BARRY PRESCOTT

basis of positive relationships between tutors, conductors and students.

For this approach to work, the studio teacher and the choral leader need to be in full agreement. Atchison has also been impressed with how Grylls has been willing to change the sound of her choirs, and she thinks that a New Zealand choral identity has finally found its home in a colourful, free-sounding vibrancy of tone with a unique accent.[12]

With the increased influence of Māori and Pasifika voices, and the more soloistic yet blended colours possible through using complementary vocal values in studio *and* rehearsal, Aotearoa New Zealand has made its own tradition.[13]

The chief sources of directors and assistant conductors have been training courses, the national choirs, and the leaders of The Big Sing choirs. There has also been the arrival of skilled and experienced migrants.

The most fruitful of the sources has been alumni of the New Zealand Youth Choir. A 1999 informal survey of the occupations of former Youth Choir members identified 26 music teachers, including nine who were leading choirs.[14] Although there appears to have been no research on the subject since then, anecdotal evidence suggests that, now, several hundred Youth Choir alumni are active choral conductors, singers, accompanists, administrators and choral composers.

An example of the influence of alumni of the New Zealand Youth Choir is Isaac Stone. His story, reinforcing many of the issues raised in this book, demonstrates how a wide range of experiences shapes an exceptional choral leader. It also underlines the importance of key influences.

To conclude a chapter on how New Zealand's choral music has flourished over the last 20 years, it is pertinent to highlight an activity that has brought cohesion, focus and a sense of celebration to the world of choristers, conductors, coaches and choral audiences over that time: The Big Sing, known in its early years as the Secondary School Choir Festivals. These regional and national choir competitions, open to any secondary schools wishing to take part, have been unifying because all New Zealanders — Māori, Pasifika, Pākehā and other ethnic groups — can feel involved: from the young person whose only interest had previously been pop, rock, hip-hop, alternative (or whatever had been on their playlist), through the disabled and those shut out of musical opportunities by lack of money, to the army of adults as carers, organisers or leaders, along with sponsors, local authorities and the public providing support. Three ways in which The Big Sing competitions have been a focus for the choral community have been the need for workshops to help each new generation of singers and directors; the prodding of choirs and schools to take part; and the annual need for new compositions and arrangements, although, it has to be said, not all directors arrive at appropriate balanced choices for their groups. The Big Sing began life as a 'Vocal Section' of the Westpac School Music Contest in 1978, grew into Choir Festivals and became the full responsibility of the New Zealand Choral Federation (NZCF) from 1988.

In a 2012 Doctor of Musical Arts dissertation, part of which is devoted to the history of The Big Sing, Matthew Leese identifies several choral directors that stand out in the period 1988 to 2005.[15] His analysis highlights the crucial role of the director for a choir's excellence to be recognised. Further, in two cases, it demonstrates the almost immediate improvement that a highly skilled director can have upon arrival in a new school: Terence Maskell led choirs from six schools to a total of 16 Finale appearances, and Roger Stevenson led five different choirs to 14 Finale appearances.[16]

Dr Leese also discusses three issues: the comparatively low participation by groups from many of the regions; the low involvement of schools in low socio-economic communities; and the under-representation (at least until 2011) of Māori, Pasifika and other ethnic groups.

TOP Fortissimo, from Dilworth School, winners of the Auahi Kore (Smokefree) Award for the best performance of a work using Māori text, 2015.
PHOTOGRAPHER RICHARD ARMISHAW

BELOW LEFT Programme for The Big Sing, 2014.
AUTHOR'S COLLECTION

BELOW RIGHT Elizabeth Crayford, coordinator of The Big Sing Festivals since 2007, in 2019.
PHOTOGRAPHER LUKE PILKINTON-CHING

The story of the rise of choral activity in this country has not been one of unmitigated success. While great results have been achieved, they have not necessarily involved the whole nation. It was conspicuous that greater heights were attained in the schools' festivals when more Māori and Pasifika students took part after 2011. They had found barbershop singing — witness groups like Tawa College's Musical Island Boys; now they were finding mainstream choral singing with a vengeance.

A great deal of work was done on the Secondary School Choir Festivals from 1997 to 2000, when Craig Pollock was chairman of the national committee responsible for the festivals.[17] In 2000, the festival was rebranded as The Big Sing, and a student choral composition competition was introduced. In 2002, oversight of the organisation passed from the Wellington committee to an advisory panel under the direction of the NZCF. Various modifications were made in format and content, including the introduction of the Auahi Kore (Smokefree) Award for the choir giving the best performance of a work using Māori text.

The NZCF Big Sing, is, in 2019, New Zealand's largest choral festival, and it has caught the attention of about a third of all secondary schools. In 2012, prominent Australian music educator and music arranger Andy Mison was encouraged to attend the Finale in Wellington. He admitted to being bowled over by the excellence of the singing, and wondered why they couldn't do it in Australia. Why not indeed? Mison was discovering something special to New Zealand. We knew of no similar choral event anywhere in the southern hemisphere.

There are administrative reasons, also, for the continuing success of the regional and national festivals — the hundreds of voluntary helpers who appear every year to run efficient events throughout the country. Elizabeth Crayford has marshalled these helpers since 2007, taking over from Rachel Tipping, who had been Wellington-based coordinator of The Big Sing Festivals for the previous 10 years.

The enthusiasm of students taking part in The Big Sing has helped to build or rebuild choir singing traditions in participating schools and their surrounding communities. The fostering of singing talent has produced national and international soloists: alumni such as Madeleine Pierard, Anna Pierard, Anna Leese, Jonathan Lemalu and Simon O'Neill. A list of more recent names would contain the Sol3 Mio trio of Pene and Amitai Pati and Moses Mackay, and the winner of the 2018 Lexus Song Quest, Joel Amosa. The festivals have also fostered outstanding conductors such as Sue Densem, Rowan Johnston, David Squire and Andrew Withington, as well as the superb singers with whom they have worked. A particular pay-off has been for Finale-level choirs to travel overseas and have their excellence recognised

Finale of The Big Sing, conducted by Andrew Withington, 2018. PHOTOGRAPHER RICHARD ARMISHAW

there. An example is the choir tours that David Hamilton made to Australia and Finland.

Sometimes New Zealanders don't hear about or recognise a success story in their midst. The Big Sing Finales are an example of this phenomenon. The rise in standards at the national festivals since the start of the new millennium has largely gone unnoticed by the general public. Certainly, the media has not always shown interest. But it is a baffling and frustrating state of affairs for the choral fraternity. In sporting terms, it is like being unaware of the existence of elite secondary school rugby sides.

However, among the young cognoscenti, the live-streamed Gala Concerts receive thousands of hits each year, which speaks volumes about their popularity. Their followers keep connected with the Finale season each August, following on social media. In 2018, the compère, Nick Tipping, reported that over 100,000 people from around the world were live-streaming the concert. Especially from 2012 to 2018, the top choirs at the National Finale Gala Concerts have been recognised as being at a high international level. Tecwyn Evans, world-travelling conductor, says that nowhere else is there such a high quality of choral music in a similar competition. At one Finale, Sue Densem led a Burnside High School Senior Chorale performance of 'Let the River Run' by Carly Simon. Since being placed on YouTube, it has drawn comments such as: 'Well done to this choir and their obviously excellent teacher . . . from an English opera singer wowed by the excellent tradition of choral singing in New Zealand.'[18]

Furthermore, the repertoire of the Finale choirs has often been challenging and new. Over this period, Densem has won several Platinum Awards, conducting, for example, her Senior Chorale in Ivan Hrušovský's *Rytmus*, and a movement from Czech composer Zdeněk Lukáš's *Requiem* (1992) a cappella. In the same year, Densem also prepared the choir in music by Brahms, Bob Chilcott, David Childs, Ēriks Ešenvalds and Ward Swingle.[19]

In 2017, Rowan Johnston, also a multiple Platinum Award winner, prepared Choralation to sing Ešenvalds' *Stars*, and 'Undarmoi and Kalervoi' by the great Estonian composer Veljo Tormis, for which they were awarded the A Cappella prize. They then added a choral arrangement of the 1930s popular song 'It's Only a Paper Moon'. In addition to their choral expertise, many members of Choralation were experienced as vocal soloists, playing in instrumentalist chamber music ensembles and singing in barbershop groups. It is no wonder that the choir came across as a powerful and flexible artistic group.[20]

The sense of celebration and excitement that is obvious at The Big Sing Gala Concerts — even before the evening programme begins — is a constant reaffirmation of their worth. They are inclusive, broad-ranging events.

TOP LEFT Sue Densem, winner of several Platinum Awards and conductor of a chamber choir at the University of Canterbury. PHOTOGRAPHER MIKE CUTFORTH

TOP RIGHT Rowan Johnston, director of Choralation, 2017. PHOTOGRAPHER GRANT HUTCHINSON

BELOW Voicemale (Westlake Boys' High School) participating in the Second Leonardo da Vinci International Choral Festival in Florence, July 2018, where they won top marks for various categories as well as the Grand Prix award. LEONARDO DA VINCI INTERNATIONAL CHORAL FESTIVAL

PARDUBICE

15

Five national choirs and a world symposium

The New Zealand Youth Choir (formerly the National Youth Choir), the New Zealand Secondary Students Choir, Te Roopu Waiata Māori (the National Māori Choir), the New Zealand Male Choir, and Voices New Zealand — these five national choirs show the breadth and excellence of choral music in New Zealand, which underpinned the successful bid for the World Symposium on Choral Music in 2020.

Since the foundations of the National Youth Choir in 1979, Professor Peter Godfrey had been its principal guest conductor. He became the sole conductor in 1983, following Sir David Willcocks directing it in 1980, my leading it in Auckland in 1981, and both Godfrey and I conducting it on the 1982 tour. The Godfrey period saw a 1984 choir recording become a finalist for Classical Record of the Year. He experimented with dividing the full choir into two, and this move was successful, with the Chamber Choir winning the youth section of the European Broadcasting Union's Let the Peoples Sing competition in 1986. The jury said of the choir: 'With its marvellous voices, it is among today's top young ensembles . . . choral singing here is not an end in itself, but a spiritual achievement.'[1]

However, there was unease about the two-choir policy, with its potential for divisiveness, and the policy was disbanded after a couple of years. These years also saw the beginning of an increase in Māori and Polynesian membership.

A 1988 tour was built around the Eighteenth International Youth and Music Festival in Vienna — one of two overseas competitions the choir took part in, and they won first prize for best choir at the festival. The chairman of the judging panel said that the choir was outstanding: 'They bring an understanding for the need for phrasing . . . the meaning of the words . . . they also have a beautiful blend of tone.' He also mentioned the balance between parts, and control of rhythm.

Godfrey publicly commented that 'the 1988 National Youth Choir has shown European conductors and singers that its standards and qualities are at least equal to theirs'.

Attendance at the Europa Cantat Choral Festival in Hungary was a useful cross-cultural experience, with Deputy Conductor Brigid McLafferty noting how the Cantat drew together 'diverse political ideologies, religious and ethnic groups into an inspired whole'.[2]

From 1989, Karen Grylls was director of the choir. She oversaw the choir's name change to New Zealand Youth Choir (NZYC) and introduced Scandinavian and French music, with a consequent shift away from the emphasis on English repertoire. In 1992, the choir won the youth choir section of the Let the Peoples Sing competition, and the Silver Rosebowl for best choir in that competition.

An American tour planned for 1993 included Bub Wehi's 'Kua Rongo' (a welcome song that was to become important in the choir's repertoire) and an invitation to sing with the Mormon Tabernacle Choir.[3] In addition, the choir was selected to represent the Pacific/Australia/New Zealand region at the World Choral Symposium in Vancouver that year, even though they had represented the region at the previous Symposium and, strictly speaking, were not eligible to attend.

They were the joint choir-in-residence with Te Waka Huia at the 1997 Sing Aotearoa, continuing the special relationship begun in the Sydney Opera House the year before. When, in Ōhakune, the two choirs sang 'Hinemoa' and 'Tīmatanga' together, the effect was 'immediate and explosive'.[4]

From the already auditioned choir, a group of 44 was chosen to tour Europe in 1999. The choir set out to do as well as they possibly could in two competitions: the Choir of the World competition at the International Musical Eisteddfod in Llangollen, Wales, and the European Grand Prix for Choral Singing in Trencianske Teplice, Slovakia. In rehearsals, Grylls was meticulous in developing the skills needed to compete successfully against the elite European choirs that they would meet, including using the International Phonetic Alphabet to master the sounds of songs in foreign languages. In the event, the choir won the Mixed Choir Class in Llangollen, and the following day nine judges gave the choir the Choir of the World award — the equivalent of a Rugby World Cup. This time the choir made Television One news.

The NZYC went on to win the four-choir contest in Slovakia. Local composer Ivan Hrušovský was complimentary about the choir's rendition of one of their star pieces: his difficult *Rytmus*, which wisely had been in the choir's concert programmes from the start of the year.

One of the choir's recordings, the CD *Gaude*, released in 2004, was nominated a finalist in the Best Classical Album category at the New Zealand Music Awards the following year. In July 2004, on their tour of Europe, the choir achieved highest marks in several categories at the Forty-third International Choral Competition in Gorizia, Italy.

In 2011, David Squire became the fourth musical director of the NZYC. He came to the position with many notable successes behind him, including winning the Platinum Award at the 2008 The Big Sing Finale with his chamber choir The Fundamentals from Rangitoto College — the first time a mixed-voice choir had achieved this award.

Squire had been in the NZYC, as well as in Voices New Zealand Chamber Choir and the innovative V8 Vocal Ensemble (as a founding member of both). He studied singing with Isabel Cunningham, Glenese Blake and Beatrice Webster. A trained teacher, he gained a Master of Music (Hons), studying with Karen Grylls and Juan Matteucci. He had marked success in the instrumental field as well as choral, conducting the Westlake Symphony Orchestra (Westlake Girls' and Boys' High Schools) for more than a decade, and establishing the Auckland Youth Big Band. He has often been involved in session and recording work, and he toured with George Benson as a backing vocalist

ABOVE National Youth Choir (director: Karen Grylls), Choir of the World 1999. NATIONAL YOUTH CHOIR

LEFT David Squire, fourth musical director of the New Zealand Youth Choir, 2015. PHOTOGRAPHER BROOKE BAKER in 2010. Squire was awarded a New Zealander of the Year Local Heroes Medal in 2011 for services to music education.

Two years after his appointment, Squire took the NZYC on a celebrated tour of the United States and Canada. When the choir performed in the 2014 New Zealand Festival of the Arts in Wellington, the *Dominion Post* commented, 'this concert was a timely reminder of the quality of choral singing we have in this country'.

In 2016, the choir attended the International Festival of Academic Choirs, at Pardubice in the Czech Republic, with choirs from the Czech Republic, Poland, Russia and four from that mecca of choral music, Latvia. NZYC won all four classes they entered, as well as a special prize for Outstanding Vocal Culture. Then, with an entirely new programme, and in front of seven adjudicators, they were awarded the Grand Prix. They travelled to Le Quesnoy, a small town in northern France which had been liberated by the New Zealand Division near the end of the First World War, to participate in their memorial services. On several occasions the choir has sung at the Anzac Day National Memorial Service in Wellington.

Recently, Squire has been leading the group to present short concerts with other choirs and institutions, including an informal concert in February 2018 with the Auckland Graduate Choir (directed by Terence Maskell). In September 2018, a concert in the Wellington Opera House featured the choir with FilCoro (Wellington Filipino Choir), Wellington Young Voices and the Wellington Youth Choir.

Many alumni of the NZYC have enjoyed national and international success as soloists and conductors. Internationally recognised musicians are among those who acknowledge their debt to the New Zealand Youth Choir.[5]

The international standing of the New Zealand Secondary Students Choir (NZSSC) has come about because of the expert skills and personalities of its first three directors: Roger Stevenson, Elise Bradley and Andrew Withington.

Roger Stevenson, head of music at Havelock North High School, who had been assistant director of the inaugural choir in 1986, was appointed musical director the following year. Prior to this he had been involved in national secondary schools' holiday choral courses since 1978, when he sang the baritone solos in Brahms' *Requiem* at the Palmerston North course.

Stevenson led the NZSSC in several visits to a choir festival in Hawai'i, always returning with gold medals. Alumnus of the choir Simon O'Neill, now an internationally acclaimed tenor, recalls his experience of being steered towards auditioning for the

TOP New Zealand Youth Choir winning the Grand Prix in Pardubice, July 2016. NEW ZEALAND YOUTH CHOIR

BELOW The Graduate Choir New Zealand, conductor Terence Maskell. THE GRADUATE CHOIR NZ

Secondary Students Choir by Robert Aburn, music teacher at Ashburton College and foundation member of the National Youth Choir:

> NZSSC was the catalyst for my vocal development. I am so grateful to Roger Stevenson and his wonderful colleagues. . . . We went to the 1990 Pacific Basin Choral Festival in Honolulu, Hawai'i. Two years earlier, I'd been part of the Canterbury Youth Band attending the Pacific Basin Brass Festival (playing the euphonium) so I knew how fun it was going to be. We sang the hell out of our repertoire and the judges rewarded the incredible level of polish Roger demanded from us. We performed a spiritual, 'The Solid Rock', with the great Robert Wiremu as soloist. I felt like I was part of a mid-Alabama State Baptist church choir! I was in awe of Robert's voice, it was an honour to be in the backing choir.[6]

Stevenson also took the NZSSC to Singapore, and then, in 2000, to Canada at the invitation of the Canadian Government. A special tour from Ottawa to Edmonton was organised for them as part of the Millennium Celebrations.

Elise Bradley was engaged as musical director of the choir late in 2000. While head of music at Westlake Girls' High School, Auckland, she had received a National Excellence in Teaching Award for Secondary Teaching. Her Key Cygnetures choir had been awarded the City of Vienna prize at the Internationales Jugendmusikfest and the Award of the City of Vienna at the Summa Cum Laude International Youth Music Festival. She was a member of Voices New Zealand Chamber Choir.

Roger Stevenson had earlier taken the NZSSC to Brisbane, and Bradley took the group to a conference in the same city in 2002. The Australian secondary school choir directors present were (again) extremely impressed with the group's level of achievement. They found it hard to believe that such remarkably fine singing could result from just two weeks' rehearsals.

Bradley then led the group to the International Choral Kathaumixw in Canada in 2004, where they took out first place Youth Choir, first place Adult Mixed Choir and first place Folk and Cultural Traditions. In 2006, they were presented with The World's Choir award at the Hong Kong International Youth and Children's Festival. The same year they won Champion Mixed Voice Youth Choir at the World Choral Games in China.

In 2007, Bradley was appointed artistic director of the Toronto Children's Chorus in Canada when the founder-conductor Jean Ashworth Bartle stepped down. That

TOP LEFT Elise Bradley, 2016. Bradley was musical director of the NZSSC 2000–07. TORONTO CHILDREN'S CHOIR

TOP RIGHT Andrew Withington, director of NZSSC 2008–18. PHOTOGRAPHER STEPHEN COMPTON

BELOW The NZSSC Canada Tour, 2016. NZSSC ARCHIVES

TOP Rim D. Paul and Te Roopu Waiata Māori (the National Māori Choir), 2013. NATIONAL MĀORI CHOIR ARCHIVES

BELOW Te Roopu Waiata Māori (the National Māori Choir). NATIONAL MĀORI CHOIR ARCHIVES

Bradley won this position ahead of an international field of excellent applicants speaks volumes about the quality of the various forms of training and professional development she had received in this country, as well as the environment that influenced her growing up here. Her practical vocal pedagogy insights have been recognised by invitations to several World Symposia on Choral Music. She led a national 'Kids of Note' course in Auckland in 2016 amid hopes that this would lead to an ongoing national children's choir, and she brought the Toronto Children's Chorus to New Zealand as choir-in-residence at Choral Connect 2019. In 2018 Bradley was made a Member of the New Zealand Order of Merit (MNZM) for services to music.

Andrew Withington was appointed artistic director of the choir in 2008. He took the choir to Canada in 2010, and at the International Choral Kathaumixw the NZSSC was awarded first place in the Adult Mixed Choir class and second place in both the Youth Choir Class and Folk and Cultural Traditions. They also received The People's Choice Award.

Six years later, NZSSC returned to Kathaumixw as the guest choir, and Withington chaired one of the juries. They were a guest choir at Hong Kong and Shanghai events in July 2018. The choir tour that moved Withington most profoundly, however, was the visit to South Africa in 2012 for the Ihlombe Music Festival.

In down-to-earth fashion, Withington tells of his own failure to get into the NZSSC when he auditioned as a sixth former (Year 12). There were no problems later, however, with a successful audition for the New Zealand Youth Choir. He has since sung regularly with Voices New Zealand Chamber Choir. Withington obtained a Master of Music (Hons) in Choral Conducting with Karen Grylls, and completed a doctorate on the topic of approaches to teaching choirs to sing in 'Just Intonation'.[7]

The idea of Te Roopu Waiata Māori (the National Māori Choir) was the brainchild of composer, arranger, television and recording artist and producer Rim D. Paul, in 1989. As leader of Māori showbands Hi-Quins and Quin Tikis, musical arranger for four decades for Howard Morrison (later Sir Howard Morrison), and an internationally recognised entertainer, he drew on wide support in the music industry.[8] As a choral conductor, lecturer and Māori leader, he could see that such a group would play a useful part in the New Zealand sesquicentennial celebrations the following year.

The choir was formally established as a 1990 Commission initiative. Senior Māori involved in kapa haka groups, church choirs and community choirs were supportive, particularly because it was hoped that the formation of the group would lead to choral singing being revived in Māori communities. It aimed to attract both older generations and younger people, singing a 'joyous' style often heard in Māori gatherings after the traditional waiata, poi, mōteatea and pātere were sung.[9] Te Roopu Waiata Māori, led by Rim D. Paul, performed with distinction and added to a sense of closer Māori–Pākehā relationships at the first of the New Zealand Choral Federation's choral fiestas, Sing Aotearoa at Ōhakune in October 1990.

After a break of 10 years, the choir was brought together again. This time it was to launch a CD, *Songs of Inspiration*, expressing the mood of many Māori at the time. Guests at the launch, held at Parliament Buildings in November 2000, included representatives of Te Māngai Pāho (funder of Māori initiatives in music, radio, television and new media), Creative New Zealand, and composer Morvin Simon, who had earlier been chairperson of Te Roopu Waiata Māori.

An 80-voice choir sang on the main stage at WOMAD (World of Music, Arts and Dance) in Taranaki, 2013, collaborating with the band The Yoots in a special commission. The choir also took part in Sing Aotearoa in Rotorua the same year. A 2014 event with hymns and songs to mark 'two hundred years of church music in Aotearoa New Zealand' did not eventuate because of lack of financial and other support, despite two years of rehearsals that Rim D. Paul undertook in Rotorua.[10]

The New Zealand Male Choir was formed to perform at the Welsh Millennium Celebrations in 2000. An invitation for a New Zealand male choir to attend a Festival of Welsh Massed Male Choirs was accepted in 1998, and 72 choristers gathered in Nelson in October the following year. They rehearsed for an inaugural concert at Nelson College and for performances in Wales in 2000.

International invitations were soon extended to the choir, but the group had little profile within New Zealand. To boost this, it was decided to undertake concert tours throughout the country on a regular basis. These have occurred almost yearly ever since, covering the country from Kaitāia, Dargaville and Whangārei to Gore and Invercargill.

The choir has travelled twice to the United Kingdom, where it competed in the International Eisteddfod in Llangollen, Wales, and made appearances at St George's Chapel at Windsor Castle, Notre Dame and Mozart's Chapel in Salzburg. In 2010, their 11 concerts were in venues as varied as York Minster, a rugby club grandstand, and the penthouse reception room in New Zealand House, London. In 2015, they sang in four Canadian cities. The choir has also travelled within Australia.

TOP The New Zealand Male Choir in Whanganui prior to the Australian Tour, May 2018. PHOTOGRAPHER MARK BRIMBLECOMBE. NEW ZEALAND MALE CHOIR

BELOW Joe Christensen, director of the New Zealand Male Choir, 2016. DUNCAN BROWN PHOTOGRAPHY

Voices New Zealand Chamber Choir publicity photo (director: Karen Grylls). CHARLES BROOKS PHOTOGRAPHY

The choir's repertoire, in Māori, Welsh and English, includes songs from the traditional male voice repertoires, waiata, hymns, spirituals, opera choruses, arrangements from musical theatre, ballads and New Zealand compositions.

The New Zealand Male Choir is now an auditioned choir of 60 with the stated aims of supporting and encouraging choral singing in New Zealand schools and communities. Undoubtedly, good fellowship and the joy of singing more than compensate for the considerable commitment and the expense of regular travel within New Zealand and overseas. Proceeds of concerts are shared with community organisations such as Rotary, Lions, parent–teacher associations and hospice trusts.

The choir's five directors have been Pete Rainey, David Qualtrough, Angela Cresswell from 2002 to 2007, Robert Aburn from 2007 to 2015, and Joe Christensen from 2016 to the present.[11]

Christensen studied voice and opera performance to postgraduate level at

the Queensland Conservatorium of Music. He has sung with Voices New Zealand Chamber Choir, performed as a soloist throughout New Zealand and Australia, and conducted choirs at Karamu High School, Hastings (where he was head of music). He directs the Hastings Choral Society and four other groups in the Hawke's Bay region, and has been closely involved with the New Zealand Choral Federation.

Male choirs have contributed to the New Zealand choral scene since earliest times. Three of the oldest are the Royal Dunedin Male Choir, 1878, the Christchurch Liedertafel Male Voice Choir, 1885, and the Wanganui Male Choir, 1898. Other active groups include the Taranaki, Wellington and Nelson Male Choirs.

In the same year that the New Zealand Male Choir was founded, the New Zealand Youth Choir's graduate arm, Voices New Zealand, made its debut, performing Bach's *St John Passion* with the New Zealand Chamber Orchestra in Auckland and Wellington. In a press announcement, Karen Grylls spelled out why Voices New Zealand was necessary:

Karen Grylls, 2019. PHOTOGRAPHER LUKE PILKINTON-CHING

> Voices New Zealand has grown from the internationally recognised excellence of the Youth Choir. 'We have had increasing invitations to perform, and many of our singers are committed to finding a way to keep singing challenging choral repertoire of a professional standard once they leave the Youth Choir. Voices New Zealand aims to provide that platform,' says Karen.[12]

At the 1998 Tolosa International Festival in Spain, the choir sang 'Tīmatanga' by the Wehi whānau in the folklore section of the competition and received the prize of first equal for the performance.[13] The choir came second equal in the polyphony section, and was awarded a trophy for 'the best performance of a Basque song'. The esteem in which the organisers held this unknown New Zealand conductor and her new choir was shown by Grylls being invited back to be an adjudicator at the following year's festival.

Back home, however, the New Zealand media still greeted the country's latest choral conquering heroes, as an Auckland commentator, Heath Lees, said, 'with a deafening silence'. Had it been a sports team's victory that had gone unreported, wrote Lees, 'we'd have had a national scandal on our hands'.[14] Little had been learned in the two decades since the Dorian Singers' triumphs had gone virtually unnoticed. The nation's newest national choir would have to grow thick skins and develop a gracious resilience.

Voices New Zealand has also recorded for international recording companies and distributors Atoll and Naxos, and it performs at national festivals and at international choral symposia. The choir has appeared regularly with the New Zealand Symphony Orchestra and the Auckland Philharmonia Orchestra, and they sang with the King's Singers at the 2018 International Festival of the Arts in Wellington.

It is the kind of slightly cheeky, ambitious enterprise that suits the New Zealand psyche: apply to have a prestigious global choral jamboree come to New Zealand in 2020 and expect the application to succeed. 'Faint heart ne'er won fair lady' was proven once again; there was jubilation in choral circles when the successful bid was announced. The twelfth triennial World Symposium on Choral Music — 'the world's most prestigious, non-competitive choral event' — was granted to the New Zealand Choral Federation in July 2016.

New Zealand conductors and singers have attended and given presentations at world symposia since their inception in 1987 in Vienna, Austria, and the New Zealand Youth Choir and Voices New Zealand Chamber Choir have been chosen to sing at a number of them. Informal contact with officials of the International Federation for Choral Music (IFCM) over several years made them aware of New Zealand's interest in staging the event, and then Grant Hutchinson and John Rosser of the New Zealand Choral Federation formally presented NZCF's credentials as potential symposium hosts to members of the IFCM Executive Committee in Macau, in late 2015. John Rosser compiled a 50-page bid document with the help of the Auckland Conference Bureau and submitted it in early 2016.

Bids for the event were received from North and South America, Africa, Eastern Europe, Russia and the United Kingdom, indicating the strength of interest. When the IFCM reported on its decision, the 'energy of New Zealand's choral community' to mount such a huge undertaking was a factor. Also mentioned was the fact that we have a supportive network of singers, conductors and composers 'that, per capita, rivals the best choral centres of the world'.[15]

Members of the World Symposium on Choral Music 2020 Artistic and Administrative Committees during June 2018 meetings in Auckland. From left: Ki Adams, Tim Sharp, Jean-Claude Wilkens, Jonathan Velasco, John Rosser, Lisa Davis, Gábor Móczár, Juliet Dreaver. PHOTOGRAPHER CATHRYN WYLLIE

The New Zealand symposium would have been impossible without significant government support, and achieving major events status was a crucial next step in the process. For Rosser and his team, this meant another six months of hard work preparing comprehensive business plans and submissions for both the Ministry of Business, Innovation and Employment (MBIE) and Auckland Tourism, Events and Economic Development (ATEED) to achieve the first significant grant of this kind to a single arts event. This was an encouraging sign of recognition of the potential economic and social benefits of the choral art form.

Auckland will host the eight-day symposium in July 2020. The theme of People and the Land — He Tangata He Whenua — will focus the attention of delegates on the connection and tensions between people and land, between urban life and the natural world: exploring the relationship humans have with the land that supports them, the sense of identity they derive from it, and the tensions that may arise out of it.[16] It is hoped that the theme will be unpacked and interpreted freely and with flair by participating choirs and presenters. Partnership with local Māori from the early planning stages has been a priority for organisers. Both New Zealand and overseas visitors can confidently expect a bicultural experience in sight, sound and soul, taking intercultural choral collaboration to unprecedented levels and, it is hoped, sparking new conversations and connections in the New Zealand choral music scene as one of its legacies.

A feature of the planning for the symposium is the unusually high international standing of the teams of overseas choral musicians giving assistance. The new IFCM board places great importance on the New Zealand symposium. The overseas members of the Artistic Committee at the June 2018 meetings in Auckland were Tim Sharp (United States), Executive Director, American Choral Directors Association and Vice-President, IFCM; Jean-Claude Wilkens (Belgium), CEO, A Coeur Joie (French Choral Association) and past Secretary-General, IFCM; and Jonathan Velasco (Philippines), world-renowned clinician and President, Philippine Choral Directors Association.

Visiting members of the Administrative Committee were: Emily Kuo-Vong (China), President, IFCM; Gábor Móczár (Hungary), President, European Choral Association and Vice-President, IFCM; and Ki Adams (Canada), renowned music educator and IFCM board member. New Zealanders were John Rosser, Karen Grylls and Peter Walls on the Artistic Committee, and Juliet Dreaver, Christine Argyle and Lisa Davis (Ngāti Whātua, Ōrākei) on the Administrative Committee.

The World Symposium will be something new for New Zealand: a festival with 24 of the brightest and best of the world's choirs, and more than 40 eminent choral musicians offering practical workshops and seminars, exhibitions and, very likely, colourful choral entertainment on the streets of central Auckland. The winning of the bid for the symposium was not just a feather in New Zealand's cap. Competing for and winning the rights to hold the 'Choral Olympics' was a ratification of Kiwi excellence: recognising the blossoming of the best in New Zealand's choral garden. Another pivotal moment in the choral story of Aotearoa New Zealand is in the making.

16

How has the best become so good?

In discussions on how some Kiwi choral singing has become consistently excellent, there is a tendency to immediately focus on individual conductors and the choirs they have trained. While the work of exceptional leaders is justifiably applauded, there are broader influences in the choral scene that have helped to produce that excellence and determine the shape and nature of singing in choirs. Widening the lens, we find three themes: background factors that have had a steady effect; turning points that have taken centre stage for a time; and seismic shifts that have pushed some singing into a high-quality zone.

Curiously, the country's temperate climate has been a significant factor in choral music's success, because it attracted influential choral specialists to these shores. When frail health forced Robert Parker to leave England's cold climate he decided to come to New Zealand. Stanley Oliver immigrated to Wellington because he was tired of the freezing Canadian weather. Peter Godfrey decided to get away from the icy conditions affecting England every winter. Other choral musicians also came for health reasons or for a 'better life' — usually understood as a healthy lifestyle, a more congenial climate and an egalitarian society.[1]

Another background determinant has been the consistency of the English influence. For the first 150 years, virtually everything choral was English — from the early settlers and the repertoire they brought, the appointments to cathedrals, the 1911 visit of the Sheffield Choir, the four educators imported in 1925, through to the milestone year of 1958 when three influential musicians impacted the country in the same year: Englishman Peter Godfrey arrived in Auckland; Englishman Bill Walden-Mills became National Adviser in School Music; and New Zealander Maxwell Fernie returned to work in Wellington after his successful years at Westminster Cathedral, London.

Anglophile aspects of choral singing have continued to dominate, or at least affect, our choral life in many ways. Peter Watts, a deputy conductor of the New Zealand Youth Choir, and director of Auckland Choral Society for 20 years, studied in London; Englishman Simon Ravens stayed in New Zealand long enough to establish The Tudor Consort; our choirs travel to Britain; the King's Singers come here to offer workshops and sing with Voices New Zealand Chamber Choir. We no longer regard England as 'the home country', but we are still loosely tied to her musical apron strings.

A further background factor is the generally high level of musicianship of those who win places in the New Zealand Youth Choir, Secondary Students Choir or Voices New Zealand. We now take for granted that the sight-reading of these people will be first class and that they will accurately and sensitively memorise their music. Most of the credit for these high standards should go to private tutors, secondary music teachers and sound rehearsal procedures in the better choirs. When taking up an appointment with the Trinity College Chapel Choir in Melbourne in 1989, Godfrey came to the conclusion that the musicality and sight-singing of those undergraduate students did not compare favourably with the abilities of students on this side of the Tasman.[2] Having easy access to piano lessons, and to band or orchestral tuition at secondary school (free since 1945), has enabled singers to raise their aural and reading skills and extend musical understandings.

Another feature is a changed attitude to the vocal capabilities of those who sing in choirs. It took until the 1970s for it to be seen as normal for each choir member to acquire singing skills through individual or small-group tuition. This was soon seen as hard work; Sir Donald McIntyre once quipping that 'singing is only marginally easier than shovelling rocks uphill'. The idea that conductors should be knowledgeable about the voice was a fairly easy battle to win, and the influence of conductors who have been trained singers and therefore able to show choir members how to sing well was noted. However, two advances were crucial in helping choirs to take vocal development seriously: the availability of group vocal tuition since 1977, and the incorporation of vocal coaching into choir rehearsals.

In concerts and competitions the world over, the beauty, resonance and distinctiveness of vocal tone marks the excellent choir, and it is now not enough for singers, young or old, just to do their best. A greatly increased number of New Zealand choirs now understand the primacy of training each individual vocal instrument.

Yet another of the complex factors quietly determining the success of choral singing is the assortment of traits and attitudes that push New Zealanders to punch above their weight. The 'number 8 wire' adaptability is well entrenched, as is ambition not limited by imaginary class barriers.[3] But as hard-working and innovative as we might be, we don't take ourselves too seriously. This casually self-deprecating trait has often suited our choral brazenness and high hopes, as has been the willingness to accept failures. When the Dorian Choir were demoralised in 1975 by the New Zealand media not recognising their overseas successes, they recovered quickly and looked ahead.

All of this is unsurprising if New Zealand is perceived as an energetic and enterprising nation, obviously with achievements in the sporting world but also in the social and arts spheres. In proportion to the population, New Zealand has had an unusually high number of international singers in opera and related fields, including Rosina Buckman, Inia Te Wiata, Dame Kiri Te Kanawa, Sir Donald McIntyre, Heather Begg, Rodney Macann, Jonathan Lemalu, Madeleine Pierard and Simon O'Neill. Also, like the Baltic and Nordic countries, New Zealand has, according to the International Federation for Choral Music, a choral network that rivals the best choral centres of the world.

A 'can-do' attitude only works if there is a critical mass of experiential confidence from which optimistic goals and daydreams can spring. In the case of choral singing, it is best found when administrators and sponsors know what a good choir is like from the inside. Being active choir members themselves enables them to tell whether a conductor can effectively rehearse quality repertoire, and whether voices will be capable and willing to deliver.

Besides the many background factors that have positively affected New Zealand's choral growth, there have been pivotal moments marking a distinct change in direction and a striking improvement.[4] The last 200 years has been full of turning points big and small, some almost buried in the mists of history; for example, Robert Parker's 59-year development of Wellington's choral scene, and the Bradshaw phenomenon in Christchurch, for 35 years from 1903. There are more recent examples: Victor Peters, a figure now almost unknown, successfully set about turning around a pervasive complacency in the ranks of amateur music-makers and introduced demanding contemporary repertoire; Stanley Oliver with his Schola Cantorum 'opened the door on a great deal that is beautiful in music, apart from that most commonly known';[5] Vernon Griffiths, a man for the 'common people', from his internationally acclaimed music scheme in Dunedin provided the country with dozens of good choral arrangements easy to sing and teach.

There are also the excellent singing broadcasts of E. Douglas Tayler and Tom Young; Auckland having its choral music rebuilt by Austrian Georg Tintner (then carelessly losing him six years later); St Mary's Anglican Church in Parnell, Auckland, which was careful to retain Peter Godfrey long enough for the choir to build a strong reputation, and for him to have a huge following.

Bill Walden-Mills, an overlooked choralist, surely gets a prize for the turning point with most domino effects. His Madrigal Course in New Plymouth in 1966 led to National Holiday Choral Courses, the Secondary Students Choir, the National Youth Choir and, through our best conductor, Karen Grylls, to Voices New Zealand Chamber Choir.

A few School Music Contest officials in 1977 could claim a close second prize for choral innovation. Their willing implementation of a vocal section in their instrumental contest in 1978 has led, 40 years later, to The Big Sing Festival, the New Zealand Choral Federation's flagship event. The NZCF itself has been a major force in developing a strong and vigorous choral morale.

Added to this is Godfrey's first conducting class in 1982; then 18 summer conducting schools and winter Choral Connects, which brought together hundreds of leaders for training.

Of the many personalities that have floated in and out of the narrative, one has been particularly influential: Rodney Eichenberger. From 1985, he and his past students, Jerry Blackstone, David Childs, Faye Dumont, Julie Jackson-Gough, Christopher Kiver, Jo-Michael Scheibe, myself and others, embraced a conducting methodology developed by him. There's been a gradual turning away from that system since, but many fundamental gestural understandings and other insights remain from his teaching and materials.

Some turning points were carefully planned; for example, the 2011 launch of an NZCF Association of Choral Directors (ACD). The subsequent ACD conventions, known as Choral Connect, have become more than mere turning points. They have been more like earthquakes — low on the Richter scale but still keenly felt.

These seismic shifts are not easy to explain because there is a paradox involved. Unexpectedly, the exhilaration of success is usually combined with a moment of stillness.

There were still points when the audience at the Auckland University Festival Choir's first concert in New York heard the sound of the choir and were stopped in their tracks; when the Dorian Choir, in England on their first tour in 1975, read their first reviews; when the three-day festival and competition Te Matatini opened in 1972. Others were when Sir David Willcocks conducted the first National Youth Choir in *A Child of Our Time*; when the audience heard Te Waka Huia and the National Youth Choir producing a new choral sound in the Sydney Opera House in 1996; in 1999, when Karen Grylls included in the National Youth Choir repertoire some of their new-found Māori taonga, and they won 'Choir of the World' in Wales. Or when an NZCF regional committee decided to accept responsibility for the Schools' Choral Festivals, meaning that NZCF now has a public event which is the envy of international observers. Also, when Jerry Blackstone, one of America's leading choral conductors, gave a concert at Choral Connect 2014, including classics by Billings and Josquin (*Ave Maria Virgo serena* — one of the great motets of the fifteenth century), Brahms' *Sehnsucht und Warum*, Ēriks Ešenvalds' *Long Road*, and Moses Hogan's arrangement of 'I Can Tell the World', all performed with passion and attention to detail by, I believe, the best choir Blackstone ever had. Blackstone gave a talk at the same event on the 'soul' of conducting and its practical outworkings, the role of the conductor in caring for the wellbeing of a group of often disparate people, knowing that an inspirational conductor can have a profound effect on lives. Another still point was at the 2017 Auckland Choral Connect, when Ēriks Ešenvalds presented his haunting commissioned work *Spring Rain*, helped by Holy Trinity Cathedral's magnificent acoustics for a cappella singing.

Finally, there is a question to ask: What has choral singing done for society? In particular, has it been available to *all* New Zealanders? Has it been socially responsible? And has it been respectful of all traditions in our country?

The view that group singing strengthens the heart of society is not new, but it has attained a new standing in recent years. Besides helping us learn 'to enjoy a positive kind of patience', and playing its part in 'educating, shaping and reshaping us emotionally',[6] making music together requires us to behave cooperatively.

Research in other countries indicates the many physical, psychological and social benefits of adults singing in choirs. Similarly, children get better grades in school and become better team players with more advanced social skills. The literature has mushroomed in recent years. Recent research suggests that singing in a choir is 'the new exercise'.[7] All of this has applied to the New Zealand scene in various ways.

Whether mixing with supporters of rugby or other sports, being in a school gala crowd, playing in the school playground, or taking part in a civic ceremony, feelings are heightened when in a group. The same applies to group singing. It reminds us of the others around us. We hear their voices. We are encouraged by the conductor to move in a 'dance of sympathy', synchronising with them.[8]

The New Zealand national anthem talks of 'the bonds of love'. Many of our choirs have demonstrated a unified and supportive bond. There has been a respect and affection for the conductor and other members that approaches familial and interpersonal love. For some, choral music has mysteriously developed a spiritual dimension to their lives; for others, it is their way to growth in aesthetic sensitivity.

The big moments, the still points and everything to do with choral music have been for anyone to enjoy. In an egalitarian society, where there is little deliberate attempt to promote social status; professional-level and volunteer choirs can thrive side by side. Occasionally tension has grown between a very good 'professional' chamber choir and an equally good volunteer group; misunderstandings or plain envy will never be far away. But the vast majority of choirs in the world are composed of volunteers. This grassroots activity is what makes choral music-making the most popular universal art form. All this amateur activity provides the base from which elite, specialist and new kinds of choirs can spring.

Curiously, no one knows the number of people involved in choral singing in New Zealand. Sometimes there are claims made, particularly in comparison to the number of active participants in certain popular sports, but no one seems to have done the research. It is rather surprising that Creative New Zealand has no statistics on the subject; for example, in their *Creative New Zealand's Support for Music 2013 to 2017*, there is no mention of the number of groups in this sector of the arts community.

All-comers choirs have been directed by well-known conductors, and massed choirs have been common for community and church events. Huge events have meant that community choral music has built much social goodwill, such as the crowd-pleasing Waka Odyssey, which opened the 2018 New Zealand Arts Festival, when 35,000 people gathered around Wellington Harbour to enjoy the occasion.

New genres and styles have appeared to cater for new community interests: barbershop, gospel, modern folk, world music, workplace choirs, choral pop groups, a cappella, to name a few.

Other services and events in the choral field made available to everyone include free group vocal tuition in every secondary school (providing there is a suitable tutor); choral workshops and clinics spread around the country; and affordable conducting tuition since 1986.[9] The Choral Federation is providing resources to bring certain regions up to national standards for The Big Sing Finales.

There has been relatively little choral music on television apart from *Praise Be*, which ran for 30 years; the Māori Television series on The Big Sing Finales; the *Naked Choir* in 2016 (featuring a cappella groups); and some English-based programmes.[10] The amount of kapa haka on Māori Television far outweighs the amount of European-based choral music on other television channels. Organisations and individuals have played the game, working hard to make the popular choral art accessible to all New Zealanders, but the media have sometimes dropped the ball.

Particularly over the last 30 years, there has been an increased awareness of the benefits of group singing for *all* groups in the community. It has become increasingly common to hear of caring groups going into hospitals and hospices, prisons and detention centres and disabled people's communities. Choirs have sometimes been formed within these institutions. New Zealanders are said to often support the underdog, so it is not difficult to get volunteers to assist people who are disadvantaged and need a helping hand.

Choral music has linked up with music therapy specialists to good effect. The CeleBRation Choir set up by the University of Auckland as a social singing group for people with neurological conditions such as stroke, aphasia or Parkinson's disease is one such example of this development.

Because 21 per cent of the population is now 60 years or older, and this proportion is projected to grow significantly, the needs of senior citizens have become more pressing and the number of groups of older singers has markedly increased. There are dozens of choirs in retirement villages, and more resources and expert staffing will be needed for this work in the future.

Around the world the topic of the number and role of women conductors

Combined Wellington choirs rehearse for Waka Odyssey, which opened the 2018 New Zealand Festival of the Arts before 35,000 people on Wellington's waterfront. PHOTOGRAPHER KOROI HAWKINS, RNZ is sometimes raised as an equality concern, and it is interesting to consider this issue briefly in the context of choral music in New Zealand. I am not aware of any discrimination against women choral conductors here, and I was always impressed that there were more women at Conducting Summer Schools than men.[11]

About 30 per cent of New Zealanders today are Māori, Pacific Islander or Asian, but for much of the last 200 years, settlers of English/European stock made up 90 per cent of the population. There was a tendency for colonists to ride roughshod over Māori customs and culture, including their music. But while the strong English tradition brought to this colony dominated all choral activity at the start, in time there developed a greater interest in the singing of tangata whenua. Composer Alfred Hill was always respectful of Māori culture, including te reo, and some composers and arrangers since Hill have consulted whānau and kaumātua to work collaboratively with them. The musical interests of other ethnic groups have also received attention, particularly in recent years.

Fruitful results have come through a reworking of established traditions, both Māori and Pākehā. The choral classics 'Kua Rongo' and 'Tīmatanga' were the result of a respectful partnership of the New Zealand Youth Choir (directed by Karen Grylls) with Te Waka Huia, Ngāpō and Pimia Wehi, Aroha Cassidy-Nanai and others over many years. Graham Hoffman, ahead of his time, was a model for how such a relationship should work. Because of people like him, we in the choral sphere are better able to celebrate unity in diversity. With more Māori and Pacific Island singers in the New Zealand Secondary Students Choir, the New Zealand Youth Choir and in school groups, and being surrounded by waiata, kapa haka and Pasifika songs, New Zealand choirs now have a unique sound. It is richer, warmer, more resonant and animated, and even more interesting than one could have imagined.

Afterword: Where to from here?

One photo says it all: a high school choir, en route to a choir competition in Australia, singing in an airport to New Zealand's Prime Minister and her new baby. A new generation of singers, seizing the moment to celebrate by performing 'Wairua Tapu', written and composed by Māori arts leader Ngāpō Wehi, and now widely sung by New Zealand choirs.

But even with all its achievements, Kiwi choral singing still has a fair distance to go. While remarkable progress has been made by New Zealanders over the last 200 years, there are challenges for the future.

There is a lack of respect for the choral art form from some others in the musical field — especially orchestra members and administrators. Choirs are often seen as 'amateur' in a pejorative sense, lacking in musical honesty and being content with sub-par performances. It's not the professional-level choirs they are thinking of; nor the beginning groups or choirs of seniors or disabled which are justifiably indulged or excused. It's the many others that, as school reports used to say, 'could do better'.

Sometimes the criticism from outside is unwarranted, unfair or uninformed. However, there's a germ of truth hanging in the air. Comments like, 'They do their best in the circumstances' or 'At least they enjoy what they do' seem to offer excuses for work that is only second-best. We have even got used to it.

But is second-best acceptable? I think of the occasion in South Africa in 1998 when Desmond Tutu and Nelson Mandela were presented with the report of the Truth and Reconciliation Commission, and a superbly trained choir sang choral versions of

Prime Minister Jacinda Ardern and baby Neve with members of Nelson's Nayland College choir at Wellington Airport, August 2018. ROSS GIBLIN/STUFF freedom songs. The effect was electrifying and explosive. A second-best performance would have been a damp squib.

All occasions and audiences deserve the best, and the means of markedly improving choirs' performances are now widely available. Choral singing can be enormous fun, but it also calls us to sacrifice something of ourselves to meet its artistic demands. These demands start with the basics of singing in tune and developing beautiful tone. Choristers and directors need to dream their dreams of 'best-ever' performances. 'Let choirs sing well,' C. S. Lewis once wrote, 'or not at all.'[1]

Another major issue, voiced by some critics, is the worth of the music being sung. Variety in programming is essential, and the selection of repertoire is a demanding, ongoing challenge. But the choices that some conductors make on behalf of their singers could be seen as pandering to the lowest common denominator of taste, being consistently too light. It takes time to unearth great music from within the many choral genres, and finding the kind of excellence that will suit their choir will always remain a prime responsibility of the leader of a choral group.

At this point the cynics leap in, asking, 'But who determines what "great music" is, and what about beauty being in the eye of the beholder?' Many conductors tend to opt out of such discussions, preferring to stick with their personal views on what constitutes good and bad music; they just want to get on with the job.

But being surrounded by well-sung, substantial music is important if a mature, enlivened and respected environment for choral music is to be maintained.

Among smaller concerns is the question of who determines future directions of choral music. Future developments are very much the domain of trained, experienced choral conductors, who should be asked to take a leading role, and can be called upon to give advice. This consultation might range from a recommendation to close down a choir after it has achieved its purposes, to finding more long-term, generous sponsors, or actively growing larger communities of supporters.[2] If an even higher proportion of New Zealanders (including children and seniors) is to be presented with choral singing opportunities, new infrastructure and guidance will be needed. This should not be left to well-meaning, even benevolent, individuals who understand too little about the choral world.

Heightening public awareness of the breadth and depth of choral activity in New Zealand is another task to be addressed. At present choral activity is mostly invisible in online media and also in published material.[3] Choir programmes and choir-oriented films on television have been more common in overseas countries than here (the notable exception being Māori Television). Imaginative strategies and strikingly fresh initiatives will be needed to rectify the situation and catch the interest of the media and production companies. We will continue to fly under the radar unless our advocacy is better and good contacts are fostered. The coming of the World Symposium to Auckland in 2020 will provide an opportunity for a giant leap forward in public understanding of the place of choirs in this country.

If community choirs are looking for a new challenge, it may lie in contributing directly to the needs of their communities. Some, in addition to the musical joy that they bring to audiences and new members, have already joined in various compassionate ventures. However, most choirs would not see community service as part of their 'core business'. But assisting the emotionally stressed, the deprived and marginalised in practical ways, including providing food and supportive friendship, can fit well with groups of outgoing musicians. The collective strength of energetic artists is a formidable thing.[4]

A project that could combine community care with a musical aim would be the teaching of singing skills to seven-, eight- and nine-year-olds in lower socio-economic areas. String instrument skills have been taught, free, at Porirua East schools for over five years by Elizabeth Sneyd and others as part of the Virtuoso Strings music programmes. Sneyd, the 2018 National Music Teacher of the Year, has shown how expert intervention can make a difference to the most disadvantaged children and their families in our society. What has been unexpectedly encouraging are the flow-on effects to the self-esteem and morale of the young learners and their families.

In a similar way to the teaching of instrumental skills, vocal skills (not choir singing), could be appropriately taught in disadvantaged communities by enthusiastic specialists.[5] Graded instructional sight-reading materials could be introduced at a later stage, and singing exams later still. Although the project would entail careful planning and negotiations with the school principals involved, in personal and social terms it would be eminently worthwhile and welcome in many parts of the country.[6]

There is the potential for growth in many parts of the choral sphere. At the same time, there is clearly much to celebrate and be grateful for in the story of choral singing in Aotearoa New Zealand. The sensitive pursuit of excellence has paid off. And probably the best is yet to come.

The New Zealand national anthem suggests we have been meeting in the bonds of love. This sentiment is also echoed in the words of the traditional community song 'Vive L'amour' (Long Live Love):

A friend on your left, and a friend on your right,
Vive la compagnie!
In love and good fellowship, let us unite,
Vive la compagnie!
. . . Vive l'amour,
Vive l'amour, vive l'amour,
Vive la compagnie!

And here is my hope: that the strength of aroha nui (deep affection, love, compassion) will enfold and energise the whole choral sphere in its glorious variety.

Guy E. Jansen
May 2019

Glossary

a cappella	Italian term, meaning solo or ensemble singing without instrumental accompaniment
bel canto	Italian term, meaning 'beautiful singing', referring to the smooth, lyrical and agile vocal style particularly associated with Italian opera in the eighteenth and early nineteenth centuries. Bel canto singing is widely considered the most desirable tone and technique for classical singing
cantata	a secular or sacred composition for solo voice, or solo voices and choir, in multiple movements such as recitative, aria and choral movements, accompanied by instruments
canticle	from the Latin *canticulum*; a hymn, psalm or other Christian song of praise with lyrics taken from biblical or holy texts other than the Psalms
chromaticism	a compositional technique interspersing the primary diatonic pitches and chords with other pitches of the chromatic scale
glees	originating in England in the seventeenth century, a secular, unaccompanied composition for three or four (mostly unaccompanied) voices, largely homophonic (chordal), and intended as entertainment music. During the second half of the nineteenth century, many collegiate all-male singing societies formed in the United States adopting the name 'glee club'. Today, such ensembles (male and female) perform a wide range of repertoire

harmony	the simultaneous combination of notes, to produce chords
madrigal	a secular vocal music composition of the Renaissance and early Baroque eras
microtonal	a microtone being any interval smaller than a semitone
minor third	a musical interval that encompasses three half steps, or semitones
motet	a sacred choral composition in a language other than English (mostly Latin) dating back to the medieval era. Since the late fifteenth century, the term most commonly refers to a polyphonic setting of texts from the scriptures, often sung unaccompanied
oratorio	an extended, mostly accompanied musical setting of a typically sacred text. Musical elements closely resemble opera (arias, recitatives, choruses), though without costumes, scenery or action
plainsong	unaccompanied, monophonic melody associated with sacred Latin texts of the early Western church. Chants incorporate free rhythm corresponding to the accentuation of text
polyphony	music in two or more often independent parts, most closely identified with sacred music of the Renaissance
quarter tones	a pitch that is halfway between a semitone
SATB	acronym commonly used to identify an ensemble of high and low voices: soprano, alto, tenor, bass
sight-reading	the reading and performing of a piece of music or song in music notation that the performer has not seen before
sight-singing	reading and singing music at first sight
tempo, tempi	musical speed or pacing, often indicated by metronomic designations representing a particular number of beats per minute. Also common are descriptions of character such as *allegro, andante* etc.
tonic sol-fa	a technique for teaching sight-singing, invented by Sarah Ann Glover (1785–1867) of Norwich, England, and popularised by John Curwen, who adapted it from a number of earlier musical systems. Each degree of a scale is referred to by a syllable, e.g. do, re, mi
triad	a chord consisting of three notes

Notes

Introduction

1 This mainstream tradition was rooted in the vocal method called bel canto ('fine singing'), which was developed in Italian opera in the eighteenth century, and was particularly popular in the nineteenth century when Rossini favoured singers with a 'naturally beautiful voice that was even in tone throughout its full range [and] careful training that encouraged effortless delivery of highly florid music'. (O. Jander, *The New Grove Dictionary of Music and Musicians*, London: Macmillan, 1980). The bel canto sound is the preferred timbre for most Western-trained singers, while the method provides a foundation for a wide range of singing styles.

2 Philosopher and musician Dallas Willard reminded me of this emphatically in a conversation at the University of Southern California, March 1984.

3 Two outstanding examples are Bach's opening double chorus: *Come ye daughters, share my mourning,* the contralto aria, *Have mercy, Lord (Erbarme dich, mein Gott)*, and the famous chorale *Be near me, Lord.* The magnificent Barber and Ešenvalds pieces are sung *a cappella* as is Brumby's miniature written when he was 18 years old.

4 Peter L. Berger, *A Rumor of Angels: Modern Society and the Rediscovery of the Supernatural* (New York: Doubleday, 1969).

5 John Rutter, *The Importance of Choir* (blog, 31 March 2015), /blogs.jwpepper.com/index.php/john-rutter-the-importance-of-choir/

6 Elizabeth Kerr's review of Elizabeth Salmon's *Peter Godfrey: Father of New Zealand Choral Music* (Eastbourne, Wellington: Mākaro Press), in *New Zealand Books: A quarterly review*, 115 (Spring 2016).

7 John Mansfield Thomson, *The Oxford History of New Zealand Music* (Auckland: Oxford University Press, 1991), 91.

8 Quoting Adrienne Simpson and Peter Downes, *Southern Voices: International Opera Singers of New Zealand* (Auckland: Reed, 1992).

9 James Belich, *Paradise Reforged: A History of the New Zealanders, from the 1880s to the Year 2000* (Auckland: Penguin, 2001).

10 G. M. Byrnes, *The New Oxford History of New Zealand* (Melbourne: Oxford University Press, 2009). Philippa Mein Smith, *A Concise History of New Zealand*, 2nd edition (Cambridge: Cambridge University Press, 2012). Mein Smith mentions state patronage of the arts, an art gallery and visual artists, the formation of a national orchestra, 'a flowering of art that expressed Māori and Pacific identity', and a Māori film, but nothing about a prestigious 'Choir of the World' award of 13 years earlier, or choral singing's rise in popularity since the 1970s.

11 The only choral piece mentioned is a waiata with a melody not of New Zealand origin. It is perhaps understandable that the book, authored by Robert Hoskins, Dugal McKinnon, Norman Meehan and Allan Thomas, omitted the subject because of its specific intended use by senior secondary school students. Yet, it is one more publication that downplays the substantial presence of choral music in this country.

12 Peter Lineham, *Sunday Best: How the Church Shaped New Zealand and New Zealand Shaped the Church* (Auckland: Massey University Press, 2017).
13 Thomson, *Oxford History.*
14 W. L. Renwick, *Emblems of Identity* (Wellington: Department of Education, 1978, 1987).
15 G. M. Trevelyan, 'The Present Position of History', in *Clio, a Muse and Other Essays* (London: Longmans, Green & Co., 1913).

1: The heritage of Māori song and the birth of a new tradition

1 Radiocarbon dating related to human presence in Aotearoa points to first arrivals somewhere between 1210 and 1385 AD.
2 Rawinia Higgins and Arini Loader, 'Waiata tawhito — traditional Māori songs', Te Ara — the Encyclopedia of New Zealand, http://www.TeAra.govt.nz/en/waiata-tawhito-traditional-maori-songs (accessed 9 January 2018).
3 Sir Āpirana Ngata, *Ngā Mōteatea* (New Zealand Board of Māori Ethnological Research, 1928–29).
4 T. S. Kāretu, 'Māori Choral Music', *Dossier, International Choral Bulletin* (April 1996): 5.
5 Dr Mervyn McLean of Auckland University first notated the microtones of a significant number of mōteatea in *Traditional Songs of the Maori* (Auckland: Reed, 1975). Microtone intervals cannot be found on piano keyboards which are tuned to 12 semitones per octave.
6 Anne Salmond, *Between Worlds: Early Exchanges Between Maori and Europeans 1773–1815* (Auckland: Viking, 1997), 79.
7 *The Cambridge Companion to Choral Music*, ed. Andre de Quadros (Cambridge: Cambridge University Press, 2012), 179.
8 My argument is that the musical organisation was horizontal, not vertical; that the variant of the chant consisting of the third below and unisons was heterophony ('two slightly different versions of the same melody being performed at the same time'). Or, if not that, then a type of polyphonic stratification.
9 Quoted in Salmond, *Between Worlds*, 450.
10 Kāretu, 'Māori Choral Music', 6.
11 T. S. Kāretu, *Haka! The Dance of a Noble People* (Auckland: Reed, 1993).
12 Allen Curnow, 'Landfall in Unknown Seas', poem commissioned by the New Zealand Department of Internal Affairs to commemorate the 300th anniversary of Abel Tasman's arrival in New Zealand. Later, Douglas Lilburn wrote music for string orchestra to accompany the poem.
13 *Ngā Mōteatea, The Songs. Scattered Pieces from Many Canoe Areas. Part 1.* Collected by Sir Āpirana Ngata (Auckland: Auckland University Press, 2004), xxxvi.
14 Samuel Marsden, *The Origin and History of Missions*, Vol. 1 (Boston, Massachusetts, 1838), 579.
15 New Zealand was the fabled land of birds. Its biota was so strange that it would be dismissed as science fiction if the fossil record was not there to prove it. Some 70 species of birds were found nowhere else in the world.

2: Colonial music and choral beginnings

1 Quoted by Rosalind Halton, 'From Hailstones to Hallelujah: The First Handel Commemoration', in *A World of Popular Entertainments: An Edited Volume of Critical Essays,* eds Gillian Arrighi and Victor Emeljanow (Cambridge: Cambridge Scholars Publishing, 2012).
2 'Art of the United Kingdom', www.en.wikipedia.org
3 Jens Peter Larsen, 'The Development of Handelian Oratorio and *Messiah*', *Handel Studies, American Choral Review* (New York, 1972).
4 'Queen Victoria', www.biography.com/people/queen-victoria-9518355
5 Glees were three-part or four-part unaccompanied songs on convivial English texts, usually for male voices, but often including parts for ladies as guests.
6 Pip Howells, 'Regional cultural life — Early regional arts and culture', Te Ara — the Encyclopedia of New Zealand, http://www.TeAra.govt.nz/en/regional-cultural-life/page-1 (accessed 8 October 2017).

7 These included St John's Church in Christchurch, the Wellington Primitive Methodist Society, and Knox Presbyterian Church in Dunedin.
8 *Wellington Independent*, 18 July 1857.
9 *Wellington Independent*, 29 June 1853.
10 Guy E. Jansen, 'The History of School Music in New Zealand' (unpublished master's thesis, Victoria University of Wellington, 1966).
11 'General History', *An Encyclopedia of New Zealand,* ed. A. H. McLintock (Wellington: Government Printer, 1966).
12 John MacGibbon, *Piano in the Parlour* (Wellington: Ngaio Press, 2007).
13 Directing 11 singers with a baton, outdoors, is an unusual sight. Overbye, who was sometimes addressed as Professor Overbye, later served in the New Zealand Medical Corps in the First World War.
14 Adrienne Simpson, *Hallelujahs and History* (Auckland: Auckland Choral Society, 2005), 41–8; Betty Brooke, *Century of Music, 1855–1955: The Story of the First 100 Years of the Auckland Choral Society* (Auckland: Auckland Choral Society, 1955), 8.
15 John Mansfield Thomson, *The Oxford History of New Zealand Music* (Auckland: Oxford University Press, 1991).
16 Peter Barton, 'Choral Colonists', in New Zealand Choral Federation, *In Tune: The First 10 Years of the New Zealand Choral Federation* (Auckland: NZCF, 1995), 23.
17 Earthquakes have played havoc with the cathedral's structure. Hopefully current plans to save the main body of the cathedral will be successful, and the nave with its generous acoustics can be restored.
18 *Wanganui Herald* (II, 195, 16 January 1868).
19 J. Cuthbert Haddon, *Modern Musicians* (Boston: Le Roy Phillips, 1913), 257.
20 Ibid: 258.
21 Quoted by John Mansfield Thomson in a chapter in Shirley Tunnicliff, *Response to a Vision: The First Hundred Years of the Nelson School of Music* (Nelson: Nelson School of Music, 1994), 41.
22 Ibid: 40–1.
23 Ibid: 45.
24 Ibid: 52.
25 Jansen, 'The History of School Music in New Zealand', 3.
26 *Appendix to the Journals of the House of Representatives*, 1898 (Session E-1), 91.
27 S. P. Braatveld, 'A History of Music Education in New Zealand State Primary and Secondary Schools 1878–1989' (unpublished PhD thesis, University of Canterbury, Christchurch, 2002).

3: Visits by overseas choirs

1 Lynn Abbott and Doug Seroff, *Out of Sight: The Rise of African American Popular Music 1889–1895* (Jackson: University Press of Mississippi, 2002), 13.
2 *New Zealand Herald* (XLVII, 14560, 23 December 1910), 6.
3 Nadia Turbide, 'Charles Elbert Edwin Harriss: The McGill Years' (Master of Musical Arts thesis, McGill University, Montreal, 1976).
4 https://archive.org/stream/drhenrycowardpio00rodgiala/drhenrycowardpio00rodgiala_djvu.txt
5 Nick Strimple, *Choral Music in the Twentieth Century* (Portland, Oregon: Amadeus Press, 2002), 292.
6 Schola Cantorum concert review by H. P., *The Dominion* (2 December 1948).
7 At its height, the Sheffield Choir was probably the leading amateur chorus in England, and its world tour is still remembered as one of the most remarkable events in British choral history.
8 J. A. Rodgers, *The Pioneer Chorus-Master* (London: Ballantyne Press, 1911).
9 Meaning: to add an extra task to something already difficult. In Greek mythology, giants attempting to storm the Heavens piled Mount Pelion upon Mount Ossa.
10 Rodgers, *The Pioneer Chorus-Master*.

11 Coward was knighted in 1926 and died in 1944 aged 94. Today, very few in the choral community appear to have heard of him.
12 He had hoped to have rehearsals with every local choir taking part in tour concerts. *Evening Post* (26 July 1910), 2.
13 *New Zealand Herald* (XLVII, 14560, 23 December 1910), 6.
14 M. W. Leese, 'British Influence on New Zealand Choral Traditions' (unpublished doctoral dissertation, University of Illinois at Urbana-Champagne, Urbana, 2012), 43.
15 *The Press* (6 July 1911), 6.
16 *The Triad* 18, 3 (10 June 1911): 4.
17 *The Triad* 18, 5 (10 August 1911): 9, 10, 11.
18 Ibid: 11, 12.
19 Ibid: 4, 5.
20 Leese, 'British Influence', 43.
21 Christopher Fifield, *Ibbs and Tillett: The Rise and Fall of a Musical Empire* (Aldershot: Ashgate, 2005), 88–9.
22 Quoted by J. M. Thomson in a lecture on the Sheffield Choir, 1987 (Alexander Turnbull Library, Wellington audio tape, MTL MSC001 455).

4: Thirty turbulent years from 1914

1 Nancy Swarbrick, 'Choral music and choirs — The first century, 1840s to 1940s', Te Ara — the Encyclopedia of New Zealand, http://www.TeAra.govt.nz/en/choral-music-and-choirs/page-2 (accessed 17 April 2018).
2 Early members of the Christchurch 'Group' included Louise Henderson, Ngaio Marsh and Evelyn Page.
3 Ministry for Culture and Heritage, New Zealand History: https://nzhistory.govt.nz/culture/the-1920s/1929
4 In Leipzig he played second violin with the Gewandhaus Orchestra under such conductors as Brahms, Grieg, Tchaikovsky and Max Bruch.
5 Yuen Ching Lam, 'An Analytical Study of Alfred Hill's String Quartet No. 2' (Master of Arts thesis, University of Otago, Dunedin, 2006), 6.
6 Lam, 'An Analytical Study of Alfred Hill's String Quartet No. 2', 7.
7 J. M. Thomson, *Distant Music: The Life and Times of Alfred Hill 1870–1960* (Auckland & Melbourne: Oxford University Press, 1980/82).
8 Adrienne Simpson, *Hallelujahs and History* (Auckland: Auckland Choral Society, 2005), 73.
9 Ibid: 78.
10 Ibid: 82.
11 Ibid: 90.
12 Ibid: 95.
13 Paper by Michael Brown presented at 'New Horizons: New Zealand Folklore Symposium 2007', organised by The Stout Research Centre for New Zealand Studies, Victoria University of Wellington.
14 Nancy Swarbrick, 'Choral music and choirs — The first century, 1840s to 1940s', Te Ara — the Encyclopedia of New Zealand, http://www.TeAra.govt.nz/en/choral-music-and-choirs/page-2.
15 From a review by Alan Armstrong in *Te Ao Hou — The New World.*
16 'E Hara Te Waea' ('Love Never Dies') can be heard on the website: excavated shellac.com/category/new zealand
17 From AudioCulture (www.audioculture.co.nz).
18 M. Alexandratos, *The Discographer Magazine*, vol. 3, no. 6 (June 2016): 14.
19 M. Willyams, 'Singing Faith: A History of the Waiata Maori Choir, 1924–1938' (Master of Arts thesis, University of Otago, Dunedin, 2012).
20 Armstrong, review.
21 *Cultural Arts 1*, 1 (April 1937). It is not known how many other competitors there were!
22 *New Zealand Free Lance* (25 October 1939), 43.
23 Allan Thomas, 'Centennial Music', in *Creating a National Spirit: Celebrating New Zealand's Centennial* (Wellington: Victoria University, NZETC), 232.

24 Ibid: 241.
25 *New Zealand Listener* (16 August 1940), 17.
26 Robin Hyde, 'Journey from New Zealand', 1938.
27 P. Norman, *Douglas Lilburn: His Life and Music* (Christchurch: Canterbury University Press, 2006), 103, 104.
28 The pentatonic mode is one of the traditional styles in ancient Chinese music. Its five tones are the 1st, 2nd, 3rd, 5th and 6th degrees of the Western diatonic major scale, e.g., the black keys of a keyboard. Lilburn's use of this mode would have reminded the choirboys of Chinese compositions.

5: Significant choral leaders of the time

1 'Frail health forced Mr Parker to leave England', according to the editorial in the Wellington-based *Cultural Arts* 1, 1 (1937). In Christchurch his health still 'gave anxiety'.
2 John Mansfield Thomson, 'Parker, Robert', *Dictionary of New Zealand Biography*, first published in 1993. Te Ara — the Encyclopedia of New Zealand, https://teara.govt.nz/en/biographies/2p6/parker-robert (accessed 18 October 2018).
3 Ibid.
4 Parker's important contributions to the national Music Teachers' Registration Board are detailed in John Jennings, *New Zealand: A Jubilee History of the Music Teachers Registration Board of New Zealand* (Wellington: Music Teachers' Registration Board of New Zealand, 1978).
5 Thomson, 'Parker, Robert'.
6 *Cultural Arts* 1, 1 (1937): 1.
7 Judith White, 'White, Harold Temple', *Dictionary of New Zealand Biography*, first published in 1996. Te Ara — the Encyclopedia of New Zealand, https://teara.govt.nz/en/biographies/3w11/white-harold-temple (accessed 29 September 2018).
8 Ibid.
9 John Drummond, 'Galway, Victor Edward', *Dictionary of New Zealand Biography*, first published in 2000. Te Ara — the Encyclopedia of New Zealand, https://teara.govt.nz/en/biographies/5g3/galway-victor-edward (accessed 29 September 2018).
10 In 1948, as organising professor of music for the University of New Zealand, he vehemently disagreed with the marking standards at Victoria University College. Drummond, 'Galway, Victor Edward'.
11 Lin Saunders in 'Bradshaw, John Christopher', Te Ara — the Encyclopedia of New Zealand, A. H. McLintock, 1966. Saunders, who became music critic of the *New Zealand Herald* for 53 years from 1940, was regarded as one of New Zealand's most respected music commentators, particularly on choral performances.
12 *The Press* quoted in F. K. Tucker, *J. C. Bradshaw, A Memoir* (Christchurch: Caxton Press, 1955).
13 Philip Norman, compiler, *John Ritchie at Ninety* (Wellington: Nota Bene, 2011).
14 Nancy Swarbrick, 'Choral music and choirs — The first century, 1840s to 1940s', Te Ara — the Encyclopedia of New Zealand, http://www.TeAra.govt.nz/en/choral-music-and-choirs/page-2 (accessed 3 February 2018).
15 Frederick Page, *A Musician's Journal, 1905–1983*, ed. and arr. J. M. Thomson and Janet Paul (Dunedin: John McIndoe, 1986), 43. The work was repeated the following year.
16 *Cultural Arts* 1, 4 (21 July 1937): 2.
17 From an interview with Jack Body.
18 JAVS Online, 2003, http://violaspace.com/avs/ks/site/JAVS%20Online/Summer%202003/Balling/Balling.htm.
19 Because of anti-German sentiment during the First World War, the name of the Auckland Liedertafel was changed, and in 1926, with a royal charter, it became known as the Royal Auckland Male Choir.
20 Luscombe's compositions were among works by New Zealand resident composers performed during the Centennial celebrations. Another was Stanley Oliver's *A Delightsome Land*. Subsequently, Luscombe won the Philip Neill Composition Prize, and had two orchestral works performed by the National Orchestra conducted by the composer.

21 Natzke, a 27-year-old bass, one-time blacksmith from Freemans Bay, Auckland, had already made a big impression here and in England. Trinity College, London, had granted him a full scholarship when Anderson Tyrer cabled a recommendation to the College: 'the finest voice I have ever heard'.
22 Guy E. Jansen, 'The History of School Music in New Zealand' (unpublished Master of Arts thesis, Victoria University of Wellington, Wellington, 1966), 46.
23 Ibid: 55.
24 Ibid: 47.

6: Bonanzas unheralded, unsung, 1925–45

1 Guy E. Jansen, 'The History of School Music in New Zealand' (unpublished Master of Arts thesis, Victoria University of Wellington, Wellington, 1966), 61.
2 Ibid: 83.
3 Up to 80,000 copies of pupils' booklets of broadcast songs were issued by Radio New Zealand each year. The broadcasts continued for half a century from 1932.
4 Professor of Education at Victoria University, Colin Bailey, once remarked to me that this rather delicate, sensitive man, frustrated by lack of support for his idealistic programme, went to California and there died of a broken heart. There is still a mystery about Tayler's death when he was only 46.
5 Hollinrake's Department of Music soon became the country's largest. Graduates included choral leaders H. C. Luscombe and Ronald Dellow. Richard Hoffmann became an amanuensis to Arnold Schönberg; Layton Ring was an internationally recognised early music expert; and Ossie Cheesman, arranger, composer, concert pianist, conductor and leading figure in light music, had a popular choral group, the Cheesman Singers, which contributed to television programmes in the 1960s.
6 Roger Hollinrake, *The Life and Times of Horace Hollinrake 1904–1955* (Oxford: Mayfield Press, 2009), 1.
7 Handel's 'Lascia ch'io pianga' is followed by 'The Lass with the Delicate Air', Schumann's 'Merry Peasant' rubs shoulders with three waiata, and the book is closed out with a two-part Mozart song, and a page of 12 rounds.
8 A setting of George Herbert's poem.
9 David Grace in Hollinrake, *The Life and Times,* 33.
10 Conducting colleagues in the festivals included the imaginative teacher Ramsay Howie.
11 Quoted in Hollinrake, *The Life and Times,* 50.
12 Vernon Griffiths, *An Experiment in School Music-making* (Wellington: NZCER, 1941).
13 In Griffiths' opinion, the London committee which had appointed him had sought a man whose beliefs were in sympathy with those of the likes of Walford Davies, Cecil Sharp and Gustav Holst: someone who believed that culture is rooted in everyday life and enshrined in folk song and dance, who believed in the musical heritage of the British race, and who was willing to work among the 'common' people (taped interview with John Ritchie, Ngā Taonga Sound and Vision, reference number 321491, 1960).
14 In 1942, Callaway was appointed head of music at Dunedin Tech when Griffiths left for Christchurch. After overseas studies, including conducting at the Royal Academy, he returned to the school as musical director in 1949 before being appointed reader at the University of Western Australia in 1953.
15 An indication of the calibre of assembly singing at Nelson College is provided on tracks of *A School Makes Music — Nelson College,* LP recording MA-2 (A. H. & A. W. Reed), e.g. 'Firmly I Believe and Truly' to the tune 'Stuttgart', with organist Barrington Brinson, a pupil at the school.
16 Letter to Callaway, 15 November 1954. Footnote 67 in Rachael M. Hawkey, 'Vernon Griffiths (1894–1985): His Life and Philosophy of Music Education as Demonstrated in his Collected Papers' (PhD thesis, University of Canterbury, Christchurch, 1993).
17 Griffiths and Callaway, and other prominent school principals and music teachers, pushed the Education Department to pay more attention to the successful Dunedin Tech scheme. According to Walter Harris, supervisor of teaching aids in the Department from 1941, the Griffiths

Scheme was not taken up by the Department because of the expenses involved in the training of teachers, provision of instruments and appointment of a national supervisor of music. Further, it seemed that there was little interest among principals at the post-primary level to develop music in their schools. (Letter from Harris, 7 July 1953, Hawkey, 'Vernon Griffiths', 69, Vernon Griffiths Papers 22:10.) The seminal Thomas Report in 1944 was enthusiastic about developing secondary school music, and music teacher training might have been seen as a timely development. But Griffiths' national 'blueprint' was not officially favoured, and it is also possible that a number of departmental inspectors had little personal interest in music.

18 *The Pupil's Own Song Reader: Twenty-five Songs* (Christchurch: Whitcombe & Tombs Ltd, 1943), No. 6 and inside cover.

19 Other repertoire featured melodies by Dowland, J. S. Bach, Beethoven, Haydn, Schubert, Schumann, Chopin and Brahms and British folk tunes.

20 Jenner also adjudicated and composed, and for many years was music critic for the *The Press*. He did not seek honours or a high personal profile but was elected a Fellow of the Royal Academy of Music in 1950 and was made an MBE in 1962.

21 Thomas Garland had made his broadcasting debut in 1923 on 1YA in Auckland. At that early stage of public broadcasting he ran a weekly children's session under the name 'Uncle Tom' and organised many of the station's religious broadcasts. He became a licensed minister in 1934.

22 Bill (William) Renwick and his family had a high regard for Scrimgeour. In a fascinating book, *Scrim, the Man with a Mike* (Wellington: Victoria University Press, 2011), Renwick tells of his parents listening to the Friendly Road programme regularly and how he enjoyed hearing its theme tune, 'The Stranger of Galilee', week after week through the bedroom door. 'The Old Rugged Cross', 'The Angelus' and 'Finlandia' were other pieces in the choir's repertoire.

23 Alexander Turnbull Library: Eph-A-Radio-1933-01.

24 The broadcasting of Parliament was Michael Joseph Savage's highest priority in radio broadcasting.

25 These included Yvonne Hitchings in 1960 and Joan Stevens in August 1963 and later Robert Matthews, Val Drew and Wilbur Manins.

26 As described by Judith Tait, a retired teacher who vividly remembers Young's broadcast programmes. S. Braatveld (PhD dissertation, University of Canterbury, Christchurch), 247.

27 The New Zealand Broadcasting Service, Educational Broadcasts to Schools, 1940: 119.

28 S. Braatveld, PhD dissertation, 246.

29 Another in the photo is Patricia Murray (née North) who has been deputy conductor of the Festival Singers, conductor of the Capital Choir, a member of four other choirs, and a choral activist.

30 S. Braatveld, PhD dissertation, 249.

31 Ibid: 10.

32 *The Dominion*, 28 December 1938.

33 *New Zealand Herald*, 11 March 1937.

34 *The Dominion*, 28 December 1938.

35 *The Dominion*, 2 June 1939.

36 *New Zealand Free Lance*, 25 October 1939.

37 Foundation members who stayed included Molly Atkinson, Olga Burton, Muriel Hitchings, Owen Bonifant, Harry Brusey, Roy Hill and B. R. Lankshear. Later recruits, many of whom became leading musicians, included Merle Gamble, Sybil Phillips, Joan Wood, Mattie Fearnley, Gwyneth Brown, Susan Rhind, E. K. Braybrooke, Grahame Lilly, John Dellow, Joe Miller, Peter Nisbet and Hal Radford.

38 Repertoire, for their first public appearance after nearly eight months of rehearsals, ranged from Dowland to Vaughan Williams, with Holst's difficult 'Ode on a Grecian Urn' judged to be one of the treasures of the evening.

39 *Evening Post*, 29 November 1955.

40 'Peace In Our Time', review in the *Evening Post*, 2 June 1939.

41 Ibid.

42 Tanya Buchdahl Tintner, *Out of Time: The Vexed Life of Georg Tintner* (Perth: University of Western Australia Press, 2011), 41.

43 Ibid: 40.
44 Ibid: 45.
45 Tintner's compositions included fugues, songs, a sonata for violin and piano, and he started an opera. Five years later he completed a six-voice choral work and an overture for full orchestra.

7: After the Second World War: A new world beginning

1 I am indebted to Nancy M. Taylor, 'The Arts Survive', in *The Home Front Volume II* (Wellington: Historical Publications Branch, Department of Internal Affairs, 1986) for much of the coverage of this section.
2 Taylor, 'The Arts Survive', 1215.
3 Rachel Barrowman, *A Popular Vision: The Arts and the Left in New Zealand 1930–1950* (Wellington: NZETC/Victoria University Press, 1991), 220.
4 David Walsh, 'A Survey of Orchestral Activity in New Zealand' (unpublished thesis), quoted in Taylor, 'The Arts Survive', 67, 68.
5 Taylor, 'The Arts Survive', 1213.
6 Allan Thomas, *Music is Where You Find It: Music in the Town of Hawera, 1946 — an Historical Ethnography* (Music Books, 2004). Louis Fox's Methodist choir sang hymns and short excerpts of Mozart, Bach and Gounod; the Presbyterian choir might do a cantata at Easter and a section of *Messiah* at Christmas. H. C. A. Fox had been trained in 'the heartland of brass banding in Yorkshire'.
7 F. L. W. Wood, *Understanding New Zealand* (New York: Coward-McCann Inc., 1944), 156–7. Wood was professor of history at Victoria University from 1935 to 1969.
8 Wood, *Understanding New Zealand*, revised edition as *This New Zealand* (Hamilton: Paul's Book Arcade, 1952), 126.
9 Ibid.
10 In February 1943, the *New Zealand Listener* made inquiries into the effects of the war on amateur musical societies.
11 *New Zealand Listener*, 17 April 1942, 12.
12 The purpose of the Thomas Committee, appointed by the Minister of Education, was to make recommendations regarding the choice of subjects for the schools. Fortunately, the committee was aware of the findings of the English Spens Report (1938) that had carefully considered the place of music and the arts in the curriculum.
13 Aided by the provision of instrumental tuition in schools, this was a period of a rapid catching up by instrumental music. It could be argued that for the next 30 or more years instrumental music overtook choral music-making in popularity and public esteem.
14 Director of Education Dr Clarence Beeby wasn't a music enthusiast, and he told Professor Fred Page that he considered private music teachers were already doing a great deal for music, but that the arts and crafts had had no such support (from conversation between Page and the author, 1967). At this distance it is impossible to say whether a music appointment around 1946 might have triggered new growth in choral singing.
15 Joy Tonks, *The New Zealand Symphony Orchestra, The First Forty Years* (Auckland: Reed Methuen, 1986), 115 ff.
16 Walden-Mills' leader in the auditioning work was Ashley Heenan, musical assistant to several conductors of the New Zealand Symphony Orchestra, a dominant personality and keen promoter of the National Youth Orchestra. Later he was conductor and musical director of that youth orchestra for 10 years.
17 Kapa haka is a high-energy combination of dance, song (unison and in harmony), body actions, rhythm and harmony that tells a story — historical or contemporary — in a precisely choreographed manner. It requires years of rehearsal and fitness training.
18 Authority (mana) is given to different tribes (iwi) to host Te Matatini. The University of Waikato is a strategic partner in the organisation.
19 According to Sir Tīmoti Kāretu, whakaeke and whakawātea can be sung, chanted or be in the form of a haka or ngeri (short haka with no set movements). Some teams tend to combine them all in both whakaeke and whakawātea, while some prefer to sing instead.

8: The main cities take centre stage

1 The male choir was founded by Samuel Moyle. Subsequent conductors included Jesse Timson (25 years), Dr Victor Galway (17 years), singing teacher Ernest Drake, Gilmore McConnell, voice specialist Val Drew (a record 26 years), Harry Madden, and composer Richard Madden (from 2001).

2 Jenny Burchell, interview with Charmian Smith (www.odt.co.nz/entertainment/arts/highs-lows), 17 October 2013.

3 Peter Adams, commenting on the choir's 'extremely high standards', pointed to their success with Bach's *Christmas Oratorio*, Francis Poulenc's *Gloria* and Stravinsky's *Symphony of Psalms*. Subsequent conductors of the choir included Peter Warwick, Raymond White and Peter Adams.

4 Peter Adams, in *New Oxford Companion to Music*, ed. Denis Arnold (Oxford/New York: Oxford University Press, 1983), 113. Donald Cullington succeeded Byars and in 1978 instituted a Southern Cathedrals' Choir Festival for the three cathedrals still maintaining the tradition of male choirs.

5 Madden's evergreen carol, 'I Sing of a Maiden', has enjoyed widespread national and international success.

6 Peter Lineham, *Sunday Best: How the Church Shaped New Zealand and New Zealand Shaped the Church* (Auckland: Massey University Press, 2017), 151.

7 Griffiths' arrangements gave a certain gravitas to choral singing in many secondary schools. In 'bass-tune' verses, three free parts were added above the tune. For adolescent singers, Griffiths suggested light forward tone, humming, and vocalising on vowel sounds. He believed that every singer should be able to see the printed music. Much of the music had already been sung successfully at the Dunedin Technical College.

8 *Dominion Song Book No 8: Twelve Well Known Songs* (Christchurch: Whitcombe & Tombs Ltd, n.d.) — resilient arrangements to be sung confidently by staff and students alike. See Rachael M. Hawkey, 'Vernon Griffiths (1894–1985): His Life and Philosophy of Music Education as Demonstrated in his Collected Papers' (PhD thesis, University of Canterbury, Christchurch, 1993).

9 One exception is his work for mixed-voice choir and brass band: *Peace and War* (words: Bernard O'Brien).

10 Griffiths had contributed enormously to the musical life of Christchurch through organising the first children's music classes in 1929. When revived by Robert (Bob) Perks, they grew to over 1000 participants and included a Saturday morning choir.

11 Not particularly known as a choral composer, Ritchie wrote over 80 choral pieces or compositions involving a choir, including a 'Kyrie' and a 'Gloria' from the Latin Mass. A number of pieces were for male voice choir.

12 Other recordings followed in the series: the Choir of St Mary's Cathedral, Auckland (Peter Godfrey) and Durham Street Methodist Church Choir (Wallace Woodley).

13 For example, Holst's *The Hymn of Jesus,* Vaughan Williams' *Serenade to Music*, Berlioz' *Childhood of Christ* and Purcell's *Come Ye Sons of Art*.

14 From conversation with Russell Kent, 29 December 2016, and from John M. Jennings, *Song of the Music Makers* (Christchurch: University of Canterbury, 1989). The irony of this situation is that George Martin formed and led the Christchurch Junior Choral Society for many years, influencing for good hundreds of choral singers who were all loyal citizens. I worked with Martin and found that this imposing musical figure was also humble, respected and socially responsible.

15 Newson, in directing the festival for 21 years, teaching at the training college and giving leadership in music education politics, contributed much to generations of primary school-age choristers.

16 This seven-minute memorial to the victims of the Holocaust, written in 1947 for narrator, men's chorus and symphony orchestra, was a radical choice of Hawkey's because of the use of 12-tone rows in the composition.

17 Included were prominent conductors Guyon Wells (Hamilton Civic Choir), Ernie Williams (Carter Chorale, Rotorua), Ian Menzies (New Plymouth City Choir), Don McIvor (Palmerston

North Choral Society), Geoff Thorpe (Christchurch Liederkränzchen) and Janet Christie (Southland Choral Society).

18 *The Dominion*, 2 December 1948.

19 *New Zealand Arts Year Book* (1950).

20 *The Dominion*, 19 November 1951.

21 Ibid.

22 Oliver was also very influential as chairman of the Music Teachers' Registration Board for 10 years which operated by Act of Parliament (the first country in the world to have such a system), and for a longer time was president of the Federation of Societies of Registered Music Teachers of New Zealand.

23 *Evening Post*, 15 August 1962.

24 I write as a humble former player, coach and referee of lower-grade rugby union and fan of the All Blacks. The book was choir accompanist Clement Howe's compilation: *Schola Cantorum, Fifteen Years of Musical Adventuring, 1936–1950* (Wellington: Wright & Carman, 1951).

25 *Southern Cross*, 2 December 1948.

26 *Auckland Star*, 11 June 1951.

27 Ibid.

28 The choir was the first New Zealand musical organisation to sing on the *BBC Third Programme*.

29 *Evening Post*, 15 August 1960.

30 Plaudits for Oliver's spectacular results continued to come. Malcolm Rickard, after returning from hearing many English choirs in 1955, ranked the Schola higher than the London Bach Choir under Paul Steinitz. Simon Tipping, *Orpheus: Portrait of a Choir* (Palmerston North: Dunmore Press, 2002), 17.

31 Tipping, *Orpheus,* 5.

32 Brusey was an efficient and admired musician. In 1955, when he was director of music at St James' Anglican Church, Lower Hutt, and deputy conductor of both the Royal Wellington Choral Union and the Schola Cantorum, he organised 13 other Wellington choirs to sing the Beethoven Ninth with the Orpheus Choir and the National Orchestra under James Robertson. This was the Orpheus' first of over 18 performances of the work.

33 Tipping, *Orpheus,* 94.

34 As a student at Victoria University, Hills had his first taste of conducting with the university Glee Club. A violinist, he took music credits with Tom Young at Wellington Teachers' College and became deputy conductor of the college choir. He taught music at Hutt Valley High School and later was appointed deputy principal, and 'spent 28 winters coaching a rugby team'. After he retired from the Orpheus, he became a member of the St James' Church choir.

35 James Shelley, 'Annual Report of the New Zealand Broadcasting Service (1946–47)', *Appendix to the Journals of the House of Representatives*, 1947, Session I, F-03.

36 The *Evening Post* listed all the choir's repertoire for over three years. While it featured many madrigals, glees and English part-songs, the repertoire ranged widely, from Beethoven's 'Creation's Hymn' and a chorus from Verdi's *Aida*, to the 'Eriskay Love Lilt', 'The Road to Mandalay' and 'London Song', which 'proved to be a topical hit, reflecting the spirit of the well-bombed city'. The accompanist was John Randall.

37 Oliver was appointed choirmaster at St Mary's after Fernie's death. Awarded a QSM for his 20 years' work with Cantoris and the National Early Music Schools, he is a prominent conductor, singer, viol player and musical entrepreneur. Organ student Allen James, who studied with Fernie, later became organist at the La Chapelle Royale Protestante de Bruxelles, and professor at the Conservatoire Royal de Mons. Other organ students included Rosemary Collier and Nicolas Kynaston who had been a choirboy at Westminster.

38 Kiwi Records LD-5, Wellington; album notes and direction by Fernie. Volume II followed.

39 After the first rehearsal, Fernie was heard to remark, 'Never heard such awful singing in my life.' Angela Ballara, unpublished biography of Maxwell Fernie (1990), 40.

40 Ibid: 40.

41 The Gramophone Newsletter, https://www.gramophone.co.uk/review/rachmaninov-all-night-vigil.

42 Ballara, unpublished biography, 43–4.
43 *New Zealand Listener*, 29 January 1983.
44 L. Taylor, article for Maxwell Fernie Trust (www.maxwellfernietrust.com).
45 Fernie was elected an Associate of the Royal Academy of Music and a Fellow of the Royal College of Organists, and was awarded an OBE and the Papal Cross pro Ecclesia et Pontiface. Wellington City organist for 27 years, he was a teacher of organ and singing at Victoria University. I was honoured and fascinated to be a voice student of his in 1968.
46 Trust Records, http://www.trustcds.com/php/artist.php?ID=20
47 Roger Hollinrake, *The Life and Times of Horace Hollinrake 1904–1955* (Oxford: Mayfield Press, 2009).
48 Ibid: 62: 9:6.
49 Ibid., 83.
50 Interview by Tanya Buchdahl Tintner, 26 October 2004 (*Out of Time: The Vexed Life of Georg Tintner*, Perth, WA: University of Western Australia Press, 2011), 102.
51 *New Zealand Herald*, 15 October 1953.
52 Betty Brooke, *Century of Music, 1855–1955: The Story of the First 100 Years of the Auckland Choral Society* (Auckland: Auckland Choral Society, 1955), 8.
53 Adrienne Simpson, *Hallelujahs and History* (Auckland: Auckland Choral Society, 2005), 112.
54 John Hopkins with William Cottam, *The Point of the Baton: Memoir of a Conductor* (Melbourne: Lyrebird Press, 2009), 75.
55 Desmond Mahoney, *Auckland Star*, 14 September 1961.
56 *Auckland Star*, 13 October 1960.
57 *Auckland Star*, 14 September 1961.
58 During the Second World War Godfrey had been a captain in the King's Rifles, returning to Cambridge after the war to continue his studies as the John Stewart Scholar in Sacred Music.
59 In Elizabeth Salmon's oral history: *Peter Godfrey: Father of New Zealand Choral Music* (Wellington: Mākaro Press, 2015), 217.

9: The worth of investing in young people, 1966–86

1 The 7-inch reel-to-reel tape playing at 7.5 ips is held by Ngā Taonga Sound and Vision, Wellington.
2 Madrigals by Campion, Ford, Dowland, Orlando Gibbons and Pilkington, and part songs by Mátyás Seiber, were performed.
3 The programme consisted of three choruses from Handel's *Samson*, Vivaldi's popular *Gloria*, an eight-part *Jubilate Deo* by sixteenth-century Venetian composer Giovanni Gabrieli and brackets of madrigals sung by three mini-choirs.
4 Some people thought that the Wesley event was Rickard's concert, but in fact Walden-Mills and Rickard shared the conducting of the combined choir works. By not putting his own name on the printed programme under 'National Holiday Choral Course for Secondary Schools' as the choir's director, Walden-Mills unwittingly gave Malcolm Rickard the top billing. Madrigal group conductors were Barry Hogan, HOD Music at Pukekohe High School, Noel Lynch from Onslow College and Walden-Mills.
5 These were conducted by leading music educators Max Stewart, Fleur Stark, Elizabeth Mintz (Kerr), David Wood and Laughton Pattrick.
6 I was on a Winston Churchill Travelling Fellowship during which I heard, as well as the Durham choir, David Willcocks' Bach Choir in London, and in Montreux, the award-winning Tapiola Children's Choir (conductor: Erkki Pohjola) and Eric Ericson conducting music by Frank Martin, Lidholm and Ligeti.
7 Later, I proposed a Board of Reference to tap into professional-level advice. The task of chairing the board was split between Renwick and me. The members of the board, Spencer Russell, Helen Young, Peter Nisbet and Robert Field-Dodgson, met for the first time about two weeks before the choir's first rehearsals.
8 Mr Wellington later became a fan of the choir, speaking warmly at the farewell concert in Auckland in July 1982.
9 Radio New Zealand were particularly helpful with news releases and interviews. Beverley

Wakem, Controller of Programmes, had promised the same kind of support as given to the Youth Orchestra and the Music Federation's schools' contest.

10 A rather unwieldy but intriguing course orchestra was formed for a session in the first week of rehearsals.

11 Many choirs are vexed by choir uniform issues, sometimes long-running disagreements threatening to tear the fabric of a group's goodwill. No such serious problems occurred under the strong, wise and gentle leadership of NYC costumiers like Marjorie Charlton and her teams.

12 From those arriving on that first day, five were still in the choir nine years later: Sarah Castle, Juliet Dreaver, Ewen Griffiths, Nicola Jansen and Martin Snell. Sectional tutors were Brigid McLafferty, Elizabeth Beverley (Salmon), Roy Tankersley, Simon Tipping and David Wood; the accompanists were Rae de Lisle, Barry Nalder and John Hendren.

13 Before taking up a scholarship at York University, Christopher Norton had been an award-winning pianist, an outstanding composer-in-schools and, from 1976 to 1978, associate conductor of the Festival Singers of Wellington. Sounz (the New Zealand Music Centre) lists his 15-minute work for solo voices, semi-chorus and SATB choir as being of 'advanced difficulty'.

14 If the third vibrated, it meant that singers were pitching the note slightly differently.

15 It has been fashionable to claim that baroque music cannot be sung in a sufficiently light, articulated fashion by very large choirs. However, Willcocks' rhythmic sense and musical intelligence enabled him to train such choristers to perform successfully the difficult, fast semiquaver runs in the final choruses of Handel's *Dixit Dominus*, as well as make Bach's *Singet dem Herrn* dance.

16 There's a fascinating account of a vivid Mick Jagger impression in the oral history of Willcocks by William Owen, *A Life in Music: Conversations with Sir David Willcocks and Friends* (New York and Oxford: Oxford University Press, 2008), 216. Marianne Faithful and Jagger had just finished some recording sessions with the Bach Choir. The famous maestro's jiving and singing impersonation of the rock star was said to be extraordinary.

17 Schütz studied under one of Italy's greatest composers, Giovanni Gabrieli, and then under Claudio Monteverdi. Later, J. S. Bach borrowed some of his methods.

18 I had promoted this Tippett work partly because of its use of the five spirituals. I thought that because they had arisen within a folk culture, the spirituals would appeal to many in the choir, members having grown up in the time of the modern folk music movement.

19 Post-1980, having Sir David Willcocks back in England vouching for the good standard of the National Youth Choir was obviously a factor in the choir receiving exciting invitations for the 1982 tour. That a British Youth Choir was formed quite soon after his return is a tribute to how impressed he was with the New Zealand version of youth choirs.

20 It has been performed only twice since — late on the choir's 1982 European tour.

21 Simon Tipping, *Choir of the World* (Palmerston North: Dunmore Press, 2002), 33, 34.

22 Hamilton's *Lux Aeterna* and *Stabat Mater*.

23 The Choir of King's College Cambridge, http://www.kings.cam.ac.uk/choir/about/history.html.

24 Peter Godfrey is the only person to have been a chorister, choral scholar and director of music at King's College, Cambridge since the fifteenth century.

25 Three-time visitor to New Zealand, the conductor Simon Halsey wrote of Godfrey's sojourn at King's, that they all 'felt secure with Peter because we knew he was making music for the right reasons — for the glory of God, in daily services. I learned a great deal from his integrity'. Elizabeth Salmon, *Peter Godfrey: Father of New Zealand Choral Music* (Eastbourne, Wellington: Mākaro Press), 137.

26 It was very unfortunate that recording equipment was not available for the Wells concert early in the tour because the choir responded beautifully to the acoustics and the magnificence of the building.

27 Malcolm Seymour, *Wells Journal*, 29 July 1982.

28 William Renwick, ed., *Creating a National Spirit: Celebrating New Zealand's Centennial* (Wellington: Victoria University Press, 2004), 20.

29 'Forever Tuesday Morning' (Andrew Fagan and the Mockers) arranged by Nicola Jansen for mixed choir and backing group. Helen Reddy, sister of Tim Reddy, a member of the Mockers, was a member of the course. At the time of writing, the original song is still heard on national radio. Roger Stevenson was the associate conductor.

30 Contrary to more recently expressed views, the new choir was not conceived as a training ground for the National Youth Choir.
31 A number of these later contributed substantially to the upswing of choral music in the country's towns and cities. They included Jacqui Coats, Katherine Hodge, Joanne Hodgson, Igelese Ete and Greg Neil.
32 Peter Boag, whose passions were maths and music, had possibly discussed it with his wife, Elisabeth, who had been a member of the Dorian and Phoenix choirs. She has said that 'we shared ideas (except Plato's notion that music is an even higher form of knowledge than mathematics)'. Email correspondence, 22 November 2018.
33 In later years, the music staff at schools attended by Youth Choir or Secondary Students Choir members were advised that the new vocal tuition provision was implemented with the national choirs and holiday course participants in mind, but, also, that any student was eligible to receive tuition — even if not in a school choir.
34 An itinerant was a peripatetic tutor, either full-time or part-time, using hours allocated to the schools visited. This flexible scheme allowed even small rural schools to employ voice teachers — if they were available. The vocal part of the scheme was subsequently implemented in parts of Queensland.
35 By the end of 1978, 45 Tawa College students were learning voice under this scheme.
36 Soloists such as Anthea Moller, Roger Wilson and Denise Wilson were employed as tutors.
37 Stacia Gregson, Nancy Mitchell, Roy Tankersley and John Hendren, along with Madalene Bowers from within the Department of Education.
38 These were the accommodation officer, Heather Jones, and sectional tutors: Daryn Edmundson, Elizabeth Curtis, Jenny Calder, along with Heather Keith, who also acted as registrar.
39 See Simon Tipping's comprehensive book on the history of the National Youth Choir from 1979 to 1999: *Choir of the World* (Palmerston North: Dunmore Press, 2002), for the names of many sponsors, experienced advisers and other supporters who were important to its development.
40 The Bank of New South Wales changed its name to Westpac in 1982.
41 Viennese émigré Arthur Hilton and New Zealander Joan Kerr were founders of the contest. It has a long list of talented alumni, including pianist Michael Houstoun, John Chen and former New Zealand String Quartet violinist Wilma Smith.
42 Elisabeth Airey, born and educated in Wellington, remained with the Music Federation until 1997, including a lengthy period as general manager after Arthur Hilton died.
43 John Mansfield Thomson, *Into a New Key: Origins and History of the Chamber Music Federation of New Zealand, 1950–1982* (Dunedin: John McIndoe Ltd, 1985), 8, 138.
44 Page 3 of Minutes: Wellington Cathedral Choir Room, 2 p.m., 8 December 1985. Margaret Cull, Peter Godfrey, David Wood, John Knox, Guy Jansen, Peggy Haworth and Patricia Murray were other members of this group of 27.
45 Letter from the Music Federation's Education Services Manager to Dr G. E. Jansen, Curriculum Officer (Music), Department of Education, 19 November 1986.

10: The perplexing question of conductor training

1 William Owen, ed., *A Life in Music: Conversations with Sir David Willcocks and Friends* (Oxford and New York: Oxford University Press, 2008), 10, 34, 35, 38, 39, 41, 42, 72, 74.
2 Ibid: 267.
3 Ibid: 241, 242. His stance was the same all his life. He said that he didn't think he'd learned anything from books on conducting, but 'a great deal by watching people'.
4 Ibid: 241, 242. Willcocks is correct about Toscanini's lack of lessons. However, he omits to mention the legend's photographic memory, a phenomenal ear for orchestral detail and sonority, and a brilliant intensity that made him one of the greatest conductors of all time. Toscanini's career began one evening when in an opera orchestra as a teenage cellist with no conducting experience, he was persuaded to step in as conductor of *Aida*. He led a magnificent performance completely from memory. Quoting the stunningly exceptional case of Toscanini doesn't help Willcocks' argument.

5 New Zealand Choral Federation, *In Tune: The First 10 Years of the New Zealand Choral Federation* (Auckland: NZCF, 1995), 12.
6 *New Zealand Herald*, natlib.govt.nz/records/307198477
7 Mary Crowe and John Rosser, National Youth Choir members at the time, took part in the class. The music used was *Sing in Harmony*, a four-part a cappella collection from various periods of music history — appropriately accessible and challenging literature for singers and conductors launching a serious endeavour.
8 Among those who have completed postgraduate work with Grylls are Tim Carpenter, Naomi Chye (Singapore), Lachlan Craig, Megan Flint, Nick Forbes, Rowan Johnston, David Squire, Andrew Withington, and others on a more casual basis. Now Professional Teaching Fellow and vocal coach at the School of Music, Robert Wiremu studied at Victoria University, the University of Auckland and Queensland Conservatory of Music. Along with collaborative work with Dame Kiri Te Kanawa, Simon O'Neill and others, Wiremu has been artistic director of the V8 Vocal Ensemble, training the group for two performances of Berio's *Sinfonia* with James Judd and the NZSO. He was formerly voice clinician for the New Zealand Youth Choir and Voices New Zealand Chamber Choir.
9 'Karen Grylls — a personal perspective', *In Tune,* 14.

11: We're all going on a summer holiday: Conductor training in action

1 Larry Livingstone, formerly Professor of Conducting, and Music Director of the University of Southern California orchestras, has succinct and useful comments on this in a 2007 YouTube video entitled *Conducting Philosophies* (https://www.youtube.com/watch?v=pRJKcxcVC7g).
2 The prestigious music school drew many fine students from throughout the United States. Some of those in my classes were Mack Willberg, now conductor of the Mormon Tabernacle Choir and Orchestra, and a leading choral arranger; Professor Jerry Blackstone, director of choirs and chair of the conducting department at the University of Michigan for 30 years to 2018; and Jo-Michael Scheibe, currently Professor of Choral and Sacred Music at USC.
3 The USC choral programme was built by Dr Charles Hirt from 1941 to 1976. USC was the only school that I could find which offered all my subjects in depth: conducting (both choral and orchestral), choral literature, choral arranging (with distinguished American composer Morten Lauridsen), vocal tuition and vocal pedagogy, musicology, music education and church music. I developed great respect for the six searching preliminary exams that I had to pass, including theory, harmony and American-style analysis. Other bonuses were having Dallas Willard, director of the USC Philosophy Faculty, as one of the assessors of my dissertation; visits from eminent choral figures such as Roger Wagner and Paul Salamunovich; and the vibrant cultural life of LA. The total fees and expenses incurred in attending this private university were around a quarter of a million dollars in today's terms, but it was a worthwhile investment.
4 The 24 included Elise Christensen (later Bradley), Masterton; Cherie-Ann Stayner, Nelson; and several ex-National Youth Choir members: Susan Raine, Tom and Peter Rainey, Stephen Rowe and Stephen Rowley. James Allington, later to become conductor of successful Wellington College choirs and an assistant with the National Youth Choir, went to Australia, where he became director of music at elite private schools, Barker College and The Scots College in Sydney, and is now director of music at the NSW Department of Education and Communities.
5 As part of a busy academic and entrepreneurial life, Faye Dumont had formed the Melbourne Youth Choir, taking the group to France in 1978 where, in Paris, they sang Duruflé's *Requiem* to the elderly composer. She then planned a mind-boggling travelling pageant of 7200 children for Prince Charles and Lady Diana, who were visiting Melbourne later in the year. The Australia-New Zealand Foundation funded Dumont's return travel to the summer school.
6 Peter Godfrey said of himself that he'd had 'the necessary experience of dealing with people and choirs before coming out to New Zealand', having run a local parish church choir and conducting a Women's Institute choir for five years. At the time of the first summer school,

Godfrey had a national reputation as New Zealand's leading choral specialist: working with the Dorians, the University Singers, Auckland and Wellington cathedral choirs, as well as the Orpheus and National Youth choirs. There is little doubt that some people came to the first school purely because of Godfrey's involvement.

7 Simon Tipping, *Choir of the World* (Palmerston North: Dunmore Press, 2002), 61.

8 Conductors at the first polytechnic course included Rosemary Russell, Roger Powdrell, Greer Garden and Elise Christensen, who was later to become director of the New Zealand Secondary Students Choir and is now director of the Toronto Children's Choir. She made the return trip over the Rimutaka Hills from Masterton each evening.

9 Organising committees of successive schools strongly suggested that assistance be sought from employing authorities: boards of trustees, church committees, etc.

10 Karen Grylls was a protégé of Peter Godfrey's. She remembers, at their first meeting, Godfrey challenging her to conduct a Samuel Barber piece with the Auckland University Singers. She was 'overwhelmed' and 'felt like the most unlikely person for the job!' Subsequently, Godfrey suggested she pursue conducting study overseas. 'Peter Godfrey 1922–2017', *Applause Magazine* 23 (November 2017): 29.

11 This judgement call of the veteran music reviewer Lin Saunders was probably not far off the mark, considering that the *Svenska Dagbladet* (the Swedish daily paper published in Stockholm) held that the choir was 'undoubtedly one of the best choirs in Sweden . . . maybe even the best'. Through workshops and concerts in Wellington, Christchurch and Auckland, Ericson introduced a new range of repertoire, including Swedish classics. Videos of an Auckland workshop, now at Ngā Taonga Sound and Vision, show some striking qualities of choir and conductor. Ericson was not averse to using popular items, e.g. Norman Luboff's arrangement of 'Yellow Bird'. Ericson's breadth of interest is exemplified in a superb YouTube video of him guest-conducting the a cappella vocal jazz quintet *The Real Group* in their album Stämning (https://www.youtube.com/watch?v=_WevOIW-CK0).

12 Murto said that vocal training was the top priority for Dominante. He said that the work of the choir's two voice production teachers and the work of their predecessors, form the basis of the Dominante sound.

13 Twenty years earlier, in 1971, the Tapiola Children's Choir (ages 9 to 18) which began in Espoo, Finland, had become one of the world's leading choirs, winning the main prize of the BBC Let the Peoples Sing competition.

14 The pōwhiri — the Māori welcome involving speeches, dancing, singing of waiata and hongi (pressing of noses) — is a centuries-old tradition in Māori culture, symbolising the arrival of one tribe onto the sacred ground of another. We were honoured that the Ngāti Pōneke Marae agreed to welcome delegates in this dignified ceremony.

15 'Māori way of doing things'; derived from the Māori word tika meaning 'right' or 'correct'. Custom, etiquette, protocol.

16 Singer-songwriter Hirini Melbourne wrote songs in Māori (inspired by bird calls) that became influential in kōhanga reo (preschool language-learning nests). Bands such as Herbs borrowed the reggae rhythms of Jamaica, but their music reflected life in the South Pacific.

17 The previous year the National Youth Choir had recorded an entry for the BBC's Let the Peoples Sing and won the Youth Choir section. It had also won the Silver Rose Bowl award for the best choir overall from 26 choirs entered. Later in the same year the Youth Choir represented the Pacific Basin, with groups from China and Japan, at the Third World Symposium on Choral Music in Vancouver.

18 In late 2014, the Fiji Broadcasting Corporation announced, 'Fiji-based composer Igelese Ete will be providing his vast knowledge of Pacific music in a Disney movie titled *Moana*'.

19 Julie Jackson, a lecturer at Waikato University, conductor of the Hamilton Civic Choir and the Waikato High Schools' Choir, was completing a PhD in music education at Florida State University with Rodney Eichenberger. David Childs, MMus (Florida State), was head of music at Havelock North High School and was planning to undertake a DMA in Choral Music at Louisiana State University. Christopher Kiver, MMus (Florida State), acting director of choral

music at Brisbane Grammar School and conductor of several community choirs, was later to earn a DMA, Choral Music from University of Michigan with Jerry Blackstone.

20 Five years earlier, McLeod had set a new direction in composition with *He Iwi Kotahi Tatou*, 'for Māori and Pākehā choirs'. McLeod became a member of Ngāti Rangi, and regularly wrote hymns for Māori churches. Among the 100 attendees some were very influential in their local areas; for example, Colleen Marshall, Nelson; Di Lenihan, Invercargill; and Andrew Withington in Christchurch.

21 With David Willcocks, John Rutter had produced the hugely popular books *Carols for Choirs*. He then went on to pen further imaginative and singable arrangements and original carols. His freelance, professional London choir, the Cambridge Singers, had been founded in 1981 for recording purposes, and many of his elegant settings and compositions appeared on 30 critically acclaimed albums. Later he was awarded a CBE and a Lambeth Doctorate of Music.

22 The design and production of the enrolment brochure and handbook were important parts of their work. Created by Nicola Kiver, this design captured, in the background, a conducting diagram which had been the school's logo, as well as highlighting the five all-important sponsors. It set a benchmark for future schools' brochures.

23 Dr Grylls and Jacqui Simpson established the chamber choir Voices New Zealand as the graduate choir of the National Youth Choir in 1998.

24 Many current and future leaders in Australian choral music took part in that strand, e.g. Kate Albury (SA), Kym Scott (WA), Paul Holley and Carole Parker (QLD) and Owen Nelson (NSW).

25 At the final night's concert in Mayne Hall on campus, the young choir sang a crowd-pleasing programme ranging from a Torres Strait Island song arranged by Stephen Leek, Mozart's *Laudate Dominum* and modern folk songs from several countries, to Chilcott's moving 'Can You Hear Me?'. This was Birralee and Julie Christiansen's first public appearance. They have since represented Australia at Anzac ceremonies in France and Belgium. Christiansen was later awarded an OAM.

26 Carl Crossin, whose Adelaide Chamber Singers were invited by the Association of British Choral Directors (ABCD) to sing at their 1996 convention, studied conducting in the USA and Britain, and had been conductor of the National Youth Choir of Australia for its 1998 and 1999 seasons. A programme of his in the Adelaide Bank 2004 Festival of Arts in St Peter's Cathedral featured works by Hildegard of Bingen, Victoria, Arvo Pärt, and the Tallis 'Spem in Alium'.

27 The anthem, based on Psalm 145:15, was popularised in New Zealand by Peter Godfrey, who used it as a grace here and overseas with the New Zealand Youth Choir, most of whom knew it from memory, as well as with the Dorian and other choirs. It was a tradition that helped to mould a singularity of purpose among all involved in choir music.

28 Debra Shearer-Dirié, originally from Western Australia, holds a DMus in Choral Conducting from Indiana University, conducts Fusion, Vintage Voices and the Brisbane Concert Choir at St Andrew's, and is on the council of the Australian National Choral Association.

29 The differences between the United States and New Zealand were, of course, huge. ACDA had many thousands of members, whereas New Zealand might have been aiming for a paid-up membership of 300 to 400 in a new NZCF Association of Choral Directors.

30 This quartet's first performance, which provoked a riot, has been called one of the turning points in the history of music. The final movement, a setting of a Stefan George poem, 'Entrückung', began with the line 'I breathe air from another planet', and Schönberg floated into a new solar system away from the gravitational pull of the tonal system. Asked to identify himself during the First World War, Schönberg gave his name. 'Are you the notorious composer Arnold Schönberg?' he was asked. 'Yes,' he replied, 'somebody had to be.'

31 Dr André Thomas, a former colleague of Rodney Eichenberger at Florida State University, has recently received the highest award conferred by the American Choral Directors Association, the Robert Shaw Choral Award.

32 The term kaumātua refers to the elected elders who are keepers of the knowledge and traditions of a Māori subtribe or tribe. Female elders are also known as kuia.

12: A world in union: The New Zealand Choral Federation

1 The Māori word mana means authority, influence, prestige or honour.
2 Auckland Choral, Wellington Orpheus, Royal Christchurch, Christchurch Harmonic and Dunedin Schola Cantorum.
3 Simon Tipping, *Orpheus: Portrait of a Choir* (Palmerston North: Dunmore Press, 2002).
4 21 October 1981 to Professor Godfrey from G. E. Jansen, Education Officer, Music, Department of Education.
5 Letter from David Wood to Margery Charlton, 20 July 1984.
6 This group had a flexible membership. Some of the main players were Diana Cable, Joan Clayton, Linda Dawkins and Simon Tipping, along with members of Wellington's Festival Singers: Margaret Arthurs, Andrea Blanchard, Patricia Murray, Frank Carter, David Wood and myself.
7 Letter from Margery Charlton, 21 June 1984.
8 Having returned from USC only a matter of weeks before, I was understandably keen to win support for an invitation to Eichenberger and his celebrated choir. Robert Shaw, musical director/conductor of the Atlanta Symphony Orchestra and doyen of American choral conductors, held that the USC choir produced the finest choral singing he'd ever heard from a university or school of music ensemble.
9 James Allington, Marie Brown, Nicola Jansen and John Rosser were selected by the conference committee from the 29 who applied.
10 Their itinerary also featured performances in Auckland, Queenstown, Christchurch, Havelock North and Tokoroa. The *New Zealand Herald*'s Lin Saunders enthused, 'For sheer beauty of sound nothing in Auckland concerts over many years has quite equalled what was heard at St Patrick's Cathedral last night' (Friday, 26 July 1985), 10.
11 The programme also included Dr Ronald Smart leading his Sydney Conservatorium Chorale in a lunchtime concert and workshops that were highly significant for the future of artistic choral singing in the country. These were led by Flora Edwards, 'Caring for Your Voice'; Godfrey, 'What Makes a Conductor?'; Wood, 'Administering a Choir', Tipping, 'Learning Music and Preparing for Auditions', and myself, 'Know Your Choral Repertoire'.
12 Nan Anderson, Peter Barton, Don Whelan of Christchurch; Judy Berryman, Rosemary Collier, Patricia Murray, Monika Smith, Margaret and Bevan Werry, Bill McCabe, Roger Williams of Wellington; Margo Knightbridge, Ronald Dellow, Barry Hobman and Bob Armstrong of Auckland; Guyon Wells of Hamilton; Joan Whelan of Whanganui; Barbara Nicholls of Taupō; Gwenyth Logan of Dunedin; Juliet Cooke of Greytown; and Ruth Eckford of Masterton, to name but a few. Also on the list are the names of ex-National Youth Choir members, other younger singers, local Wellington choristers together with Peter Pocock and others from Australia, and, finally, Peter Godfrey, who offered himself on this occasion as a baritone.
13 *NZCF Newsletter* 1, 1 (November 1985): 7.
14 The administrator was Margaret Cull. Nancy Blake and Marilyn Reynolds were coordinators of the Secondary Schools' Choral Festivals recently brought into the NZCF fold.
15 David Willcocks, personal letter to author, 25 August 1988. Willcocks was 'very impressed by the standard of performance and dedication of the many young choral singers with whom he had come in contact' during his two-week stay in New Zealand. (He had been invited by the NZSO to conduct 60 members of the National Youth Choir and the New Zealand Secondary Students Choir, trained by Peter Watts and Roger Stevenson, in a broadcast performance of Lilburn's *Prodigal Country*.)
16 Terence Maskell, Margaret Lange, Stephen Rowe, David Crooks, David Hamilton, Morag Atchison, Deborah Orr, Brigid McLafferty among others
17 David Willcocks, personal letter to author, 25 August 1988.
18 Megan Flint, *The Big Sing: An investigation of its impact on the development of choral music in New Zealand secondary schools* (research project, University of Auckland). In those days it was relatively easy to obtain sponsorship funding. I made a visit in 1991 to the offices of Smokefree New Zealand in Pipitea Street, Wellington, picked up an application form and had a brief interview.

19 While in Dunedin in 1991 with Bel Canto and Dame Malvina Major for the Mozart Bicentenary Celebrations, I had made a point of meeting with key choral leaders, including Carole Randall, to ensure that if the festival were offered to that city for 1993, there would be sufficient and willing resource people to see the project through.

20 Graham Hoffman, by then NZCF general manager, strongly opposed this plan. But at the beginning of February 1993, three days before moving to a new position at The University of Queensland, I informed Hoffmann in a private meeting that the festival would be going ahead in Dunedin that year. As chair of the Secondary Schools' Festivals Committee, I also sensed that the Wellington committee (which included Felicia Edgecombe, Shona Murray, Jill Goddard [deputy principal of Wellington East Girls' College] and Lois Coplon, with Judy Berryman as secretary), had had its fair share of organising the national festivals over the previous five years.

21 Lois Coplon, executive officer of NZSSC for 10 years, resigned in 2001 after disappointment with decisions on the restructuring of the organisation of the festivals, including the standing-down of the Wellington-based Secondary Schools' Choral Festivals committee. Neil Denney took up the position for two years, working from the Auckland NZCF office, followed by Shona McIntyre-Bull.

22 Graham Hoffman had proved his organising ability with the first Sing Aotearoa in 1990 at Mount Ruapehu. He was persuaded that Māori should have a leading role as partners within the Choral Federation, and he worked closely with Greg Tata, Bub Wehi, Tīmoti Kāretu and local iwi (tribes). The impressive planning of the Ōhakune event is a notable part of Hoffmann's legacy. He was assisted in later Sing Aotearoa festivals by Marijke Batenburg, who also served for a period as chair of the NZCF National Executive.

23 During the 14-year period (January 1989 to May 2004) Pollock was retained as a pro bono consultant to NZCF. He also provided strategic marketing and development advice and services to the Auckland Philharmonia Endowment Trust, Auckland Art Gallery Toi o Tāmaki, Te Papa, the NZSO/Tainui (as CEO of the joint venture company First To The Future Limited) and Plunket — in the lead-up to that organisation's centenary.

24 Hoffman and Pollock, in New Zealand Choral Federation, *In Tune: The First 10 Years of the New Zealand Choral Federation* (Auckland: NZCF, 1995), 5.

25 Hoffman formally stepped down from his position as general secretary of NZCF and adviser to the International Federation for Choral Music in September 2007. Karen Grylls acknowledged Hoffman's outstanding contributions to NZCF when she informed the International Federation for Choral Music of his death on 1 June 2008. Grylls was an IFCM board member, 2003–9.

26 The first Governance Board members were: Karen Grylls, John Rosser (chair), Michael Littlewood (secretary, soon to be involved in Auckland University's Retirement Policy and Research Centre), Richard Madden (choral composer and conductor from Dunedin) and myself.

27 These were in conjunction with the Federation's Regional Committees.

28 Shona McIntyre, 'Recent developments in training for beginner directors', *In Tune*, 12. Realising her harsh judgement, McIntyre added that she was loath to criticise 'the genuine attempts of teachers unskilled in the nuance of choral music' who were doing their best.

29 These leaders were brought to New Zealand (with their choirs) when I had appropriate facilities at hand in the Head Office of the Department of Education.

30 Others who have been involved are: Karen Grylls; Simon Halsey (chief conductor of the 64-voice professional Berlin Radio Choir, and a colleague of Sir Simon Rattle) Ben Parry, Simon Carrington and The King's Singers from England; and Jo-Michael Scheibe from the United States.

31 Graham Hoffman, Greg Tata (convenors), Margery Charlton and Melody Witehira (NZCF Research), 'Aotearoa Sings — the 1990 and 1993 Sing Aotearoa Festivals', *in In Tune,* 15.

32 Ralph Ward, New Plymouth, in NZCF Secretary Margaret Cull, *Newsletter (November* 1990): 'I can vouch for the veracity of this tall story about choral singing on the snowy slopes of Mt Ruapehu (alt. 2797 metres). Mild confusion reigned for a short time when it was found that Swiss conductor Willi Gohl had been delayed and would only arrive on the *second* chair lift. It was an honour to be asked to deputise for this event on New Zealand's largest active volcano — probably the pinnacle of my career?'

33 Cull, *Newsletter* (November 1990): 4.
34 A hāngi is the Māori method of cooking a main meal using heated rocks buried in a pit oven.
35 Julian Raphael, community musician and educator who leads several daytime Sing for your Life groups in Wellington, presented this 'sing for your health' topic at the 2016 festival.
36 Guy Jansen, Grant Hutchinson, Helen Jackson, Noeline Cuzens and Steph Gilks, *Reference Manual for Convenors and Committees of the National Choral Clinics, 2008* (Guy Jansen on behalf of the NZCF Governance Board, 2008), 28 pp.
37 The clinic convenors were already very busy as conductors, NZCF regional representatives and leaders in their communities, e.g. Gayle Dowsett (Whangārei); Max Stewart (Hamilton); Joe Christensen (Hastings); Noeline Cuzens (Wellington); Pete Rainey (Nelson).
38 Christine Argyle, who conducted Anthem choirs at three matches in Wellington, recalls the thrill of performing to a packed stadium: 'Just before going onto the field, someone said to me, rather casually, "I suppose 35,000 is the biggest audience you've ever conducted in front of?" I hadn't really thought of the numbers involved until that moment!'
39 The 1990 symposium took in those three cities within the one week. It was inspiration in abundance. One afternoon in Russian-held Estonia, 5000 people came out to sing for us in the huge soundshell in central Tallinn.
40 The value of being involved is exemplified in my being invited to the Fourth World Symposium, Sydney, 1996, with a choir (The University of Queensland Chamber Singers) to be the resident choir for Stefan Parkman's conducting masterclasses. The four set pieces included Poulenc's *Un Soir de Neige* and Per Nørgård's avant-garde *Wie Ein Kind*. Parkman expected singing perfection. My choir was the only Australian university group invited to participate in the symposium.
41 Examples are: organ builder and keyboardist Roy Tankersley's postgraduate studies in baroque music in London; Karen Grylls' groundbreaking studies in musical analysis and conducting at the University of Washington, Seattle; David Hamilton's short trips to Finland to study Finnish choral music and promote his compositions; Susan Densem's vocal studies and specialist choral and opera experience in Brisbane.
42 Rosser was a devoted Dorian Choir member, and deputy conductor of Godfrey's Auckland University Singers.
43 *Peter Godfrey — an inspiration*, www.nzcf.org.nz (4 October 2017).
44 NZCF, *Breve* (May 2012): 1. As NZCF chair at the time I was privileged to preside over this jovial occasion, which was typically begun by Godfrey conducting 'Oculi Omnium', with everyone singing from memory.

13: The flourishing of a rich choral culture, 1972–99

1 Margery Charlton was already well known to Godfrey as parish secretary at St Mary's Cathedral from 1956 to 1963. She was an experienced public servant and Chamber Music Society organiser. Stephen Park, *A Story of Service to New Zealand Choirs — Margery Charlton. . .*, Papers Past (National Library of New Zealand).
2 Ronald Dellow headed up the Auckland Bach Cantata Society in the late 1970s. Composer John Rimmer quotes a twelfth-century Chinese poem when asked to describe Dellow's management of musicians: 'If you want to be a leader, walk behind the people rather than in front of them.'
3 Letter from Jim Bjorge quoted in Elizabeth Salmon, *Peter Godfrey: Father of New Zealand Choral Music* (Wellington: Mākaro Press, 2015), 109.
4 C. S. Cooper, 'Dorian Choir's Finest Hour', *New Zealand Herald,* 15 May 1975.
5 C. S. Cooper, 'Elated Choir on Eve of Homecoming', *New Zealand Herald,* 19 June 1975.
6 Ibid.
7 Godfrey on LP cover: *The Dorians Sing* (Tartar LP record TRL – 029, 1983). This, the last recording that he made with the Dorian Singers, contains music that he loved to share with audiences, e.g. 'Kyrie Eleison' and 'Heilig' from Mendelssohn's *Lutheran Mass,* and Robert de Pearsall's 'Who Shall Win My Lady Fair?'.
8 Philip Hope-Wallace, *The Guardian*, 30 August 1977.
9 *The Times*, 29 August 1977.

10 *The Daily Telegraph*, 27 August 1977.
11 Knightbridge was the group's organiser for many years. Anthony Blaschke conducted the choir in its very early stages and was followed by Peter Watts. Watts later relinquished the position to Anita Banbury, who still conducts the group.
12 Tankersley, among other roles, is a past chair of the Wellington Branch of the RSCM, a frequent conductor of combined choirs on the television programme *Praise Be*, and chair of the Manawatū/Whanganui NZCF Regional Committee.
13 Cantoris was founded by Andrew Baines in Wellington. In Christchurch, Scuola di Chiesa was established by Brian Pritchard for the performance of seventeenth- and eighteenth-century music; Martin Setchell founded the Jubilate Singers; and the 100-voice Celebration Singers sang at the open-air church service at the 1994 Commonwealth Games. Graham Parsons was the foundation conductor of the Palmerston North Renaissance Singers (since led by Guy Donaldson). The National Youth Choir included young people between the ages of 13 and 24. The diversity of initiatives over this time is striking.
14 Professor Wharehuia Milroy devised the name for the new festival: Te Mata (the face); tini (many), hence Te Matatini (many faces).
15 Tikanga: traditional values and customs; 'the Māori way of doing things'.
16 *New Zealand Herald*, 1 August 1996.
17 The following year the two groups sang together again at Sing Aotearoa, Ōhakune. The effect of 'Hinemoa' and 'Timatanga' was 'immediate and explosive' (Grylls), and 'the highlight for the weekend' according to critic Nigel Gearing. Simon Tipping, *Choir of the World* (Palmerston North: Dunmore Press, 2002), 158.
18 Glamaphones, the Wellington gay, lesbian, bisexual, transgender, inter-sex community SATB choir, began in 2011.
19 There is an annual choral celebration at the Tabernacle organised by the New Zealand Chinese Church Music Association.
20 Email correspondence with the author, 20 December 2017.
21 Publications such as *The Maorilander: Journal of the New Zealand Folklore Society*, provide information on many early songs. Phil Garland, 'the godfather of New Zealand folk music', made it his life's work to collect, interpret and preserve early folk material. Kiwi Records issued an extensive series of recordings of New Zealand folk songs.
22 Neil Colquhoun, who trained with Ernest Jenner and Barry Trussell at Christchurch Teachers' College, and became a primary school music specialist, published a book of New Zealand folk songs in 1972. It was revised and enlarged as *Song of a Young Country* (Wellington: Steele Roberts, 2010).
23 Gospel was associated with political causes in the United States more than here, and some songs go back to the slave era. 'We Shall Overcome', used in the civil rights movement, is sung by gospel choirs.

14: The new millennium

1 Supertonic, Grey Warblers, Doubtful Sounds: zany names of choirs to join the classic Australian one, Spooky Men's Chorale.
2 Stamper has an MMus in Choral Conducting from Southwestern Baptist Theological Seminary, Fort Worth, Texas.
3 See the hundreds of events advertised monthly on the NZCF website: www.nzcf.org.nz/
4 Apart from major works of the choral/orchestral repertoire, New Zealand compositions (including five of Chris Artley's) have been prepared for performance. An imaginative January 2018 programme, entitled *Choral Sounds of the Enlightenment*, exemplified three different *bel canto* styles: Mozart's *Mass in C*, Dmitry Bortniansky's Russian *Concerto for Choir, No. 24*, and Morten Lauridsen's *Shining Night*. It was led by Ebbe Munk. Jonathan Berkahn was accompanist.
5 Backhouse completed a BMus at Victoria University. He had sung in a choir while at high school, and in the late 1970s formed a short-lived choir in Wellington called Red Wings. His eclectic mix of inspiring choirs include: Addicts Rehabilitation Centre Choir, Chanticleer,

Philippine Madrigal Singers, and Taverner Choir and Consort. He appears on YouTube as soloist with Heaven Bent in Edwin Hawkins' 'O Happy Day' in 2011 (https://www.youtube.com/watch?v=_LzznNjovSo).

6 Email correspondence with Everingham, 19 July 2017.

7 SLNA website: www.songleaders.org.nz/index.php/from-our-patron (accessed 3 January 2018).

8 Also styled Young@Heart. During this tour, sponsored by Summerset Retirement Villages, director Bob Cilman held auditions for a small group of local senior singers to sing with the visiting choir. They became the basis of an Auckland choir. Singers mostly live independently.

9 Information from a survey conducted by the Retirement Villages Association in March 2018.

10 Repertoire for recent concerts by the choir at Summerset Retirement Village, Aotea, Wellington, has ranged from 'Surely' (*Messiah*), Purcell's 'Sound the trumpet' and J. S. Bach's 'Sheep May Safely Graze', to arrangements of 'What a Wonderful World', folk songs and popular hits.

11 Auckland University's School of Music now has five voice teachers involved in various ways with choral programmes: Dr Morag Atchison, Rachel Fuller, Catrin Johnsson, Dr Te Oti Rakena and Robert Wiremu.

12 The visits of internationally renowned vocal specialists Richard Miller and Marvin Keenze from 1996 validated the principles of vocal pedagogy, including free phonation, which undergirded these developments.

13 Others to adopt this close association between individual voice tuition and choral technique have included Judy Bellingham with the Southern Youth Choir, Susan Densem at Burnside High School, and Shelagh and Nick Richardson at Kristin School.

14 Simon Tipping, *Choir of the World* (Palmerston North: Dunmore Press, 2002), 190.

15 Roger Stevenson trained the most choirs invited to Finales. He was followed by Shona Murray, Terence Maskell, Peter Hercus, David Childs, Stephen Rowe and, later, Virginia Le Cren among others. The six years after 2005 saw Rowan Johnston become a dominant force, followed by Sue Densem, the ever-present Terence Maskell, Chris Burcin, David Squire and Douglas Nyce.

16 Matthew Leese, 'British influence on New Zealand choral traditions: a study of the relationship between choral festivals and societies in the United Kingdom and in New Zealand, with focus on New Zealand's high school festival "The Big Sing"' (AMusD. dissertation, University of Illinois at Urbana-Champaign, Illinois, 2012). This dissertation, and Megan Flint's later Auckland University research project on *The Big Sing's impact on the development of choral music in New Zealand secondary schools,* are important background documents.

17 Craig Pollock also created and presented 24 workshops on marketing for singing groups at NZCF's request. During these three years he also was director of marketing and development for the New Zealand Symphony Orchestra.

18 'Let the River Run', Burnside High School Senior Chorale (YouTube: https://www.youtube.com/watch?v=2hhg1U09kKo), The Big Sing, 2015.

19 In addition to school commitments, Densem directs a chamber choir at the University of Canterbury, the Christchurch Jubilate Singers and workshops for the NZCF Association of Choral Directors. She has been a soloist in opera and with choirs travelling overseas.

20 The Big Sing in its various manifestations — Westpac Contest, Regional and National School Choral Festivals, and The Big Sing — has been a prevailing and powerful force in the choral movement. For example, in 2011, Katie Macfarlane, director at the time of the Wellington Youth Choir, told me that nearly 90 per cent of her choir of 51 members, when at secondary school, had participated in an NZCF Big Sing event.

15: Five national choirs and a world symposium

1 Report, ARD West German Radio, May 1986.

2 Quoted in Simon Tipping, *Choir of the World* (Palmerston North: Dunmore Press, 2002), 91.

3 Members of the Tabernacle Choir voted Karen Grylls the best guest director to have taken part in the live television programme *Music and the Spoken Word.*

4 Grylls: conductor's report on Sing Aotearoa, 1997.

5 The current chief executive of the New Zealand Youth Choir is Arne Herrmann, and the operations manager is Emma Billings who has been part of the team for 12 years. Those previously involved in its administration have included Roger Lloyd, Barbara George, Jenny Jamieson, Jacqui Simpson, Paddy Nash and Colin Brown.

6 www.nzsschoir.com (accessed 16 April 2018).

7 The administrators of the New Zealand Secondary Students Choir have played an important role in the choir's achievements and to contributions to choral singing in this country. Early voluntary administrators such as Heather Keith were followed by Lois Coplon who served for 13 years until her untimely death in 2009. Coplon often involved other members of her family to help in the work. Student choir leaders have been a significant part of the administrative structure, e.g. Anna Dong, student leader in 2015–16, a choir member for four years and now on a scholarship at Princeton University.

8 I well remember him singing in the 1963 John O'Shea film *Runaway*, film score by Robin Maconie, and starring Kiri Te Kanawa.

9 'Māori Choir Launch CD', *Pā Kāea* (Whakatane, December 2000), 8.

10 From a phone conversation with Rim D. Paul, 26 September 2018.

11 The choir has also had a succession of talented, experienced accompanists, including Sylvia Watson of Ashburton when Aburn was director. The present accompanist, Alex Wiltshire, was one of the first professional women conductors in New Zealand, when she worked as assistant conductor for a New Zealand Opera Company production of *Marriage of Figaro*. She also shared conducting duties with Sir William Southgate for several productions of the New Zealand Ballet Company.

12 'Auckland What's Happening' ran the announcement. The Choral Federation had been working on a New Zealand Singers proposal but had not decided whether to proceed with it. The Youth Choir Board gave the green light for auditions to take place for the Youth Choir graduate arm (no name had yet been chosen) because a tour to an International Choral Contest in Tolosa, Spain was looming as a possibility.

13 Aroha Cassidy, a member of Te Waka Huia, travelled with the choir to Spain to continue preparing the choir for the haka and poi parts of the work.

14 Heath Lees in the *Weekend Herald*.

15 Announcement on website of International Federation for Choral Music (ifcm.net/the-12th-ifcm-world-symposium-on-choral-music-2020-goes-to-new-zealand/). It was gratifying to see the show of confidence that IFCM leaders had in our Choral Federation and the team of organisers headed by John Rosser.

16 http://www.nzcf.org.nz/theme-wscm2020

16: How has the best become so good?

1 Professional conductors Carl Gustav Schmitt (1881) and Maughan Barnett (1893) also came for health reasons.

2 I think that this was one of the disappointments that Godfrey experienced during the three years in Melbourne. He told me later that he felt that he had made a mistake in taking up that position.

3 Growing up on farms, I observed the use of the most common fencing wire (number 8) along with scrap materials to repair machinery and other structures. First farmers, then Kiwis generally, came to be seen as ingenious people who could turn their hands to anything. The term 'number 8 wire' came to symbolise resourcefulness, using materials readily at hand.

4 The term 'turning point' can be ambiguous, and the choice of turning points or other defining moments is somewhat arbitrary. Here I use it to mean a step-change that in retrospect has clearly affected the development of choral music. The event or action may have been hesitant or very small and its consequences may have been unforeseen.

5 *The Dominion,* 1 July 1941, 10.

6 Jeremy Begbie, *Resounding Truth: Christian Wisdom in the World of Music* (Grand Rapids, Minnesota: Baker Academic, 2007), 222.

7 J. Blumberg@YoniBlum (www.cnbc.com/2018), accessed 23 February 2018.

8 Graham Buxton, *Dancing in the Dark: The Privilege of Participating in God's Ministry in the World* (Eugene, Oregon: WIPF and Stock, 2013).
9 When visiting Trinity College of Music in London I asked how many choral conducting students there were. Upon being informed that there were two per year, I rather brazenly asked how all the hundreds of conductors for school, community and other choirs were to receive training.
10 The half-hour programme *Praise Be* began on TV ONE in 1986. Featuring choral groups and ecumenical congregational singing, the weekly audience has averaged about 70,000 people. An estimated 47,000 people sang on the programme in its first 25 years.
11 I have begun a list of some of the more than 90 female conductors who have been active in the last few years: Clare Adams, Rosemary Allison, Nan Anderson, Christine Argyle, Anita Banbury, Pepe Becker, Judy Bellingham MNZM, Christina Bevan, Elise Bradley MNZM, Marie Brown MNZM, Claire Caldwell, Eve de Castro-Robinson, Helen Charlton, Maaike Christie-Beekman, Maria Colvin, Te Taite Cooper, Mary Cornish, Jean Cumming , Noeline Cuzens, Susan Densem, Katherine Dienes-Williams, Gayle Dowsett, Felicia Edgecombe, Nicola Jansen, Hana Fahey, Judy Faris, Bev Faulknor, Pauline Fitchett, Kath Fletcher QSM, Megan Flint, Cathryn Graham, Rachel Griffiths-Hughes, Karen Grylls ONZM, Kate Hays, Naomi Hnat, Katherine Hodge, Joanne Hodgson, Penelope Hoosen, Philippa Hosken, Rachel Hyde, Glenys Kempshall, Joan Kennaway QSM, Elizabeth Kerr MNZM, Margo Knightbridge, Karen Knudsen, Gillian Lander, Elizabeth Lau, Leonie Lawson MNZM, Virginia Le Cren, Di Lenihan QSM, Dame Sister Mary Leo DBE, Tianyi Lu, Katie Macfarlane, Shona McIntyre-Bull, Brigid McLafferty, Vicki McLeod, Sarah McNabb, Lois McNeil, Jennifer Mahoney, Holly Mathieson, Sue Mepham, Nancy Miller, Jennifer Moss, Patricia Murray, Shona Murray, Charlotte Murray, Anya Nazaruk, Gemma New, Joanne Oliver, Celeste Oram, Bridget O'Shanassy, Rita Paczian, Jan Parkinson, Barbara Paterson, Wendy Patston, Ngoi Pēwhairangi QSM, Sarah Rae, Carole Randall, Margaret Ritchie, Sue Robinson, Rosemary Russell, Elizabeth Salmon, Carol Shortis, Barbara Smith QSM, Maureen Smith, Monika Smith, Ann Marie Stapp, Claire Stevens, Alison Stewart, Rachel Sutherland, Jayne Tankersley, Rosemary Tarbotton, Fiona Tibbles, Rosemary Turnbull, Felicity Ward, Pimia Wehi QSM, Fiona Wilson, Maria Winder, Sister Mary Winefride Blake QSM.

Afterword: Where to from here?

1 C. S. Lewis, *The World's Last Night and Other Essays* (San Diego: Harcourt Brace and Company, 1987), 80. Lewis loved music, particularly Wagner, in his younger days.
2 Within two years of the golden days of Godfrey and Grylls coming to an end, the Auckland Dorian Choir were discussing the difficult but, I think, correct decision to wind up the choir.
3 As I was writing this, I came across a book by Sarah Ell and Nicola Legat, *Our New Zealand: A Celebration of our National Treasures & Pleasures* (Auckland: Random House, 2013). While it has a mention of waiata and haka, and a short section on 'Our Songs', there is in its 240 pages not one reference to widespread Kiwi choral pleasures and treasures.
4 An outward-looking American ensemble, Tonality, recently formed by Alexander Blake DMA, is dedicated to promoting 'peace, social justice, and unity'.
5 Although some may object that the age of seven or eight is too early for specific vocal training, it is useful to remember that the young boys in the King's College, Cambridge, choirs over the past 100 years have not suffered vocal harm.
6 Ownership of the whole scheme would need to be in the hands of a vocal expert to monitor aspects of teaching. Personable young voice graduates who have caught the vision and are able to communicate with children could be encouraged to commit time to the venture.

Acknowledgements

I want to acknowledge the generosity of a large number of people without whom this book would have remained simply a good idea.

Primarily and centrally, special thanks to Adrienne Jansen. Her unswerving belief in this project and her editorial skills during the writing have been outstanding. She has also master-minded the compilation of the book and acted as project manager for the many tasks and people necessary for its completion. It is hard to imagine a better sister-in-law, writer and editor to work with. She has been a superb literary companion over four years: sparkling, patient, encouragingly imaginative, creatively inspiring, with wise judgement. I thank her profoundly and sincerely.

Secondly, thanks to Barry Prescott, whose superb work on the photographs has made this book the fine pictorial work that it is.

Thanks also to Sir Tīmoti Kāretu for consultation and advice on the first chapter.

Others who have contributed generously are Christine Argyle, Chris Artley, Peter Averi, Rosemary Collier, Elizabeth Crayford, Brian Dellow, Juliet Dreaver, Felicia Edgecombe, Matthew Everingham, Karen Grylls, Warwick Harvey, Arne Herrmann, the late Grant Hutchinson, Rowan Johnston, Margo Knightbridge, Peter Lineham, Michael Littlewood, Shona McIntyre-Bull, Shona Murray, Lorraine Nikera, John Rosser, Rosemary Russell, John Shrapnell, Roy Tankersley, Simon Tipping, Angela Werren and Robert Wiremu.

Thanks to the staff at Choirs Aotearoa New Zealand and to Samuel Ardell from the Alexander Turnbull Library; and many others who sent photographs and information, replied to queries, and in all sorts of ways made this book possible.

Finally, thanks to the New Zealand Choral Federation and to Creative New Zealand for their financial support.

Guy E. Jansen
May 2019

When Guy became ill, the publication of this book felt urgent. I am very grateful to the team at Massey University Press: Nicola Legat for her very quick decision to publish it; Tracey Borgfeldt for her uncompromising demands for the best, in the most encouraging and helpful way; Anna Bowbyes for her attention to detail and keeping everything on track; and Megan van Staden for such a fine design. Guy would be very proud of this book, and would no doubt have planned a celebration party, molto extravaganzo of course, in honour of this exceptional publishing team.

Adrienne Jansen
August 2019

About the author

Guy Jansen (1932–2019) MNZM studied music at Victoria University of Wellington, and later completed a Doctor of Musical Arts at the University of Southern California, with Rodney Eichenberger and Morten Lauridsen. From 1975–89, he was the National Officer for Music in the New Zealand Department of Education, with responsibility for primary and secondary school music, itinerant and out-of-hours music schemes, national in-service music courses, and much more. He initiated the formation of the world's first national youth choir, the National Youth Choir of New Zealand (ages 13 to 24), and was its inaugural musical director. In 1986 he founded the New Zealand Secondary Students Choir, and in the same year established the International Summer Schools in Conducting.

Jansen taught at the University of Queensland, where he established a master's degree in choral conducting, and subsequently he was invited to be conductor-in-residence at Wheaton Conservatory of Music in Illinois, United States. In 2011, he was made a Member of the New Zealand Order of Merit in the Queen's Birthday Honours. In 2013, he was made a Life Member of the New Zealand Choral Federation, and in 2017 he was presented with the Federation's first Distinguished Service Award.

Index

Page numbers in **bold** refer to images.

MASSEY
UNIVERSITY
PRESS

First published in 2019 by Massey University Press
Private Bag 102904, North Shore Mail Centre
Auckland 0745
New Zealand
www.masseypress.ac.nz

Design by Megan van Staden
Cover photographs: National Youth Choir recording the 'Muppet Song', May 1981 (front left); National Youth Choir, 2016, photographer Jiří Sejkora (front right); Auckland University Festival Choir, Albert Park, Auckland, 1972 (back); Peter Godfrey conducting an outdoor performance (front flap); First National Polynesian Festival Competitions, Rotorua, 1972 (back flap).

A catalogue record for this book is available from the National Library of New Zealand.

The assistance of New Zealand Choral Federation members and staff is gratefully acknowledged by the publisher.

Printed and bound in China through Colorcraft Limited, Hong Kong
ISBN: 978-0-9951001-5-2